N Sauer

D0088941

California
and Other
States of
Grace

A MEMOIR

California and Other States of Grace

A MEMOIR

Phyllis Theroux

WILLIAM MORROW AND COMPANY, INC.
New York   1980

Library of Congress Cataloging in Publication Data

Theroux, Phyllis.
    California and other states of grace.

    1. Theroux, Phyllis.   2. United States—Biography.
I. Title.
CT275.T523A33   973'.0994 [B]   79-27848
ISBN 0-688-03641-4

Printed in the United States of America

First Edition

1   2   3   4   5   6   7   8   9   10

For my family, past, present and future.

Author's Note

I have made several attempts to describe this book, only to find that the descriptions stood somewhere between a meaningless abstraction and every book that has ever been published. Then I thought of a story which seemed like a metaphor for the book itself, so I am going to introduce the book by indirection.

Several years ago, I flew with my children back home to California. The afternoon of our arrival, we went for a walk along the Carmel beach. It was sunset, the beach was particularly sharp with color, and the sun hung like a fiery communion wafer on the horizon, its last rays laying a track of gold across the water to the edge of the wet sand where I stood.

Seized with the desire to impress this scene upon my children, who were skittering like sandpipers at the ocean's edge, I gathered them together and showed them how to make a frame out of their fingers to capture the sunset like a picture. They were only mildly interested in this instant photography, and after several moments they broke away to run up and down the beach again.

"Well," I thought, retreating to a sand dune and sitting down alone, "so much for a mother's metaphysics." But then I was aware that my six-year-old daughter was plunging straight into the ocean and was already up to her knees in the strong Pacific surf.

I cupped my hands and yelled, "Wait, come back!" My daughter turned around, cast a regretful look back toward the ocean and ran to where I was sitting. "It's dangerous out there," I explained. "The water is deep." She lowered herself onto the sand, put her chin upon her knees and said quietly, "But I was only trying to step on the sunset."

This book is about trying to step on the sunset. Directly, before I knew how to swim, indirectly, before I realized that another person's sunset is not to be violated, and, finally, I understood that a sunset, by definition, always retreats before one's feet—which neither invalidates sunsets nor diminishes the worth of the desire to step toward them. Sunsets exist. The attraction toward them is inexorable. And from an early age, I waded in.

I have written about my family because it was brilliant while it existed as a unit and instructive to me when it ultimately fell apart. The convent was a time where certain insights, gathered at random and without knowing I was gathering them, came together for the first time. In other chapters, at later times, insights are altered as life inconveniently intruded upon my preconceptions of it.

In the beginning of the book, I will be an appropriately small character. Once I have woven the tapestry behind this character, she will emerge as more and more of a person in her own right. The form of the book will follow the form of my life. I'll let the sunset track itself as it will, and my hope is that the reader will recognize his or her own sunset within it.

California
and Other
States of
Grace

A MEMOIR

Chapter

I

As the plane flew over the United States, in a parabola going east to west, the packed urban sprawl, which looked like a large computer with its backside ripped open, began to recede. The land gave the eye new patterns to focus upon, natural convocations of peak and flat that can't be seen from the ground. Craters in the shape of baseball mitts, rivers spinning out fine threads on either side, like plants shaken loose of their dirt and laid with their roots to dry in the sun. At 37,000 feet you can see these things, bone-white mountains giving way to carrot-red soil, the Rockies with their tiny roads winding through them like so much loose twine flung at random.

Looking out the window was the only real diversion from the reason for the trip, and I amused myself by playing God on high, seeing all the grand schemes that the housewife shaking out her sheets below could not divine. But I knew that it was only a temporary gain of vision. I was flying straight into a can of worms. The plane would touch down and my overview would vanish. How would I handle the situation? We were flying in from all over with no knowledge of whether our father would be dead when we got there or not.

At one point during the flight, my ears began to pound, I could feel the tension building up the familiar sick fear inside and I went slightly out of control. My younger sister, Cindy, slept alongside me, her head cushioned by a pillow. She looked so unprotected and accepting of being younger in every way that I reached out and patted her head. She opened her eyes, looked at me and whispered, "Do you know how much I love you?" I said that I loved her too, and in that small exchange some of the tension dissolved. The rest was dissipated by plugging my ears into a headset and sinking into Beethoven's Ninth.

San Francisco, the fog-bound cradle that rocked me into life, lay below. I gave it the back of my hand. No one lives there anymore, except ghosts. We hustled our bags toward the Monterey ramp and within minutes were settled into a two-engine plane for the twenty-minute final leg home.

The flight from San Francisco to Monterey is unfailingly beautiful. I am never afraid of this part of the trip. We swept south along the scalloped coastline, where the olive mountains dip sharply into the water, executed a dogleg across Half Moon Bay, flew over the red tile roof of Santa Catalina School, and then made the final approach over Laguna Seca onto the runway.

As the plane touched down, the reason for coming home temporarily went away. The homecoming itself, with that sharp, excited anticipation it has always evoked, flooded over me. Who would be there? Which faces would rush from the gate? I'll say this for my family, we can play havoc with each other, but we all show up at the airport to claim a member. It's one of our strongest points, second only to birthday parties, although it struck me hard that this time my father, hustling toward the ramp, cigarette jammed into the side of his mouth, would not be there. He was plugged up with nylon arteries in a hospital, fighting to repair his heart.

We walked down the stairs and into the waiting room. My sister Wendy, brother Peter and Aunt Irene were there. This last, my aunt, was unexpected. She has no tolerance for pain, let alone death, but she was there. This must mean that my father was still alive. The expressions on their faces told me I was correct.

No time for small talk. I was determined to get to the hospital and slide into home plate before my father struck out. Such egos we have that we think we make such a difference. But there you have it—I thought I did. We tossed our bags into the trunk, said good-bye to my aunt (airports are one thing, hospitals another) and took off down Highway One.

The highway that runs inland from Monterey to Salinas is a winding road, valley on one side, the Los Laureles Mountains on the other. Salinas—a collection of frame houses full of Montgomery Ward furniture and turquoise toaster covers—lies at the end, a dusty town which sits unpretentiously on the edge of farmland that oozes like chocolate sauce in every direction.

My father had no business being stricken in Salinas, unless he was intent on winding up his life as a joke, which was a possibility. "If we go down the tubes," my mother had once said, "your father will certainly go down looking well dressed." He always had looked several portfolios richer than he was, but to be felled in a field lifting a box of artichokes onto a flatbed truck was not part of any script I had ever imagined.

"He was helping the driver," explained Wendy. "He told Dad that he had a bad back. So Daddy decided to hell with it, he'd chuck them into the truck himself. Then he felt funny, decided to check into Emergency at Natividad, and he had his heart attack in bed."

"Jeeze," I exclaimed. "He's sixty-four years old. And I imagine the driver was an old man of thirty maybe?"

"Right," said my sister. "But you know how he is. He just got impatient."

I played the probable scene over in my mind. My father saying, "Listen, give me those damn boxes, you can't ruin your back. Let the geezer do it." I settled back against the seat, feeling angry and affectionate toward my father at the same time, and looked out the window.

The spur to Salinas never fails to overwhelm me. One forgets how achingly familiar it all is, like encountering an old friend who is more beautiful than you remember. Soft green hills, gentle as bosoms, rise and fall upon each other, with oak trees growing in the creases. A California oak is a tough, comforting thing—half tree, half elephant—its gray, baggy elbows bending solicitously close to the ground, following the contours of the hill. A serving tree, all arms and generosity, no other state possesses them in such abundance, and in the spring the oaks are sharp, like cutouts, against the new grass.

Spring in California is a passing thing, as if the artist could barely work up the enthusiasm, came with insufficient supplies, went briefly over everything with a light brush and then departed. Usually the hills are brown, which easterners remark upon and are put off in their hearts. But Californians wouldn't have it any other way. Yet today the hills were lime green, the oaks polished to the last dark green leaf, and we were driving to Salinas where my strong, willful father was lying in a white room on a white hospital bed.

As the car rounded one curve after another, a few of Nature's casualties were scattered about to remind me that nothing stays unmolested. A gray, blasted oak—a lightning victim—lay in sections on the new grass, bleached to silver. Twisted, sorrowful driftwood cushioned among the poppies and lupine, it was a shocking piece of devastation. My father, the oak tree, dying in the spring. There were too many paradoxes to handle all at once. Everything had happened too fast.

Three months before his heart attack, my father and mother

had separated. It had been a long time coming, less for my father who had not been listening. But my mother had wanted it, for years really, and the last eighteen months she had devoted most of her energies to trying to figure out how to do it without damage. And then it had happened. My father moved, with Mother's help, to a month-by-month rental bungalow in Carmel Valley, they divided up the dessert dishes and candlesticks, and suddenly there were two telephone numbers in my address book.

I don't know why I hadn't been more disturbed at this sudden change. But living back East, it simply hadn't seemed real or important. Only when I thought about the living-room ecology that had been permanently altered, the three-way conversations with Mother, Dad and I all falling easily into our banter together, did I sense an upcoming loss. But it was not great. Mother was in place, and it made me realize that for the deeper, more sustaining nourishment, she had always been my choice. And that had not changed. From 3,000 miles away, in my own kitchen, I was detached from the severance, judged its impact not upon them but me, and survived it—all too well. Which shows you that you're never too old to be selfish.

The car pulled into Salinas, past the lettuce fields that make one weep for the rest of the barren country. Lettuce, kale, alfalfa, beets—"Cripes," said my father once, "you could plant a telephone book in that soil and it would sprout its own yellow pages." Anything that grows, grows better in Salinas, and the fields, newly ripped off, could still feed an army. In fact, it was this realization that had indirectly put my father into the Intensive Care Unit at Natividad Hospital.

Several years before, out of a job and restless, he had looked at those fields, put two and two together and come up with a brainstorm. "Look," he argued with the welfare bureaucrats in Salinas, "we'll take the 'culls' from the growers —doing 'em a favor when you think about it—load them into trucks, and give the poor old 'Seniors' some free food."

It was a brilliant idea, my father founded "Operation Brown Bag," and within six months he had all the senior citizens who could walk hustling food into the sacks and distributing it to themselves while my father, looking as if he'd just polished off a drink with Doug Fairbanks at Del Monte Lodge, walked around the center egging the cardiac cases on.

The growers, relieved to be the good guys for a change (after all Cesar Chavez worked the same territory), couldn't cooperate enough. It was a no-lose proposition, and my father, who always did know how to push an idea if there was no paper work involved, was just the man to pull it off. "Oh, no doubt about it," my mother had said. "It's your father's most brilliant idea yet. In time, it should definitely go national."

My mother has always had this thing about "going national." One way or another, we were all destined to serve a wider audience, at least in her mind. My brother's Elvis Presley imitations were only the tip of that iceberg, my sister's songs, my father's various businesses, her own invention, which was a logo for sweat shirts that her astrologer in San Jose told her would make it big at the appropriate time— Mother is a believer of the first magnitude, although to date no one has fleshed out her intuitions.

Pulling into the hospital grounds, I felt a chill. Somewhere in that square adobe-colored complex was my father. I was overwhelmingly anxious to see him. A great wave of protectiveness formed in my rib cage as I visualized him lying alone in bed. We pulled into the parking lot behind the Intensive Care section and my sister pointed out his room.

I jumped hurriedly out of the car, as if the emotion I held was a serum that I was anxious to donate. At least there was something I could do, was doing, for him. The very act of flying across the country would tell him something of my love. I was eager to place my arms around him, pour care around his head and reduce his fear—if there was any—by my sheer physical presence. I wouldn't allow him to die.

We walked past his window. He was asleep, his head cradled in one hand, toward the window. My God, he was an old man—a slack-jawed, white-haired old man—who filled up the hospital bed, crepuscular and fragile. We all lingered at the window for a minute, trying to link up this man with our father, the jaunty, sport-coated, loafer-wearing person who did outrageous things, like buying a Honda motor scooter for his sixtieth birthday.

My brother Peter was embarrassed by my father riding around on a Honda at his advanced age. "Could you at least wear a helmet so my friends won't see your white hair?" he had begged, which fractured my father who did not comply with the request. He continued to zip around town, helmetless, his white curly hair flying in the wind.

It was shocking to see him so collapsed and lifeless. But Wendy tried to joke a little. "It's the hospital sheets and tubes that make him look different. He always looked that way when he slept." And Wendy was right. He always did.

We walked into the Intensive Care Unit, which had a small collection of green plastic chairs and a coffee table outside the locked doors of the wing, and rang for the nurse. A couple of Mexicans were sitting in one corner, and a sad-eyed housewife type who appeared to know Wendy looked up briefly as we came in and plunged her face back down into splayed fingers. We rang for the nurse inside.

"Hi, my two sisters from the East are here," said Wendy. "Can they come in?"

"Right," said the invisible nurse. "One at a time."

I was the oldest and took the lead.

Walking into the room, I took one look at my father, who was now awake, and was relieved to find that he was all there: the grin, the twinkle, the voice. I reached out and held his face in my hands, kissed his cheek and entered into his atmosphere as greedily as any child who thought something had been taken away only to be given another chance.

It is too complicated to explain a reunion. Nothing is remembered, everything is present—the trips to Sonoma, the time we saw snow in Yosemite together, the way he used to squeeze my knee and make me laugh, the mix of bay rum, shaving lotion and tobacco. He made me feel special, made me feel miserable and, as the years went on, made me feel old. That's the way it is with fathers. Somewhere, somehow, they disappear, and all memories float unattached from the person himself, so that as I sat on the bed and looked into his eyes, I could not think what to say. But it was my father who needed to speak.

"I want you to get to know Tina," he said, with a strained look on his face. Tina was my father's girl friend of two and a half months. "The more you know her the more you'll like her."

I lied with great cheerfulness and replied that I had heard about her (which was true) and knew she was very nice (which wasn't true). I thought she sounded appalling and at least half the reason my father was in the Intensive Care Unit. But before my face could betray me, the five minutes were up, I returned to the hall and tried to get my bearings in this strange scenario.

For six days the hospital drama would take place with only one plaster wall dividing up the characters, who would move from one side to the other in varying emotional states. By eight o'clock that evening, everyone who mattered had arrived, and the family, for all intents and purposes, owned the joint.

There are six children. When John arrived, making little clicking noises in his throat to herald his arrival down the hall, we were complete. And God, it was a macabre way to have a family reunion, but as we slouched around on the plastic chairs, caught up with each other and made cracks about our appearances ("For criminy sakes, John, what's with this Fu Manchu moustache?"), I felt wonderful.

"I hadn't realized," I said at one point, "how lonely I have been for this." It was the sheer relief of being with a group of people, all of whom had the strongest bond of them all, blood, and among whom one could speak in a sort of genetic shorthand, all the references being the same. I must have felt this most of all, being the oldest, most advanced in life and the least known to everybody else there. We could thank my father for the reunion.

Each of us plays a different role with him, depending upon experience and temperament. Thus, I am forever causing my father to laugh, but rarely, if ever, do I attempt to drive any deeper. Some un-Rolfed muscle inside of me refuses to totally relax in his presence.

John has never felt psychically supported. The oldest son, the one for whom I almost had to forfeit my own chances to continue college because he was supposed to finish prep school and presumably support an expensive family, John didn't do any of these things. He lives on Stinson Beach, in a large wine barrel hauled down from Napa Valley, writes for a number of rock magazines, has published several books and is a loner. John and my father do not even laugh together. In fact, they don't do anything together, and it has always been a source of anger to my brother (who dedicated his first book to my father, who never read it) that there is no father-son connection. But he has learned not to show that anger, not out of fear but hopelessness. John is superficially cool, methodical, and rarely stays longer than a day, under any circumstances, when he visits.

Wendy, the next in line, has always been the most thoroughly involved with my father on an emotional level. It was a need which, during her adolescence, she wrenched out of him and, once the gift had been given, he was hers forever.

Wendy, in her late twenties, is a local television reporter and rather big news around the county. It doesn't take much to be famous in Salinas, although I have always thought that Wendy, once she really plugged into herself, could be famous anywhere. At one time I tried to make her give me the words and music to all the songs that she's composed over the years. Unfortunately, she forgets them almost as soon as they are composed, which I think has something to do with trying to disassociate herself from a rather frightening reserve of raw, powerful talent that might do her in if she's not careful.

Cindy, who was born eleven months after Wendy, is emotionally straightforward, unanalytical and easily persuaded to love regardless of the circumstances. Over the years she has confided in her father, turned over her ever-expanding love life for his startled inspection, and theirs is as simple a relationship as the water-bearer to a soldier. She is somewhat unsure of herself, except as pertains to her really quite fabulous body. "Pure mesomorph," somebody once said about her, which isn't nice and isn't even accurate, but at least it's something.

Peter graduated from high school and hustles orders for a local liquor store in Carmel. He is perhaps the best loved in the family, a frail boy who enrolled in a body-building program that turned him into a mountain of muscles which can barely fit through the door. Like John, he has never felt a strong bond with his father, although physically Peter is so similar, with the crinkly eyes, sideways smile, and the odd, identifying gait that I too share which sets all of us at a forward tilt as we walk down the street. Peter is the shyest, quite possibly the funniest member of the family. Tears spring to his eyes easily. He can imitate almost anyone except himself, and there is about him a halting, everyman kind of vulnerability that has always caused all of us to cherish him like a wonderful secret that can't be told outside the family.

He once asked me, after several clearings of his throat as

we walked along the beach on one of my trips home, whether I could recommend some good books for him to read. "On what subject?" I asked. "Oh, anything," he said. "I don't know about so many things except muscle-building, and I know that muscle-building is a lot of crap." I was too stunned by his humility to give much of an answer. Periodically I get postcards from Peter saying, "Greetings from here. I feel that we've met sometime before," or "Hi—thought I'd drop a line to say I love you. Pete." Peter doesn't talk much, but he packs his words with significance. In this he is unlike the rest of us, the motor-mouths who used to compete at the dinner table for time. John sometimes began a dissertation seated and would wind up standing, with one foot on his chair, like a professor. "Please, John," my mother used to say, "just the gist. I can't look at anyone this long."

As for Tony, the baby in the family, he was a curly-headed toddler, hanging onto the sleeve of an old man when the rest of us had already gone away. Tony has weathered the greatest number of storms between my parents, and because there wasn't the energy left to bring him up properly, Tony has brought himself up—right or wrong. At fifteen, he has his own job, a secret bank account, a telephone and charge cards. His comic book collection, which he hauls to Los Angeles once a year to chat it up with the dealers, is going to put him through college. He still sleeps with the same baby blanket I remembered him using as an infant.

"God, Tony," I expostulated one night, "that thing is disgusting." Tony smiled in agreement, curled his chin up under the rotten-looking rag and said, "I know. One whiff of the thing knocks me out."

Several years ago, while visiting the family, I overheard a conversation about me between Cindy and Tony who were doing the dishes together. "Do you think of your sister as your sister or just a good friend of the family's?" Cindy had asked. Well, that was sometimes how I felt. There was so

much time and distance between me and the rest. My school-
ing was different, I was married, a mother, used vocabulary
words that sprang from a classical education, and I had missed
the pot scene by a mile. Worse, I had missed it by choice. I am
sure I come across as a relic in Westminster Abbey much of
the time, and I have always felt that, by virtue of being the
oldest, I was a little feared and perhaps not loved very much
at all.

But the circumstances of this reunion pushed most of these
thoughts to one side. We were together. We had our father
to attend to, and as we huddled together on that first evening
in the waiting room, all six of us united behind my father, I
couldn't recall when I had ever felt more integrated. It was
like being a member of a club that, by definition, couldn't
admit anybody else. Which naturally led the conversation to
the subject of Tina.

Half of us had never met her. The other half filled us in.
She had met my father professionally several years before my
parents separated. No connections had been made. But then,
after my father had moved out of the house, Tina had tried
to get a job at Operation Brown Bag, and had come to him
for advice.

"As you can see," she had said, gesturing at her resumé,
"I'm overqualified."

One thing had led to another.

Tony aped her mannerisms, Peter her voice, Wendy her
total impact. Between them they spun out a portrait of a
thirty-one-year-old neurotic, talkative, pushy woman who had
my father wound around her little finger. She was due to
arrive at any minute, children being no apparent obstacle to
her self-fulfillment and I was seized with the fear that I
would do or say something extremely rude. "Keep her away
from me," I said. "I really don't trust myself."

That morning, according to Wendy, Tina had gone into my
father's room and emerged sobbing. "He was talking about

what he wanted to wear for his funeral." Wendy grabbed her by the shoulders and sat her down hard on the chair. Obviously the crying had started in Dad's room, and the thought of his heart and what Tina might do to it frightened her.

Tina had not only gone to pieces but was proud of it, as if that proved her attachment to our father. In fact, she indirectly criticized Wendy's sharp, contained cheerfulness as being inappropriate, given the circumstances. Tina was a threat.

"She's entirely capable of repeating that performance," said Wendy. "If I have to," she added, "I'm going to ask Dr. Frost to keep her out of Dad's room." Tina made Wendy mad, and as we waited for her to arrive, the rest of us got mad too.

After Tina had emerged from the "What shall I wear at my funeral?" conversation, Wendy had told Dad that she wouldn't be allowed in if she carried on that way. "She's been awfully nice to me," protested my father, "in the last couple of months." But Wendy saw that she tired him enormously, and with the family now in full force, or nearly so (my mother was in Santa Barbara, on another level altogether), Tina was about to be mooted.

"Let her down as gently as possible, will you?" said my father, almost asleep. That had been a sign to my sister that Tina was a friendship that didn't fit into the present situation. We were to be proven wrong.

Tina arrived like the exaggerated fulfillment of her description. I did not get up, and was aware that I was making her uncomfortable, but something perverse inside of me wanted her to get just that impression. Maybe she would go away. But regardless of her unpopularity—and she must have sensed that we were less than thrilled to have her in the bosom of the family—Tina fluttered around, asking for the latest medical news, making small talk about a plant she had brought and did we all see the cards that she had arranged along the windowsill in Dad's room?

Oh yes, we certainly did see the cards—all fourteen of them inscribed with ha-ha messages like "Time Flies When You're Having Fun," or the other variety, with Kahlil Gibran verse pressed against a dime-store sunset. I couldn't imagine my father, who had brought us up on Thurber and Peter Arno cartoons, receiving any of them without laughing. But then I couldn't imagine my father with another woman, especially this one.

She was a redhead, with good legs and a manner of dressing that set her smack into the Debbie Reynolds-Janie Powell school of femininity. Swinging pleated nylon skirt, stockings, very high heels. Her hair bounced on her shoulders and was obviously rolled up every night. As for her face, it was older than it should have been, there was too much makeup on it, and her eyes, which were blue and brimming with conflict, had a way of sliding away toward the ankles of the person she was talking to. My mother is small. Tina was nearly five feet eleven, if I judged her height correctly from my position sitting down. Looking up at her, as she flung her red hair nervously from one side to the other, she came across as complicated, nervous, high energy and riding a wave of emotion that caused us all to line up like a brick wall against her.

"Oh, I couldn't get here fast enough tonight," she said, "and your *father*, God love him, and He *does*, just *must* get better. Why I was so overtaken with how *important* he is—well, I just scrawled this out at a stop light, and I think it says what I *know* we are all feeling here tonight."

She plucked a piece of paper out of her purse and shoved it into my lap to read. "Your father," it began (in real ink, Palmer-method handwriting), "will live in my heart forever, and in the hearts of thousands."

I felt hysteria burping up in my throat, but I nodded as solemnly as I could and handed it on to Wendy, who handed it on to Peter and so on down the line. Tina waited, watching us with semi-lowered eyes. She had, she thought, mousetrapped us into approval. "That's nice," said John, the last to read the note. "You ever done much writing?"

By the end of the evening, we knew about everything Tina had done. It was true, she was the most overqualified human being in Monterey County. But in between listing the courses she had taken, the degrees she had possessed and the other various ways in which she had sought to nonstop improve herself in life, we were given a fairly clear picture of what the last several months, just before my father's heart attack, had entailed.

"We went everywhere your father had ever been in his whole life," said Tina. And so they had. His old hometown, the Berkeley campus, all our previous houses that we had bought high and sold low in San Francisco and Marin. They had dined at old restaurants he loved, played music that had always gotten to him, and my father had probably eaten more gourmet meals in three months than in the forty years he had been married. In fact, I'm sure of that. My mother cooks with her mind on other things.

"He would telephone me up at two in the morning," Tina reminisced, "just because he wanted to talk." That was just one example of Tina's tastelessness, her inability to comprehend that we might not really want to hear every detail of their personal life. But hear it all we did—there was no way to shut her up—and it did give me a picture that might not have been communicated if Tina hadn't been such a wide-mouthed jar.

It crossed my mind, but did not linger long enough to lodge there, that beneath the buckshot chatter, Tina was begging for entrance into our midst. The story beneath her story which she was pleading for us to reverence was that she cared deeply for my father, no strings attached, with every molecule in her being. We were the judges, to whom she was hostage, weighing her story, receiving the data, and being asked to grant her legitimacy, which she could not bestow upon herself. I did not want to be in that position. Sitting in my chair I shifted uncomfortably as if to avoid making the connection Tina was bent upon forging. I could not absorb Tina into my system that fast. Yet she was hammering away at the bars, trying to get through to all of us. "Please" was the subtext beneath her spoken words, "accept me for who I am." I should have recognized that plea. It has so often been my own. But I was silent. For many confusing reasons. Tina, not knowing how to fill in the blanks, kept on talking.

"He remembers everything," she breathed adoringly, "about you children, and oh, how he loves each and every one of you."

How lonely he must have been, I thought. The idea of my father telephoning Tina night after night from his rented bungalow to talk about his life tugged at me. The separation from Mother had done that. He had been displaced, without props or body heat to define him, and he had used Tina like a tape recorder, spilling his life into her ear in a desperate attempt to tell himself that he still existed. Tina would mirror his experience, exclaim over it, tie it all together for him again. But the strain of trying to get it all down was too much. There had been signs, even before his heart attack, that he was not well.

Two weeks before his heart attack, Mother had called me. She knew about Tina and had found within herself a surprising well of jealousy and grief. Of course, she knew that she had engineered the separation and had considered the possibility that Dad might find a woman. But she had hoped for more. Specifically, that he would not find it so difficult to tolerate himself as himself. "He came over on Easter Sunday with a present, and he looked so tired, with the look of a man who wanted to be handed his pipe and slippers." That was Mother's premonition. Tina supplied others.

"He started to go back to the Catholic Church," she began to weep. (My family had had a mass conversion at one point that didn't take.) "Going to Mass every morning. He told me that he was tired of his body, that he wanted to die." Her voice trailed off, she put her face into her hands, and I realized something new. She really did care about him. I just didn't know how to fit that knowledge into everything else.

My feelings for my father took on new strength. I wanted to protect him from Tina, from himself, from death. And as she talked on through the night ("He lived the history I only studied," she said dramatically at one point), I had a great desire to sneak into his room, insert myself beneath his shoulders and cradle him through the night. It had been such a hard and lonely time for him.

All of us sat in the plastic, sweating chairs, captive to Tina's relentless enthusiasm for telling about "the relationship." I tried to cut her off at one point by directing the conversation toward the future.

"You have a lot of energy," I said obliquely, "and a long life ahead of you that will be full of challenges." (Let her interpret that in the most positive way.)

Tina's mouth trembled, she caught her lower lip with her teeth, and a fresh sob welled up in her throat. "Oh, please don't tell me that I've done anything wrong. I've already been hurt so much in my life."

I was taken aback, both because she had caught the message so fast and because suddenly she became a little girl curled up on the couch asking me to stay my hand, not to hit her. I felt ashamed. I hadn't meant to evoke that reaction. I changed my course.

"I know it's been very hard for you," I said slowly.

"You don't know how hard," she flung back. "To see him bouncing across the street only yesterday morning, waving to me and saying he'd meet me for lunch, and the next minute to get a call saying he's in the Intensive Care Unit—almost dead."

I was suddenly squarely on Tina's side, a yank that took

27

place against my will many times before I was done.

"It wasn't just a . . . small relationship," she continued. "I mean," she continued, new tears filling her eyes, "it was wall-to-wall joy."

Peter turned his head to the wall, Cindy stared at her with incredulity, John sprang from his chair and loped toward the coffee machine. I couldn't believe what I was hearing.

"Wall-to-wall" was, I later discovered, one of Tina's favorite expressions.

Within the week I found myself, with Tina, in Dad's Carmel Valley bungalow packing away his things for wherever he would be living after he came out of the hospital. Moving between the rooms, inventorying what had to be packed, thrown out, defrosted, given away, it didn't seem real. These were my father's things, up to and including an untidy wad of checks. I couldn't place them in this context, but Tina was bent upon giving them the context I lacked.

"I really love to cook, and your Dad just adored everything I fixed for him. One night it would be a Russian feast, the next night I'd fix him an Italian spread, and—here, see this cookbook that gives you menus by country—we would have wall-to-wall gourmet meals every night of the week."

Tina had a way of describing things that put me in the position of having to be perpetually grateful, whatever the reason.

". . . and how he loved to dance. I had a whole collection of Guy Lombardo LP's, dance music of the forties; you know, the Glen Miller things that your father remembered from back then. After dinner"—her voice swayed a little at the memory—"we'd put on a record and we would dance to them. Did you know I am a professional dancer?"

It was terribly embarrassing, for me and for my father. I didn't want to know about these things, which is generally how I felt about everything Tina spoke of, yet she would not stop, and when I tried to impress upon her, by my silence, my face, my generally flaccid way of responding, that this was very tacky of her to be carrying on, she responded by carrying on further.

Tina became reabsorbed in the packing, pacing quickly back and forth between boxes, overseer of the relics within. She did not, I intuited, really want me there at all. My presence diluted the strength of her memories, like an open window that lets the perfume out. She would snatch at things as I picked them up, as if to give them their primary definition before my hands wiped the definition away.

"Your father loved to look at his scrapbooks," she said, coming up behind me as I flipped through a stack of old leather books on the windowsill. Mother had said that Dad was quite definite about taking all of them, even those of her family in New York, when they separated. Yes, there we all were—riding tricycles, assembled around the Gallwey table at 36 Presidio Terrace for Christmas dinner, hanging over the edge of the infamous Chris Craft that my father bought, moments after John and I had landed scholarships to high school.

Mother had almost divorced him for that bit of fiscal dishonesty. My father and money—one never knew when he would zig-zag into an Austin-Healey dealership and emerge with a new car to pep up his commute. When he pulled into the driveway, the kid with a new toy, my father never did make the connection between yesterday's scholarship and today's impulse buy. In fact, the scholarship freed up a little cash that wouldn't have been available otherwise.

I walked into the closet and surveyed his clothing. The old tan corduroy sport coat, leather buttons hanging off the sleeve, was the only reminder of the Austin-Healey days. He had finally sold that car. ("Owner forced to sell. Leaving for east," the ad had said.) "What do you mean 'the east'?" I had asked. "The East Bay," he answered. "What's the real reason you're selling it?" I asked. "I'm tired of waving to other Austin-Healey drivers," he replied.

I pressed one sleeve of the jacket against my face and wondered whether he would ever wear it again.

"Your father," called Tina, now in the kitchen, "loved to have me come over and clean. Honestly, I would break my neck sometimes three times a day trying to get from Pacific Grove to here and back again." "Look," she commanded, "it must have taken me three solid days to get the inside of this oven back to where it should be."

"Very nice," I forced myself to say.

"You have no idea the energy I've put into this place," she sighed. "He just didn't know how to take care of himself." She stared down at the linoleum and said softly, "I must have scraped four years worth of old wax off these floors before it would take a new coat."

("I think," my father had once said acerbically, "that your mother is perfectly capable of walking by a banana peel on the living-room rug for a week without thinking to pick it up.")

This high-kicking, gourmet-cooking, floor-waxing paragon was total woman, every man-child's dream. "They deserve each other," I thought. It was Mother, silently picketing for love with the banana peel as her symbol of defiance, who deserved more. But as I left the apartment, an antique silver bowl, which used to sit in the middle of our dining-room table, caught my eye in a flash of sun.

It looked entirely out of place, sitting on the window ledge in a month-by-month rental. Had my father taken it to remind him from whence he had come? I did not know, but it reminded me of many things—the countless times I had polished it and set it back between the candlesticks in the dining room, where we had all sat around the table, exulting over nothing, reading bad birthday poems, urging my father to tell jokes that he picked up at the office which weren't clean enough, he claimed, to repeat. We had had an enormous amount of fun as a family at that table around that bowl. But now it was displaced, like my father—two originals without an environment.

I felt unutterably sad.

"Hi."

"Hi."

Six A.M. I awoke in my plastic chair outside my father's room in the lobby to look into the eyes of a tall string bean with a buzz cut and a holster on his hip.

"He's okay. I just checked with the nurse," he said.

Cindy, who kept vigil with me many nights during that week, stirred underneath her pea jacket and opened one eye.

"You mean my father?" I asked.

"Uh huh," he said. "I spent the night inside the unit. Got a guy in there I have to guard."

I squinted out the window. It was sunup in Salinas, the sky a fogless pale blue. "Who are you?" I asked.

"I work out of Soledad, a corrections official. One of the prisoners—just a young dude—has a heart problem. So we've got to guard him while it's being checked."

His name was Nick Jones, which just about sums him up. While Cindy and I had slept away—I was determined to stay like a guard dog for as long as it took for my father to get well—he had obviously seen Cindy curled up like a young stallion on the chair and resolved to make a closer inspection the next morning.

He sat down between us and slid his eyes over Cindy, who even half-asleep instinctively rearranged herself to accommodate this new development, and waited for us to introduce ourselves.

Cindy is long, lanky, dark skinned, and even with her hair uncombed and no Ultima II on her face, is rather sensational to look at. This Nick Jones, who was not overly bright, still knew right off. What he didn't know is that Cindy is also incredibly sweet natured, and I found, after spending a week with her, that I had failed to notice a certain subtle humor that had not gotten enough room to display itself before. That made me feel good about Cindy, and since I had already conquered the body question (hers was better), I felt at ease with her as never before.

Cindy used to worry that she was adopted. Then she turned to worrying about maintenance. All things considered, which was what Nick Jones was doing, it was worry well spent.

On the other hand—looking at Nick Jones looking at Cindy—would I really want a prison guard giving me the eye? Not really, although to Cindy's credit she was not exactly overwhelmed either. But Cindy has always taken a very practical view of men. Nick Jones had a car. We were hungry. Let's not project things beyond that immediate reality.

Cindy's penchant for taking life as it presents itself, versus mine for extending it to the nth degree of infinity, has produced two very different sets of lives. Cindy has run out of fingers on which to count her conquests. I am still staring at my index finger. Cindy analyzes at the end of a relationship; I can take a smile and weave the most extraordinary tapestry in my head, anticipate every beach, bed and complication, and decide that it isn't worth it. We went for coffee.

Nick Jones, speaking slowly, told us about his entire life, which was not large, over pancakes: High-school graduate, spent some time in "Nam," a prison guard for two years, married, lives in Prunedale, one child, owns a water bed.

This last bit of private information didn't surface for several days. But Cindy brings out this kind of detail in a man, and at the time it was a comfort, as was Nick, who found a way to install himself as day and night guard over his prisoner, once it became evident that Cindy needed him to see her through the large and small "setbacks" that my father suffered during the time he was there.

We never knew from one hour to the next whether my father was mending or deteriorating, but it became axiomatic to expect that soon after Tina left his room, the cardiogram would change. One night, after Tina had spent a half hour inside his room and left the hospital with tears in her eyes, my father sank into alarming fibrillation. We were helpless in the hall, and Cindy—who had been three days and nights outside the door with me—broke into tears of frustration.

Nick materialized from nowhere, put his arms around her shoulders and walked her down the corridor, whispering into her ear. I watched the two of them from the plastic chair where I sat and felt the now-familiar burp of hilarity rising in my throat. Cindy being comforted by a Soledad Prison guard, who was murmuring about how he and his wife (who wore flannel nightgowns) had an open marriage, and would she like to go scuba diving in Pacific Grove sometime? The back rubbing, the sensuality, the mix of grief and appease-ment that flowed between them, the ecstasy of sorrow being milked for what it was worth were a triumph of flesh cooper-ating with the spirit. I flipped through the pamphlets on the table, feeling like a librarian with nowhere to fix my eyes.

Riffling through the literature, something caught my atten-tion. Between the *Modern Maturities*, some loose *THOTS FOR THE DAY* provided by a charismatic preacher who made a run through the hospital once a day, was a little pamphlet entitled *Our Daily Bread*. The front of it was cov-ered with messages in small balloons. Tony's handwriting. I read them, one by one.

There were my message from Washington, Tina's number in Pacific Grove, John's phone in Stinson Beach. I gazed idly at the pamphlet and suddenly began to laugh. In one space was my message from Washington, sent, I remembered, with frantic insistence that it be delivered at once. "Don't do a goddamn thing . . . the troops are coming." Tony had got-ten the message exactly right.

I had felt desperate at that moment. I couldn't get on the plane fast enough. For after I had talked with Wendy and tried to assess how serious it was, she had told me that Dad had taken her hand in his and said with tears in his eyes, "It's so good to have the family here." That was all I needed to crack open my heart and let all that emotion out. I packed and took the next flight.

But in another circle on the pamplet was a message from Mother, who had been poised for flight to Santa Barbara with her spiritual guru the night of the attack: "Don't call before 6 A.M.," read Mother's note, "even if news is the worst."

The two messages fractured me.

"Mother," I had accused her some days later, "what do you mean, don't call before six A.M.?" Mother had defended herself. "Rose Kennedy said nobody needs bad news before six A.M. You need your sleep to be able to deal with it." We were different this way. I have always been prone to vaunting my sleeplessness as proof of my caring.

Flipping the pamphlet over to its back side, I saw the smiling face of the reverend who had authored the pamphlet. Over his head, Tony had drawn a cartoon bubble which read, "Hi, I make $150 grand selling these things . . . you'd be smiling too." I slipped the pamphlet into my pocket and grinned at the wall.

We were not the only people who kept vigil outside the Intensive Care Unit. Others came and went, sitting in chairs about the room, in various stages of shock and sadness. One woman, the housewife I had noticed the first day, was a psychic from San Luis Obispo, who would slump with her face staring into her lap, only to raise her eyes whenever I sat down beside her to tell me something else about myself.

"You're the oldest of six children," she said once.

"Have you ever had your pancreas checked?" she asked out of nowhere another time.

"You don't live here, do you?" she queried once again.

I never did get her name, but she spooked me and I kept my distance. Her eyes would follow me, all-knowing, all noncaring, as I paced around the lobby, until finally her husband inside died. "I knew he would," she said, unemotionally. I began to think that she had been praying for just that to happen. But my sister Wendy, who can pull her heart to attention within seconds, put her arms around her and said, "Oh, I know how awful you must feel. Please accept my sympathy."

"You're a Gemini, aren't you?" said the psychic.

"That's right," said Wendy. "How did you know?"

She smiled, pulled her shoulder bag over her arm and gazed at her with Rosicrucian certainty. "I was born knowing," she whispered. "Like about Ralph . . . but he wouldn't go to the hospital until it was too late."

I was glad when she didn't have a reason to come back anymore.

Several times a day a beady-eyed reverend would slink down the corridor, look balefully at us slouched around the lobby and say, "I encourage you to pray." We never paid any attention to him, and the reverend was probably right to keep right on going out into the parking lot. But he wasn't the only minister who worked the Intensive Care Unit.

The Reverend Billy Celery came through daily, and I must say that he was full of pep, which compensated for the peplessness of the poor souls he counseled. Usually Celery brought his wife, a nondescript lady in a one-button coat, who would stand to one side with an index finger laid against her nose as if this put her in touch with some kind of understanding that would disappear if she took her finger away. Her prime function was to nod.

"We were nobody [nod from wife]," said Celery to a man who was sitting dejectedly against the far wall. "But the Lord put us in the ministry, and we're still nobody [nod from wife] but now we know Somebody."

"That's right," agreed the man in the chair, apparently a parishioner of Celery's. "Know what you mean."

"And now," continued Celery, "I can feel a revival coming up. Yes, and this radio program out of Santa Cruz that the Lord led me to lead, why I'm talking to people who don't believe and stuff? But praise Jesus, what kinds of stories are called in!"

"That's right," nodded his wife.

"Why," exclaimed Celery, "there was a man who cut his finger so bad that the blood was going to gush him to death. To *death*! But the power of God stopped the blood. The doctor, he just looked, but this man, he told me over the radio phone, that the power of God had stopped it. It was a time to uplift the name of the Lord."

"Of course, I've seen cases worse than that," continued Celery, competing with himself. "I've seen people rise from the dead."

"Of such is the kingdom of Heaven made up," added his wife.

"That's so," said the fellow in the chair.

Celery was an enthusiastic man, filled with the joy of knowing what he was for, which was to talk about himself without forgetting the Lord who had made it possible.

"He didn't send me to school to change my vocabulary," he said, "but to preach the gospel."

"We don't care about our house," added his wife. "We've got our treasure laid out in Heaven."

"Oh, you start talking about Heaven and heavenly things," moaned Celery, "and I'm gone. Kings and priests and all. . . ." Celery's voice slid skyward with emotion. "Won't it be wonderful?"

Yes, he guessed it would be, nodded the man, tapping a Marlboro out of a package and looking into space.

"I know that all the prayers that all of us has prayed has helped people," Celery went on. "But the hand of the Lord does the healing."

"For sure," said his wife, rubbing her nose.

36

". . . and the Spirit can walk right through that door," Celery continued. "Lord, we pray [everybody in the group bowed to the new tone of voice] for these things to be done. I know what You can do, Lord, and if we haven't growed that far in the Lord, I know that we should commit our ways unto You."

"Psalm thirty-seven," footnoted his wife.

"Bless the Lord, and forget not all his benefits."

"Psalm one hundred and three," said his wife.

"For every valley, there's a mountain on either side," whispered Celery. (I wondered from my side of the waiting room whether they had rehearsed this together in the car coming over.)

"I heal broken hearts," said Celery after a moment of silence.

". . . if you will just give me the pieces," completed his wife.

At this point the man in the chair was dropping into his own lap, as respectful as all get out to be the object of so much pastoral concern. Celery paused, checked his watch surreptitiously and lifted his head.

"Thank you, Jesus," he breathed, and it seemed to me that this was a sincere thought. "Like I say," he smiled radiantly at the man in the chair, "I feel a revival coming up." And then they left, presumably to hook their divine wattage into Radio Santa Cruz, where Jesus was on the telephone at that very minute.

After the second full day and night standing watch outside the locked door of the Intensive Care Unit, I knew that I had to leave the hospital if only to open my suitcase and put on some clean clothes. It was not my father that needed watching, but Tina—who was ever ready to dart in when one of us wasn't looking, fill up my father's room with excessive emotion and leave, mission accomplished.

He suffered one "setback" the night after our arrival, which coincided with the time that Tina announced to him that his family hated her. We doubled the guard at the door and informed the doctor that he ought to forbid her to come.

Dr. Frost, a youngish, competent professional who was not used to such pyrotechnics in the waiting room of the Intensive Care Unit, grew increasingly irritated with this situation. In charge of my father's health, he was petitioned at every turn by emotionally keyed-up family members with an agenda that changed with each passing hour. Finally, in frustration, he said, "I'm not a psychiatrist. If I have to take much more of this, I'm getting off the case." Dr. Frost was right to be irritated. It was soap opera with a very sloppy script.

My father, who wouldn't say what he wanted, was sending mixed signals every chance he could get. On the one hand, he said he just wanted to sleep and that it comforted him to know that we were outside. No particular mention of Tina. Yet one evening, when we were all sitting in the waiting room, a frantic flurry and buzzing could be heard on the other side, and suddenly one doctor raced down the hall, slapped open the door and disappeared inside. We jumped up, peered through the glass porthole, and as we had feared, at least a half-dozen staff members were crowding around my father. I was frantic and began to buzz the intercom.

Several minutes later, the doctor who had raced in came walking out, a disgusted look on his face. "We may have to move him," he said. "Or move *somebody*."

Tina had apparently tapped on the outside window on her way into the hospital, my father had woken up, and in an impetuous mood had ripped himself away from all the monitors and tubes and was standing by the window, waving at her. Every alert system in the unit, and several more in the hospital at large, had immediately gone off.

That incident, plus the time she jumped up and did a cancan on the retaining wall outside his room, was enough for us to be thoroughly and consistently alarmed. But there came a time when I just couldn't be responsible for the effects of Tina on my father's cardiogram any longer, and I went to Mother's house in Carmel—on the day that Mother arrived back from Santa Barbara.

She was in the kitchen, and looked better than I had seen her in a long time. She had gained at least fifteen pounds, the lines had disappeared from her face, she seemed rested and happier than I've ever seen her. She was a disciple of the inner life, had been for some years, and some time ago I had confessed that on the East Coast it was possible for me to feel wise and spiritual. On the West Coast, with Mother, I realized what a deep-down fraud I was.

"I'm still in the world, Mom," I had said. "I have to come to terms with that, and it seems as if I'm not yet done with my involvement. Not scooped out enough to receive certain cosmic truths."

Nobody outside the family would know what the hell I was talking about, but Mother did and thought that I was right where I was supposed to be, cosmically speaking.

We sat in the kitchen, and I talked about Dad, omitted Tina and tried not to get into the terrible problems we were having, as the children, guarding Dad against his own excesses. Mother was visibly upset. She knew I was walking way around the problems of one central character in order to keep her from having to deal with them. But she saw no role that she could play. "He did not want me to see him," she said. "No," I countered, "that was a mix-up of communication, he does want to see you. Dad said that the nurse got the message wrong." Before my father left the hospital, Mother did visit him, while Cindy and I kept a sharp eye out for Tina, who always came when we least expected her. The thought of my mother meeting Tina in the hallway was too appalling even to contemplate.

It was a brief, gentle visit, and should not have taken place under those circumstances. Such familiarity cannot be severed between two people who have lived forty years together. Yet when my mother came out of the room, she said very little. The forty years had exhausted her. There didn't seem to be anything left to donate that wasn't already gone. "Poor dear," she said quietly, gathering up her coat. "He is so, so tired."

And he was—not just from having had a heart attack but from being the center of so much emotional friction. Yet toward the end of my stay, I got weary of being a turnstile, interpreter and guard dog. Oddly enough, it was my Aunt Irene, who finally did come once to the hospital, who fingered the villain.

On one of the countless trips into the room, where I was trying to get my father to think clearly about where he would like to live once he was finally, hopefully better, I emerged back into the hall in complete frustration. He wanted Tina to be with him, and yet where would that be? And would he like a rest home? But perhaps they wouldn't let Tina in to visit. And yes, she was hard on him, and no, he didn't want to suffer a second heart attack, but yes, he needed her, and— finally, I had excused myself from the room.

My aunt listened to this report, pursed her lips and said quietly, "I think you have to realize that your father has got us exactly where he wants us—in the palm of his hand."

I looked at my father's sister, the youngest of two sisters who had adored him all their lives, and was shocked. I did not expect such an unsympathetic statement from that quarter. My aunt Irene had been boiling over the obvious connection between Mother separating from my father and the heart attack that had followed. She was, of his two sisters, the most blindly protective, fighting his battles, worrying over his eccentricities and collapsing helplessly before his humor. Yet often when I least expected her to make an incisive statement, she did. This was one of them.

Of course, I thought! My Aunt Irene was right. We were all part of a performance, directed by and starring my father.

Three months of loneliness were being royally compensated for with a week of totally focused attention. All of us—my brothers, sisters, aunts, uncles, Tina, Mother, the doctors—were the supporting players, dipping in and out of his room, receiving messages, clashing against each other and generally providing the drama that fed my father's need to wrench reality back into the shape that had disappeared.

I blinked hard, felt an enormous responsibility slip from my shoulders and knew that it was time to go back East. Walking back into his room, I saw someone I had not seen for a long time. My grandmother. Slack with sleep, he was a wintry replica of his own mother. Do we all, at the end, sink into the bones of the generation before us? I did not know, but my father had exhausted me. If he wanted to die, I would not try to stop him anymore. I released control of his spirit to more skillful hands, kissed him softly so he would not wake up and left the room.

The plane took off over the Pacific, making one quick loop above San Francisco before heading back East. I was relieved to be up in the air again, where I could cultivate my overviews at 37,000 feet and search for truth. But all truth was eluding me, except for the suspicion that my grandmother had reincarnated herself in my father's body. I wouldn't put it past her. But what kind of a truth was that? It had been a hard, confusing week. Overviews were coming hard, although I did notice absentmindedly that the ocean looked rather like the skin on the back of my wrist. But what did that mean? My usual enthusiasm for making macromicrocosmic comparisons was gone.

I do not remember all that I thought about on that trip back East. Perhaps I was too tired to think at all, but I had the distinct sense of fleeing from a disaster that would engulf me if I did not leave right away. My memories of a different family were stronger than the reality I had just experienced.

I clung to them, like the arms of my seat in the plane. How could this family of mine have fallen apart? Where did its dissolution leave me, if not out on a limb? In lieu of giving in to loneliness, I fell asleep, with no answers in mind.

The plane landed. Time passed. My father did not die. When the dust settled, the heroine of the piece was the one character in the drama that the rest of the family had tried ineffectually to keep off the stage, Tina.

At that time I saw her as a virus which had invaded the body of the family when all its defenses were down. Yet the plain truth of it—once I gained some emotional distance from the debacle—was that Tina had saved my father's life. Jumping, dancing, weeping Tina had willed my father back into existence—something I had not been able to do myself. That in itself was reason enough to resent her, although then I viewed her in only one way, as somebody who didn't belong in our family. God, did she not belong! On the other hand, when the family was just taking form, nobody did.

Chapter
II

We were an implausible family, even by California standards, the history of our gathering-up a story of sudden intuitions and cross-country romances that blossomed against the odds. But California encouraged that sort of thing. People who couldn't beat the odds anywhere else tended to gravitate there. And in the early 1930's, when the rest of the country was a scramble of dashed hopes, dwindling fortunes and ideas that wouldn't play, California was a last soil bank of possibility, tricking off different switches in different people's minds.

I used to chafe over the terrible lukewarm blandness of the environment, the relentless, low-slung dustiness of the state, which seemed to me to be a collection of walnut groves, gas stations and Spanish street signs with no class. But my back was to the poppies; I yearned for tall cathedrals, ignoring the absurd grandeur of mountains wet with sea. And I had to leave before I understood that California was, and is, a powerful piece of real estate—although my family came less for the gold than the golf courses, and while other San Francisco families rose to prominence on the strength of shipping, timber, hotels or sustained chicanery not detailed in the Social Register where their descendants now reside, my family seemed to rise almost in spite of itself.

My father's father, who died before I was born, was a gentle Lexington-born aristocrat who left Kentucky when he couldn't afford to pay his slaves, set up a pediatric practice in Oakland, and could never bring himself to collect his accounts, which made my grandmother, who was always short of hat money, furious. My great-uncle George married a Ghirardelli heiress, liked to sing dirty songs about the Mormons, which fractured me, and was distinguished by backing a rain-making machine that never worked and a brief chairmanship of the San Francisco Ballet. He told the press that under his direction he was "going to get all the pansies off the stage."

Uncle George was the only one of my grandmother's brothers I ever knew, although there were others, long dead, who used to run around San Francisco in fancy cars and gold rings, brilliant but brief flashes in the pan who were lawyers for the Southern Pacific, ran the U.S. Mint in Nevada, married Vanderbilt wives on the rebound and made a great deal of money, which they spent one day at a time, leaving nothing for probate at the end.

Taken as a whole, my family married into money more than making much on their own. They were emotional, high-powered, egocentric and full of style. Style came effortlessly to them, in thought, word and clothing, which was an artless jumble of scarves, pearls and muted one-of-a-kind colors that neither screamed nor could be ignored. The in-laws were attracted to my father and his two sisters like moths to a lantern, although I have always thought that were it not for the people who married in, the family could not have supported the burden of its own mysticism. Everyone depended upon everyone else. Even more, our dependence was leavened with delight.

When my grandfather died, he left a wife, two daughters, Irene and Dorothy, and a son, Jack. My father's two sisters were both beautiful, emotionally inseparable, and of marriageable age. Ed Gallwey, a Harvard flunk-out and part of a line of patent-leather aristocrats dancing around New York in the late 20's, didn't know he was going to marry one of them.

The son of an Episcopal minister in Newport, Rhode Island, Ed was fatherless at three, motherless at twelve and had been reared in his grandmother's old house by two aunts, who dutifully sent him to St. George's and Harvard, thinking he would turn out to be a handsome, methodical investment banker, which was a large possibility.

He was, and is, outrageously handsome, possessing the sort of face that Kodak wants for their advertisements. In fact, Kodak found him, and one afternoon while passing through Grand Central during a college weekend, I looked up at a giant neon billboard hanging over the lobby and there he was —the perfect yellow-cardigan-sweatered executive—laughing over the eighteenth tee at Pebble Beach, with the ocean behind.

But at nineteen, my future uncle was a dandy who had fled Cambridge for the wine, women and tea dances of Manhattan. However, after a year of that life, he felt soggy with fulfillment, was disgusted with himself and began to feel the backlash of his father's Episcopal ministry against the nape of his neck. "There must be more," he thought to himself, a sentiment that has probably filled up California with more people than any other single thought.

Without informing his aunts, he sewed a hundred dollars into the lining of his coat, took himself down to the docks and slipped aboard the Panama-Pacific *S.S. Manchuria*, which was bound for Cuba, San Diego and San Francisco. While the liner slipped beyond the harbor, my uncle rehearsed his story in the lavatory, and when he was discovered by the first mate, his lie was well worked out. The captain took one look at him and knew he had seen this sort of stowaway before.

My uncle pleaded drunkenness, seeing off a friend, the wrong boat, passed out, etcetera. The story didn't wash. Then my uncle switched to a deeper theme, that he was a moral bum in search of reconditioning and had always dreamed of going to California, where he could make amends for his foolish life.

That story didn't cut any ice either, but the captain admitted that two engine-room mates hadn't shown up for duty, and if my uncle was willing to work his way across the ocean, he could stay aboard. My uncle worked his passage, got off the boat in San Francisco, wired for his inheritance and within a short amount of time met my Aunt Irene—and proposed marriage.

At almost the same time, another young man met the other unattached sister, through Ed Gallwey who was working at the Crocker bank as a clerk. One of the other clerks in the bank was a Eugene von Teuber, the eldest son of a Czechoslovakian baron who had sent him to the United States to learn about engineering prior to taking over his inherited holdings. But Henry Ford's engineering school in New York City folded just as Gene arrived, and so he cast about to find a way to prolong his stay in the country. California provided it.

One of his father's friends, a count, lived in Burlingame, a plush, landed suburb south of San Francisco, which to this day has a kind of baronial, whipped-up European formality to it, the kind that Hearst went amok with in San Simeon farther south. The count invited Gene von Teuber to come for a visit, and, incorrectly assuming that he would be plunged into Cherokee territory, he accepted eagerly. He arrived on the same weekend that Charles Lindbergh was a houseguest.

46

California was not quite the hostile territory he had envisioned, and since he did not think that Czechoslovakia was forever, given the Nazi threat, he decided to stay. He got a job in the same bank with Ed Gallwey, was introduced to his fiancée's sister, my aunt Dorothy, and fell irretrievably in love.

There was one obstacle to surmount. The baron and baroness von Teuber wondered whether my aunt Dorothy was at least part Indian, and while my grandmother, who was an unjustifiable snob, was horrified at this slur, my prospective uncle devised a solution to the problem.

Renting a movie camera, he took it and his fiancée to the De Young Museum, which was the nearest thing to a castle that San Francisco offered. He then had a friend roll the camera while he and my aunt Dorothy walked graciously around the formal gardens, chatted against fake Doric columns and waved nicely into the camera. He developed the roll and sent it to Czechoslovakia without editorial comment. The baron and baroness were somewhat mollified and consented to the marriage.

Soon after his sisters were married, my father met my mother. Mother was sixteen when she was catapulted out West. A shy, athletic girl, the lost index card in an old New York family that was preoccupied with getting through the Depression and, ultimately, getting divorced, she was put on a train with a couple of tennis rackets and sent to visit her aunt, Marion Hollins, who had gone to California a decade before in the early 20's and had established something of a beachhead in California as a championship golfer and land developer.

Marion was a large, barrel-stomached woman who never married. Most men could not handle her energy, and the East was too small for her anyway. She had taken her inheritance and left for California, which had the kind of physical and mental room that she needed to operate in.

Marion was a big thinker and big-time investor, and within

several years of her arrival, she had collaborated with Sam Morse to lay out Pebble Beach and Cypress Point, two golf courses around which Morse flung up a number of villas, stone castles and stucco wonders that are now part of what is called "The Seventeen Mile Drive."

But Marion didn't think the weather on the Monterey Peninsula was awfully good for golf. There was too much fog for her taste, and so she went on to establish a competitive fiefdom, "Pasatiempo," where I spent my first childhood summers, which was a smaller, less-exclusive in the end, version of Pebble Beach, although not at the outset.

Marion designed "Pasatiempo" to be anything but common. There were golf courses, riding stables, tennis courts and polo fields, which, as the Depression set in, forced her to open up "Pasatiempo" to anyone with money who would build a house along the fringes of the land. But poor taste drove her wild, and she seemed to lead a life that alternated between lunching with Mary Pickford and driving around the golf course in her Franklin bellowing at golfers to "put your Goddamned shirt on."

I only knew Aunt Marion toward the end of her life, when some of her prodigious energy had run down and she would allow me to beat on her stomach, like a drum, when she was lying in bed—a beached walrus who laughed when I would ask her to inflate her stomach, which was the largest I had ever seen. But she was a great scrapbook collector, and I used to pore over those thick leather albums, which she willed to Mother when she died, and piece together her life, which had almost disappeared by the time I was old enough to know what was going on.

Brian Aherne, Walt Disney, Doug and Mary Fairbanks, "Wolo" the cartoonist (who always made pen-and-ink drawings in the guest book)—Marion cultivated Hollywood for excitement just as Hollywood cultivated Marion for her hospitality, and during the Depression, "Pasatiempo" was perpetually full of famous guests, who would motor up from Hollywood trying to forget that they didn't know where they were going to get ten cents for an apple.

A formidable woman who made and lost millions, Aunt Marion usually gambled her intuitions to good effect, her most dramatic success being the Kettleman Oil Fields which nobody believed had any oil except her. But after sinking all her capital 10,000 feet into the earth, she finally brought up a steady stream of black gold that oiled the rest of her investments, and it wasn't long before Uncle Kim, Marion's brother, came West as well, to get a desk job under Marion's auspices. Unfortunately, Kim had a drinking problem. It made him incapable of holding down any job. Yet he was charming, a good golfer himself, and entirely capable of showing up for a tournament in one of two capacities—as a player or a caddy, depending upon the state of his funds. Every once in a while he landed in jail.

"I could have sworn I saw Kim on a chain gang," remarked one of Marion's houseguests, "when we passed through Watsonville." Mother's family, which always existed on the fringes of my consciousness, was full of people like Uncle Kim, who ate dog food out of squash trophies and didn't give a good Goddamn where they would be tomorrow morning. When Marion died, Kim cried at the funeral, excused himself for emotional reasons early from the church, and when everyone else got back to Marion's house, Kim was gone, along with her silver, best golf clubs and all the monogrammed sheets. His need for drink money was constant. While Marion lived, she provided it. She was a generous soul.

Marion used to worry at the height of her success that people like Mary Pickford wouldn't have a place to go once the "talkies" took over the industry. As a hedge against the "talkies," she approached a rich landowner on the Big Sur and asked him if he would sell his 10,000 acreage, for which she had a brilliant idea.

The owner, a retired executive of the telephone company, was deeply attached to his property. But there were problems. He liked to drink as much as he liked to ride horseback through the wild hills. It was difficult, in bad weather, to get to a bar in Carmel or Monterey. In order to both ride and be close to his whiskey, he had hit upon the idea of importing cases of whiskey onto his property and having them hoisted up, by ropes, into various oak trees on the place. If he happened to be hit by a desire to drink when he was riding, all he had to do was look up. Unfortunately, his memory was so bad from drinking that he could never remember which trees had the bottles. When Marion approached him to buy the property, he had given up trying to find a solution and he sold out.

"Circle M," as she called it, was supposed to be a kind of Hollywood rusticana, the sort of place where Mary Pickford could have a bean farm or milk cows in the afternoon. But Marion could never figure out how to shave off the top of the mountains to make an airstrip. The shaggy, boar-infested Big Sur property defied her plans for a golf course. The idea wound up being filed as an interesting concept, and when Marion died, my father was forced to sell off the entire parcel for a dollar an acre. Her estate was so large that the judge who finally closed the case wrote a note to my father saying, "It might interest you to know that when this case started I was only ten years old."

During the litigation, my father came across a stack of identical form letters, printed on Aunt Marion's personal stationery, that captured her flair for doing business as well, I suppose, as for finally going under:

Gentlemen:

We have received your letter of the ＿＿inst and are somewhat surprised at its tone. Evidently, you do not understand our method of handling accounts.

When we receive invoices on the 30th of the month, we put all of them into a large hat, from which five lucky winners are chosen. But in the event that we have any more of your damn foolishness, your name will not even go into the hat.

Sincerely,

When my mother got off the train in San Francisco, Aunt Marion collected her up, and she was rapidly absorbed into a life of golf, tennis and sitting on the fringes of Marion's life, which somehow found room for Mother, who was a good golf player herself. She ran around after Aunt Marion in an old sweat shirt and pair of golf cleats, an ingenue who rarely wore a dress and didn't know that there was such a thing as guile, nail polish or a vial of perfume. Reared as a tomboy primarily by her father, who liked to go shooting in South Carolina, Mother was a primitive who took my father and his family by storm. They thought she was priceless.

Several months after her arrival, Marion threw a golf tournament and my father came down from San Francisco to be part of the competition. He took one look at my mother and was amused. He took several more looks and, on the strength of his initial amusement, and a little more, he proposed marriage. "I don't know whether it's the heat in this gas station where I'm writing this letter," wrote my father to Mother who was then back East again, "but do you think there could be something more between us than just friendship?" My mother was nineteen when she was married, my father twenty-six. The match was not considered particularly good by Mother's family, but they didn't stand in the way. They had other things on their minds, although I don't know what. But my father was a Californian, which was a strikeout in itself. Nobody had ever heard of him on Long Island, although in Mother's family, geography was quite relative. They didn't know anyone in Southampton either, and my mother, who had grown up largely ignored, was as much overwhelmed by the emotional richness of my father's family as she was by my father himself. The family were extremely close, a quality that was extremely absent in her own. Everyone put their arms around her, and she was, for many years, content within that embrace.

For a long time I never considered myself a member of any family but my father's, primarily because my mother rarely mentioned her own family back East. Every once in a while, a cousin or uncle would show up, flick cigarette ashes into their trouser cuffs, and drift off again, leaving me none the wiser as to what they were all about. But I didn't have any particular reason to puzzle them out. They lived elsewhere and didn't seem particularly fond of me. And fondness was what families were all about, a conviction that has not altered in my mind.

By 1939, the year I was born, a patina of familiarity, the overglaze of belonging to one family unit, had brushed against our collective features. Looking back at all the family photographs taken around the Christmas tree, holding candles, watching Uncle Ed carve in his tuxedo, we look as we indeed felt—fortunate. The snapshots catch this, even in black and white, which is just how I felt about everyone.

There was no one more dignified than my grandmother, merrier than Uncle Gene, more accomplished than my cousin Mimi, naughtier than my cousin John. My father was the funniest man on earth, my brother the most irritating, my two aunts, separately and together, the most beautiful and opinionated, my Uncle Ed the most responsible, and my mother . . . ? I don't have clear memories of my mother then. She was simply the left hip against the right side of my head, and there was about her a contained melancholy, even when she smiled.

Appearances are somewhat deceiving. In these family photographs we look positively Edwardian with stability. And for a long time, we had our cake and ate it too. We were conservatives with the ability to laugh, apart from the mainstream but entirely fulfilled by each other. In 1939, California had not totally embraced Emerson and the laid-back transcendentalism that suffuses the state now, but my family had already come to the conclusion, at least subconsciously, that California was a state of mind.

I grew up surrounded—by aunts, uncles, cousins and definition. We moved as a unit—apart only by necessity; and during the summer we were always together. Every June the whole family packed up and left San Francisco for "Pasatiempo." I was just one of the crowd. But even then, I was beginning to separate out.

Our parents slept inside. But we children, the half-dozen, bare-legged cousins who romped and roistered away the summer months under the hot California skies, slept outside in wall beds that pulled down on the edge of an inner brick courtyard.

During the day, the courtyard rattled with our noise, was strewn with napkins and watermelon seeds and bore up under our endless sandaled traffic. But at night, after the flotsam had been swept away, when we had been stuffed into flannel pajamas and put to bed, the courtyard became separate and peaceful again.

Lying under a pile of cotton blankets, I would watch the bricks slick over with frost, and the sky prick full of stars, and the oak branches that lined the edge of the courtyard blot their elbows against the dark.

Just before I slid into sleep, my cousin Tim in the next bed would spring forward, hurl his pillow to the ground and snap back upon his mattress, like a soldier saluting the rafters. It was a nightly prearrangement he had with himself, and when I asked him why, he answered disdainfully, "Spartans don't use pillows."

So, I thought, gazing at him with respect from the pillow

I had no intention of relinquishing, he will have a straight back when he grows up and I will not. I could feel my spine curl as I looked at him. I worried about growing up a hunchback if lockjaw didn't get me first. But my pillow softened the threat. I was far too Athenian to follow his example, and the hot blankets and cold air finally worked upon Spartan and Athenian alike until both of us passed separately into the same lukewarm kingdom of sleep.

My wall bed was nearest the door, which gave out onto the driveway in front of the summer house. When the sun cracked through the oak branches and laid bars upon my blanket, I would wake up and slide my head to the edge of the mattress and engage in my own ritualistic prearrangement, while Tim lay asleep. There was something I wanted to see, and every morning when I opened my eyes, the same small miracle presented itself.

"Cockleweeds" is their proper name, although I thought they looked like bumblebees quivering on harp wires, their papery husks dangling in a bright swarm, which trembled in the morning sun. They were golden, translucent, amazing sheaves of wheat. The light drove down the shafts of the stalks, making a cool fire of the dew that collected at the roots. My eyes would contemplate the cockleweeds without searching for the adjectives that even now elude me. I would simply hang off the mattress, staring at the sight, getting my bearings, not knowing why.

By afternoon they were only weeds again—dry, dusty things, which we crushed and bent and took away in splinters on the outside of our socks as we strode through them toward the road. But at night they would suck new strength from the moon, silently repair their broken parts; and the next morning there they would be again, straight, healed and shot with fresh fire. I would lie at the edge of my mattress, silently marveling at how this could happen.

Could it be, and this is the question of a speculative, un-marveling adult, that every human being is given a few sights like this to tide us over when we are grown? Do we all have a bit or piece of something that we instinctively cast back on when the heart wants to break upon itself and causes us to say, "Oh yes, but there was this," or "Oh yes, but there was that," and so we go on? What good is a patch of cockleweeds otherwise? I don't know, but that time in childhood when I burned like a new candle, exulted over hot heels on cool lawn and hurled myself down hills in sheer astonishment over the catapulting force of the slope—these first bits and pieces must have a purpose, like the grownups who allowed us to gather them.

The grownups, the skirted, trousered parents, aunts and uncles who brought us and fetched us from our games, were our casually loved servants. As we played and punched each other in the courtyard, they glided in with trays of water-melon and glided off again to sit amongst themselves and their own complexities. We plunged our teeth into the juicy trian-gles and shot the seeds from our dripping mouths onto the bricks. But beyond the circumference of our own seeds, we understood nothing.

If we heard them talking inside at night while we lay in bed, we didn't hear woe, or cries, or pain—only the soft strum of the syllables which made up the words. The meaning of the words was of no concern to us. The speakers were our mean-ing. And so our limbs stretched in the night until we passed beyond childhood itself, each of us unaware of the transition until it was accomplished.

That summer house isn't in the family anymore. We are all grown and scattered, like the cockleweeds which I used to thresh through my fingers and throw into the air. I still sleep with a pillow. I assume that my cousin still throws his on the floor. But it's something I always forget to ask him on those rare occasions when he passes through town and we have a chance to talk. But after the house is quiet and my children are asleep, we do what we always do, which is piece our way back to the beginning. But he never had the cockleweeds, so always we come to a different understanding of things.

Chapter

III

I was born innocent, or at least my nose was clean, and as it is with anything innocent, I was open to suggestion. The eye blinked. The mind reacted. The memory, with nothing old in it, began to keep files—crisp, slim folders of brand-new information. As I watched ants crawl over my fingers, cracked leaves along their seams, felt under fountain counters for gum wads, nothing was unworthy of my attention. I was a walking picture-taking machine, although it was an unconscious, sidebar activity, like childhood itself.

Childhood is a series of unreasonably sharp snapshots saved for no particular reason: a certain bird balancing upon a shingle, the blue mosaic tiles on a staircase, a lady whom I observed from a car window and decided, quietly, to remember. She was trudging up the backside of Clay Street. She wore a red coat. That's all I know about her, but for reasons I can't fathom I decided that I would never forget her. And I haven't. She lies anonymous and immortal in my mind, useless to everyone, including me.

Other memories—brief, plotless flashbacks—don't bear going into except to suggest that even before I was a year old I was my own archivist, collecting, collating and trying to get a fix on the world, which I saw as a case that I was supposed to crack. Everywhere there were clues: milk oozing from stinkweed, tar dripping from buckets, soft, untouchable mounds that my Aunt Dorothy carried over her beltline. There was a lot to integrate, and if I was born innocent, a debatable point, I was also born with a rather desperate desire to make sense of things. Ironically, I was born in San Francisco where, underneath a thin veneer of surface intelligence, sensibility has always prevailed.

A distinction should be made. San Francisco has changed hands. Even Union Square, where I used to stuff my gum wrappers into the hedges after a trip to the dentist, is different. A second row of teeth has sprouted behind the originals in the skyline. The streets seem full of homosexual waiters. There is a cuteness about the city, a manic decorator look that hasn't missed an alley. And where San Francisco once rode the coastline like a quiet lady in a white dress, she is shot full of hormones now, a divorcée in the process of running away with her act. Or so it seems to the visitor, and a visitor—hard as that is for me to accept—is what I am now.

There are still traces of the old personality—the green and yellow Muni buses crackling along their cables, the dusty, ramshackle palm trees that used to harbor pigeons in their fronds before pigeons were banned. But now Union Square is ringed with vendors who set up their Big Sur wares in front of I. Magnin's, and a lady in busted tennis shoes stamps her feet and says angrily to nobody in particular, ". . . and I just care about my freedom *more!*" An unravelment is taking place.

Yet the old sedate San Francisco, full of law-abiding Chinamen and children taking the cable car to catechism classes, is alive in my mind. The entire city would shift from gray to silver a dozen times a day. Gulls wheeled behind the ferry that chugged to Berkeley. Geraniums filled the air with sharp orange smells, and by nine o'clock my cousin Mimi in her crisp Burke's School middy would be behind her desk, my Aunt Irene would be calling Gump's about a soup tureen, my grandmother would be taking a pinch of agar-agar for her bowels, and Mr. Kornfeld would be yelling at his son Irving for letting me touch the Post Toasties display in the market.

Life was balletically slow. Men wore hats. "Stella Dallas" tried to figure out whether she could make it as a middle-aged woman in 1945, every morning on Mrs. Van Horn's radio, and it was a clean city with clean people in it. Or perhaps it was only the fog, which raked through San Francisco every morning like a gentle, cleansing absolution, that made it seem this way.

It swept across the bay during the night, over the Farallon Islands, filling up the parks, trickling down the white flanks of the eucalyptus trees, bouncing in white gusts across the sidewalk to put a sweat on my lunch box as I walked to school. The sun was the brightness that invariably followed, the smile after a brief weep, but oftentimes the two were so intersticed that driving across the Golden Gate Bridge, one would plunge into banks of blindness only to emerge seconds later into brilliant air. I used to think that the struts of the bridge itself were responsible, that they literally sliced the sun and fog into sections. But most of the time I didn't think about the fog at all. It simply existed—a cool, amniotic fluid that I breathed, walked through, and laid a clarifying wetness upon everything I examined from one day to the next.

At night the fog reentered the city, rolling down the street like a herd of wet sheep that brushed their sides against my bedroom window and moved silently toward the Embarcadero as I tried to go to sleep. The soft, regular moan of the fog horns organized my mind, divided the dark into sections, and warned the entire Japanese fleet (which I believed to be creeping steadily toward Fisherman's Wharf) to keep its distance. I was too young to fashion my own talismans, and I would go to sleep clutching a sound.

San Francisco was laid out, in my mind, very neatly. At one end was Presidio Terrace, where my two aunts and their families lived in a double household, a world unto itself which I visited whenever I had the chance. Four blocks away, a straight shot down Clay Street, was my house, or, rather, our flat, which my mother once described as being "across the street from the residential district," which was true. Across the street was full of rich, careful people who had electric garage doors, maids and appointments to keep. There was one zoning irregularity that allowed a music teacher with the fake name of "Marjorie Lane" to have a popular music studio in the upstairs part of her house, and "Cheeri-beeri-bim" and "Flying Trapeze" used to strain through an open window as piano students, anxious to keep up with the times, stumbled through chord changes. Our front steps looked out upon the cutting edge of Pacific Heights, a vaguely rectangular swath of the city which ran parallel to the Presidio and had most of the city's rich people inside its boundaries. Beyond these points of reference lay a city I knew nothing about. I had no conception of alternative maps, or different ways of looking at the city. And my side of Clay Street, which was full of apartment buildings, flats and alleys so narrow that my mother could whistle out a bedroom window and borrow a cup of sugar without going outside, was a kind of no-man's strip, neither rich nor poor, which dovetailed with my first view of myself.

Our house was a dark, thermometer-shaped flat, with bedrooms running down a hall which bloomed into a tiny living room, and a wooden porch off that. The view was of the backside of Sacramento Street. Laundry lines. Unspectacular.

To our left were the Harrisons, a second marriage between a cigar-chomping restaurateur and a large, operatically cheerful Christian Science practitioner who used to laugh when I told her I had a cold. The Harrisons had one son, Buddy, and two daughters, "Barb" and "Bev," who were teenagers by the time I was old enough to appreciate what a bobby-soxer was.

Barb and Bev were the real thing, complete with ankle bracelets, pin curls in their bangs and dishtowels converted into bandannas that jiggled on the edge of their gum-chewing chins. They would flash by me en route to high school and a world of banana splits beyond, and I thought that their socks —which they rolled into white wienies around the tops of their saddle shoes—were the cutting edge of fashion.

Ultimately I weaseled my own pair of saddle shoes out of my parents, and, riding home on the bus from the shoe store, I attempted to achieve the "Barb 'n Bev" look, which included a rakish turn of foot, heel out, in the aisle. As I silently admired how nonchalant my foot looked, so mature and detached in its own right, an old lady feeling her way past for a seat tripped over the shoe and fell cursing upon her shopping bag.

To the right of us lived an elderly bachelor named Mr. Ridley. A thin, sparrow-small man with soft brown eyes, Mr. Ridley never emerged onto the sidewalk without being perfectly gotten up, with a hat, waistcoat, watch chain and a snow-white hankie poking out of his suit jacket.

"Hi, Mr. Ridley," I'd call from the front steps.

"Good afternoon, Phyllis," he would smile politely.

I don't know what Mr. Ridley did for employment all week, although he was quite punctual about going somewhere. But on weekends he was deeply involved with his dahlias, tall, dusty-headed flowers that dropped their brilliant heads over Mr. Ridley's snow-white own as he moved quietly among them. His garden ran alongside ours, and one day I pulled myself up the side fence to see if Mr. Ridley was there and got the shock of my life.

At first I couldn't see anyone. But then, as my eye searched harder, I saw a man, a completely naked man, stretched flat on his stomach, between two rows of dahlias. Mr. Ridley! Without any clothes. My four-year-old mind ran this startling piece of information back and forth in my brain while I stared fixedly at his withered walnut-brown bottom—such a compelling, unbeautiful truth—for as long as my fingers were capable of gripping the fence. Then I dropped back onto the ground and tried to mesh my facts.

Mr. Ridley didn't know that I had seen him in this condition, but it changed the relationship from my end. I knew something that he didn't know I knew, and from then on, whenever he tipped his hat and said hello, I would look into his face, think about his bottom and feel embarrassed, although I didn't know quite for whom.

My own garden was a jumble of high grass and tattered hydrangea bushes, uncultivated except by my fantasies, which were somewhat poverty-stricken for want of material. But there was one moment there, perhaps three seconds long, that has hung in my mind—a bit of mold that won't scrub away— which is an obscenity made more obscene because there is no real sinner in the tale. Or so I realize now. At one point, an embarrassingly late point in my life, I painfully hauled up this memory like a foul offering that, once made, would set me free like a prospective Manichaean into the light. But it didn't work, even though I found it difficult to believe that one could confess such a repulsive sin and still be denied absolution.

My mother did not cultivate women friends. Therefore, I did not have neighborhood children to play with until I was of school age. So until then I played by myself, unless you count my little brother, which I didn't. When I was in the backyard, I made tunnels in the grass, shrank down to dwarf size and vicariously crept through them, assembled dandelion bouquets, and made one attempt to dig to China. The backyard was the place where I was alone, swinging in the hammock of my thoughts.

One afternoon, however, I looked up and saw Tommy

Chiesa, a pale, not particularly winning boy of about nine who lived in the neighborhood, climbing over the fence. He came over and sat down beside me at the base of the crabapple tree.

I was honored, I suppose, being a mere four or five, that he found me interesting. He even offered to read the book I had in my lap, and for several minutes he flipped through the pages. Then he shoved the book to one side.

"Want to see something?" he asked with a smile. "Uh huh," I nodded, wondering what that was. And then Tommy unzipped his corduroy trousers, plunged his knuckles between his legs and brought out a small pink worm which I knew, with hot mortification, he shouldn't be showing to me or anybody.

"Go ahead," he said quietly. "You can touch it." I looked up into his face, back down into his lap, and struggled with conflicting desires. After all, maybe this was important but it was frightening too. I was confused but anxious to please, and anxiety won. As I reached over and put my hand on top of it, Tommy made little approving noises in his throat.

There was something wrong with these noises, and I looked up to see if my mother was on the porch so that I could say I had to go inside. But the porch was empty, and as I felt the soft floppy thing and wished I could take my hand away without being impolite, Tommy said firmly, "Put your mouth on it —or I'll tell."

So there was something wrong, but such was the mix of fear, respect and inadequacy, so totally incapable was I of escaping the authority of this pale boy with his expressionless blue eyes, that I did what he asked. Once accomplished, I jumped to my feet, the despicable secret tingling in my mouth, and ran up the back stairs. I never told anyone.

Years later, long after we had moved out of the neighborhood, I returned to Clay Street and saw Tommy Chiesa, in a soldier's uniform, in front of his house talking to his mother. Mrs. Chiesa hailed me vigorously and I was forced to go over.

While we talked, Tommy leaned silently against the car, that same expressionless look in his eyes and smirk on his lips. So, I thought, he has not forgotten. I was shamefully connected to him for the rest of my life. As soon as I could, I walked away. As I left, Tommy took a comb out of his back pocket, ran it elaborately through his greasy, black, ducktail haircut, and stared vacantly into space.

As I first perceived it, there were two worlds and I straddled them, unsure of where I belonged. There was a world of prosperity. In this world there were cups and saucers, birthday parties, grandmothers and general contentment. Order prevailed. And while this world was the one in which I lived, I did not feel qualified. I was too ungraceful, too anxious, too aware of a terrible inner disorderliness that I trailed in my wake, which made me feel like a fringe member about to lose the starch in my clothes, which never quite looked the way they were meant to look. And while I understood that the charity of my family allowed me to be part of this world, I knew that it was a tenuous residence. My only hope was to try to find something special within myself that I could capitalize upon, some understanding of my purpose, a heading that I could gratefully subsume myself under and be absorbed. Otherwise the other world would get me and the other world was, from the limited front-steps intuitions that flashed across my consciousness, where I emotionally belonged.

In this second world, people cried, shivered in garrets and wandered around like bums looking for pies on windowsills. Tragic things happened which were nobody's fault, children were run over, diseases were contracted, and there were terrible miscarriages of mercy where sorrow was not recognized, frailty was kicked in the ribs, and old men without hearing aids tried to make their way across the street without a Boy Scout to show them safely to the other side. The second world was fraught with unsafety, women in red coats who dissolved with their own insignificance, and the most tragic thing of all was that the happy world and the unhappy world were separate from each other. They were divided, like Clay Street, by a gulf of unawareness, and in my mind that was why the happy people never had the chance to help the other side across.

Ignorance, a noun I later spliced finer with the adjective "invincible," was responsible. The happy world was full of "invincible ignorance," and I saw myself as the person who would lay herself down like a plank across the street so that the happy people could walk across and fix up the other side. I would bring the bum and the pie together in a joyful explosion that would catapult me above my own bad opinion.

Exactly when I came up with this solution to the problem of existence I don't know. It was the first of many solutions, all of which were designed to help me write a caption for the one snapshot that I couldn't make sense of, myself. But early on I conceived of myself as a kind of "saviorette" who would prove that there was more to myself than met the eye. But I was always being confronted with situations beyond my capacity to solve, opportunities I wasn't allowed to take, and dramas that folded in trumpery on top of themselves, just as I was about to dash upon the stage and save everyone concerned.

There was, on the mantel above the fireplace in our living room, a large antique sword and scabbard. I was not allowed to touch it. Yet one afternoon, the front door burst open and down the hall came a large, roughly dressed stranger, who proceeded to go straight into the kitchen where my parents were unsuspectingly sitting. The stranger did not see me, but so great was my alarm that I immediately realized that he was going to kill my parents, and my only hope was to get to the sword on the mantel, creep quietly into the kitchen and plunge it into his back.

Waiting until he had gone into the kitchen, where my parents were undoubtedly being held at gunpoint and told to be quiet, I crept up to the mantel, dislodged the sword from its scabbard and walked, with beating heart, into the kitchen, the sword clutched behind my back. There were my parents bending over the washing machine, while the stranger was on his back with a wrench beneath the wringer contraption. They looked up casually as I stood behind them. "What's that behind your back?" my mother asked. I backed out of the kitchen and quietly put the sword back onto the mantel. Those kinds of bogus opportunities were presented all the time, and with the exception of "Uncle Walter," I never saved anybody, a record that stands without correction to this day.

Uncle Walter was a ninety-year-old man who lived on our block, and my parents knew him because he was somehow involved with Moral Re-Armament, an ideological movement that swept the entire family off its feet for a good number of years. But by the time I knew him, Uncle Walter was too old to be swept off his feet by anything, and he didn't do much except shuffle around the corner down the hill to Kornfeld's Market to buy groceries, and then slowly, painfully, shuffle home up the hill, his white walrus moustache buried in the top of his paper sack.

One afternoon, while walking up Spruce Street, I saw Uncle Walter bent against the wind, ahead of me on the hill. "Hi, Uncle Walter," I called. Uncle Walter halted, raised his head slowly and then tried to turn to one side to wave hello with his free hand. I was barely even with his shoulders when I realized that he was losing his balance. The wind was too strong, his back was too weak and the weight of the grocery sack pushing against his chest was combining to push him back down the hill. It was like watching a tree slowly starting to crash. There was only one thing to do.

Bracing myself against his spine, my hands gripping his waist, I got behind him and began to push. Slowly Uncle Walter got right with the wind again, his back assumed its forward tilt, and he was finally at the right shuffle-forward position to keep from tipping over. I was embarrassed to have been so physically familiar with him, but I felt proud to have done the right thing. Uncle Walter never said a word during the entire operation, but I've always credited myself with saving his life.

During those first years, when my world was chaperoned in such a way that I rarely left Clay Street, I had to scrape together what little drama was available from the sidewalk in front. Yet there was plenty. Birds needed burials, dead puppies materialized at bus stops, and every so often my mother would open the front door and find a drunk before her, having been referred to our address by me. Once I decided to collect canned food for the Red Cross and took a wagon up and down the block, asking for spinach greens, or collards, or beets, which in my imagination would be devoured by European children who were too hungry to know what they were eating. But in this last instance I was foiled by inner corruption. After several successful stops I began to get hungry myself, and when one woman asked me what I needed, I looked her straight in the eye and asked, "Do you happen to have any apricot nectar?" My mother found the supply of cans under my bed several weeks later, and the Red Cross never did benefit at all. But it would be incorrect to imply that I spent every day looking for a place to put my compassion. I was looking for a place to put myself. In the beginning, I felt like a constituency of one.

I don't remember being frightened or unfrightened by school. My mother, who had never played me false before, simply took me by the hand one morning and walked me three blocks down the street. Suddenly I was alone in the middle of a large chunk of stone, inhaling chalk dust, staring at a row of scissors winking in the sun, and watching Miss Burdette tug with a long, hooked, wooden pole at the upper windows, which gave out onto the cement playground beyond. With one clap of the erasers I had moved into another dimension. School was something larger and more meaningful than myself.

Each morning began with an outside assembly of the entire school. We stood, by class and row, as the head traffic boy hauled the American flag up the pole. If a child had been killed in traffic the day before, that sad fact was announced city-wide, by order of Mayor Robinson, who had pledged to keep fatalities down as part of his campaign platform. But usually the streets were free of blood, we would pledge allegiance, and be dismissed to our classroom by Miss Plagaman, the principal, who shook a brass bell over our heads and then stood by the double doors as we filed past, one wrinkled, authoritarian hand hooked by her thumb into her belt.

That hand was one of many wrinkled, authoritarian hands in Madison School, which seemed to be almost entirely staffed by unmarried, bespectacled women who teetered on the edge of death or crankiness. I hadn't met women like this before, but somehow they seemed to conform to the hard, no-nonsense architecture of the school itself, and while they were not exactly child-abusers, they didn't encourage undue intimacy either. They were teachers, not social workers.

I used to hope that Irma Meyers, who scared me to death, would die. My worry was that Miss O'Brien, who fascinated me, would die instead. Miss O'Brien was a tall, frail woman with chalk cheeks and sad eyes who entered the classroom every morning with an air of having narrowly beaten down the grim reaper the previous night. She always wore black and she used to grip the edge of her desk as she sat there, and I never knew whether it was out of conviction or to keep from falling down onto the floor. Miss O'Brien never spoke of a private life, but she had a way of speaking about life in general as if she really knew what she was talking about, and I filled in the blanks by imagining that she lived in a dark apartment full of parakeets, Spanish shawls and photographs of a beloved brother who had died in the war.

Yet there was one teacher who was a warm flesh-bed of positive encouragement in an otherwise bony environment, and when I entered the third grade where she taught, I promptly fell in love with her.

Miss Geanneacopolis was young, wide-hipped, and styled her hair in a pile of dark sausage curls that nested on her brow and were repeated along her shoulders. Her calves made wonderful swishing sounds as her nylon stockings brushed against each other when she walked. I adored her, and when she announced her engagement to be married—a day I hadn't counted upon ever coming—I was stricken with jealousy and hoped that her fiancé would be killed and she would be able to get out of the deal.

Unfortunately, this did not happen and Miss Geanneacopolis got married on schedule, with the entire Greek-American community dancing to that fact, while I sat in a state of furious betrayal in the upper balcony of Sts. Constantine and Alexandros Church and watched the whole thing take place.

In the receiving line Miss Geanneacopolis leaned down and kissed my cheek, and pressed a lace-net valentine with two almonds in it into my hand. That was supposed to be compensation. Then I was back out on the street, feeling as humiliated as the Japanese did when they surrendered to MacArthur.

Miss Geanneacopolis was back in school several weeks later, her stockings swishing as seductively as ever. But I knew that her allegiance to me had been siphoned off in a permanent way. She would pause, purse her lipsticked, bee-stung lips and gaze at my bowed head as I furiously crayoned at my desk, in a willed state of personality withdrawal, for I had decided that ignoring her was my only way to punish her. Yet I also knew that it was a silly weapon; I was nothing to her but a child who was part of a crowd of children. I, on the other hand, had hoped she would be mine forever, a permanent fan in the imaginary bleachers that ran parallel to my life.

Over the years a number of people have silently filed in and out of those bleachers, applauding, marveling and confirming the opinion that I was too proud to admit out loud, which was that I was, beneath my baby fat, an extraordinary person. Certainly I saw no confirmation of this secret opinion in my outer life; I was always sideways to the mainstream of things, running to catch hold of the hand of the most popular girl, who was running to catch hold of somebody else's. But when I entered school and became part of society, I realized that the important thing was to attach myself to the most powerful armada in the bay, become part of a fleet of little girls who, by virtue of our collective power, would cut through the waters without fear. In order to make the center hold, I had to be in the center of things. Friends would protect me.

Julieanne was the first one. Her mother did not like me. I was too bossy. I pushed Julieanne around. Her mother was right. Julieanne was a nose-rubbing, droopy-eyed little girl who didn't know her own mind, and was, therefore, perfect for my purposes. I was a leader in search of a follower, and I worked Julieanne like a pinball machine, which made Julieanne's mother, a cheerful, impatient woman who ran her own restaurant and talked through her teeth, mad. Finally, she signed Julieanne up for daily swimming lessons at "The Crystal Plunge" downtown, and Julieanne became unavailable.

"Julieanne has big feet," explained my mother. "Julieanne's mother is right to capitalize upon them." But what was I supposed to capitalize on? I was too young to articulate the question.

It stood to reason, although a child reasons badly, that some children were blessed and some were not. The blessed children were effortlessly popular, eternally tidy, had mothers who wore saddle shoes and cut the crusts off their sandwiches. But as if being blessed were not enough, it followed as a kind of perverse corollary that these same children were also prone toward a kind of natural meanness toward the unblessed, and it was my sorry luck that I did not know how to avoid being the sort of person who inspired the meanness. Again, it stood to reason if one is plump, wears glasses, has an unsteady personality and no identifiable best friend, that people are going to point these facts up. And every morning before school I would awake with a snake in my stomach. The snake always lay in the shape of a question mark. Would I overcome the odds?

The cloth-coated teachers with their bells and whistles on lanyards only saw the broad strokes—ropes turning, balls bouncing, dresses moving in pairs and trios across the schoolyard. But recess was open season, swarming with hunters and their victims. Friendships dissolved without notice. One could be laughed at at any time. Side-glances, elbow nudges, the way Helene looked at Barbara who notified Diane. That strange alchemy of chance and choice, the unpredictability of how the line formed going outside to play, it was all beyond me, and the agony lay in not knowing the timetable, being powerless to affect the dynamics. Some days I was queen of the mountain. On other days I was a leper at the end of the table, and I was not above grafting myself onto an existing power clique, or trying to form one, for the express purpose of creating a victim other than myself.

In the search for the center, it was more blessed to attack than be victimized, and while I greatly empathized with all those waifs in books who were victims of poverty, prejudice and injustice, that was separate from my fear of the real thing. Pauline Pezzollo, who ate garlic sandwiches and whose mother once accused my mother of not "having the guts" to be a Blue Bird Mother, or Lanetta Robinson, a negro who used to turn her eyelids inside out to attract attention, were shunned by me as much as anybody else. I was drawn to blond, superachievers who wore Pandora sweaters; I hung around them in the hope that their auras would indirectly light up my own.

Madison School seemed to contain only children with ring-worm who lived on Sacramento Street, or children who took riding lessons and came from wealthy Jewish families who took everybody to the Fairmont Hotel for their birthdays, and I marveled at these Jewish children who seemed to have me-tabolisms that parted all Red Seas and made life a dry passage across. I don't think I even knew that I was a Protestant. My best friend, Julieanne, was a Catholic.

It should be mentioned that I was not totally without weap-ons. Before Julieanne was whisked off to "The Crystal Plunge," she put me onto one priceless possession. It was not a con-sciously bestowed gift on her part, but in order to continue leading her around, I had to follow her to catechism classes at St. Edward's Catholic Church every Wednesday afternoon. For Julieanne it was another nose-rubbing obligation. For me it was my first introduction to a living God.

Up until that time, God had been a real but somewhat un-clothed concept in my mind. He was behind the fretwork of the altar at Grace Cathedral, on top of the cross that moved down the aisle in front of the minister at St. Luke's Episcopal Church. God had no connection with Reverend Woolems, who would lean over the pulpit and speak in long, elaborate sentences that had no beginning or end. But at St. Edward's the whole thing came to life. God stepped out from behind the fretwork, and I was introduced to a battery of saints, angels and courageous human beings, all of whom had done the very things that I wanted to do.

We read comic books printed out of Baltimore about cou-rageous children living in communist countries. Real-life stories and dilemmas were discussed, such as would you turn your parents in if the Gestapo came to the front door? In these discussions, children were the linchpins, and the extent of your ardor doubled your chances to prove yourself in a meaningful way.

I had fantasies of being shoved against a wall by a squad of slit-eyed Chinese soldiers, where, like little Saint Agnes ("she was so tiny that the cuffs slipped off her wrists"), I would be asked to deny my God.

"No!" I would shout. ("Then they whipped her cruelly," said the comic book. "Even the pagans wept to see her tortured this way.") And after this brave response, the communists would shoot me twelve times, the blood would soak through my white dress, and I would simultaneously sink to the cobblestones and split the heavens with my angelic reception. I used to imagine other children, in later generations, reading about me in another comic book, with a little note at the end of the story saying, "Her feast day is on March . . . ," or whatever day it was that I gave up the ghost and got what I wanted.

These catechism classes were a short-lived venture, but certain seeds were planted that took root. I used to hitch myself up over the stone wall that enclosed the garden of the Little Sisters of the Poor, who had a home for old people at the edge of Presidio Terrace, and wonder whether I might be a nun someday. Watching the sisters move like gray swallows among the benches of old people set out to sun, I tried to imagine what it would be like to beg for food, and pray to Saint Joseph in the center hallway, and humbly polish already polished stairs like "the Little Flower" in Lisieux. But even then that seemed like a rather anonymous path to holiness. It did not fill the twin needs for virtue quickly followed by reward. Then, too, I was quite fixated upon miracles and apparitions, those special signs of approval that the nun in catechism class told me came to children whose holiness caused Mary to appear to them.

In all the stories of courageous saintettes, the children who later became legends were appeared to by Mary, in one form or other. She materialized within grottos, found them while tending goats, or surprised them in the nighttime, when they were saying their prayers. But Mary did not appear to children who lived in flats, she had a preference for foreign countries, and I was neither rich enough to be a queen of great goodness nor poor enough to be a peasant who never complained. My circumstances were so lukewarm. The chance to prove that I was ready for greatness was nonexistent, and I used to pray for a saint-making disease like polio all the while chattering with fear that I just might get it. I nevertheless tried to will Mary into the United States, night after night.

Lying in bed, my eyes dilated in search of a vision, I used to try to pluck her blue cloak out of the air, find her halo where the moon on the wall left off. I had it all figured out as to what I would do if she ever came. I would rise into her arms, dissolve with borrowed sanctity, Mary would call me blessed and that would be it.

My parents could not have known that I was mentally carrying on this way behind their backs. After all, I was going to the Jewish Community Center for swimming lessons once a week, belonged to the Episcopal choir, and seemed to spend most of my time at Bathold's Drug Store reading comic books and eating the ice cream cones that doomed me to the "Chubette" department at Macy's for many years. But, in fact, I was gearing up for sainthood. I wanted to be a holy card, and the card I had up my sleeve at that time was time, which I was biding for want of an alternative.

A child, and I was no exception, cannot tell anyone these things. Children are receivers, not transmitters. Then, too, someone might laugh, a risk no child is prepared to take. But as I buried birds, rescued old men, wept over drunks, and would have thrown all my aspirations for sainthood out the window for a guaranteed weekly invitation to Susan Figel's house where nobody ate margarine, I was plump of body but lean of intent. One way or the other I was going to force Saint Rose of Lima to unpack her mantle of roses at the foot of my bed, become the "Sweet Saint of the Impossible," once I came

74

across the impossible situation to match my passion. I never found it. In the interim I had to deal with other children who hurt my feelings and Lanetta Robinson, who, with her pink, inside-out eyelids, gave me the creeps.

My mother, in those early years, was less a person than a collection of secondary recollections which don't directly define her. The squeak of a clothesline, the sound of sorting silver back into a drawer, the smell of baked potato, the closing of a door.

She was there but not there, an open, sympathetic, somewhat drifty person who moved over automatically when I crept in beside her after a nightmare. I loved her in an ungrateful, inarticulate way, knew that she was absolutely safe, and, as I look down at my own hands, they remind me of hers —small, squared off at the tips of the fingers, and beginning to lose their smoothness across the backs. They are my mother's hands, although hers were distinguishable for a gentle twitching motion of the fingers. They would often move slightly, involuntarily, as if they were punctuating a thought that she wasn't expressing. They did these little arpeggios for years and then, suddenly, they stopped.

My father, despite a personality that never has found the right size container, is nearly as indistinct in my mind. He was an important, electric presence who came home at the end of the day and was exploded against, halfway down the hallway, by me. He worked as a kind of super salesman for a small dehydrated-fruit company that was owned by Uncle Ed, and the two men commuted across the bay to the plant every day for the better part of their working lives together.

Vacu-Dry, as the company was called, was founded upon the failed invention of my grandfather's Uncle Charles, who back in the days of Prohibition figured out that it was possible to fiddle around with the grape in such a way that it could be turned into a brick for making wine in the home. He tinkered around with various chemical processes and finally worked out a way to dehydrate the grape successfully. There was only one hitch, which had nothing to do with the invention. Just about the time that Uncle Charles had amassed enough backers to put his "wine in the home" brainstorm across, Prohibition ended and knocked the great grape-brick scheme into a hat. All that was left was the process, a tiny plant in Emeryville and a lot of bills.

At that time, Uncle Ed was working as an investment counselor in San Francisco, but there wasn't much going on since this was in the teeth of the Depression. So he took some of his inheritance, bought Vacu-Dry from Uncle Charles, and expanded the company's vision to dehydrating all kinds of fruit.

During World War II, the GI's in both theaters were eating Vacu-Dry dried fruit, and my father even made business trips to Washington to talk to military people in the Pentagon, which was a strain on him.

My father is not very good at transplanting. Whenever he sets foot out of California, he is not quite himself, and there has always been about him a kind of rattled innocence that takes over when he is out of his element. After his second trip to Washington, he never went again. The reasons are unclear except that my father said, "I ran up against the Pendergast gang." I didn't know who these people were, but it involved Truman, marked decks and part-down-the-middle politicians who talked out of both sides of their mouths.

When World War II ended, it looked as if Vacu-Dry might slide downhill, but my father came up with the brilliant idea to sell dried fruit to the state's insane asylums. "They don't know what they're eating anyway," he argued, and for several years he drove up and down the state visiting various institutions to sweet-talk the dieticians into buying the product. That idea kept my uncle's company on the map.

Every once in a while he'd take me along, and while he went into his appointments, I would sit in a locked car and watch the inmates on the grounds. It was a strange world, full of sixty-year-old women playing volleyball, their gray, uncombed hair swinging in the wind. I would watch their varicose-veined legs darting around the grass, puzzle over grown men trying to chip off nameplates from buildings with sticks, and not know whether to laugh or feel sorry for these people. But I would be relieved when I saw my father come swinging back toward the car, suitcase full of samples in his hand, a grin on his face. He was good with state types, and those poor dieticians must have looked forward to my father's visits. It would have been roughly comparable to having Fred Astaire waltz through a government cafeteria, crack a few jokes and waltz out.

Vacu-Dry put out high-quality fruit, and several times almost went bankrupt on its own integrity. There were competitors, particularly during the war, and one unscrupulous company, "run by a chiseler from Sebastapol," said my father, had the nerve to rent a couple of old tennis courts, fling apples on both sides of the net, and run over the lot with a steamroller under the hot sun.

These kinds of threats were always in the offing, but my uncle's company managed to survive them, although it never quite got off the launching pad to become anything less lovable than a family business when my father was there. And while both my uncle and father worked up charts, grossed and netted their profits, and hired excellent, blameless personnel to make Vacu-Dry an excellent company, it stubbornly refused to grow beyond a certain size. When they made the mistake of trying to branch out in Florida into orange-juice crystals, the company almost went broke. Two things happened: Consumers kept consuming the silica-gel packets that were supposed to keep the orange crystals dry and getting diarrhea. The other was that Uncle Ed got mugged. The idea of Uncle Ed being mugged by anyone was unthinkable, and in Tampa of all places. "No freeze—no squeeze—it's McKee's" was closed down, and Vacu-Dry pulled its horns back into California again. Oranges didn't fly.

That small company was a part of my father's life for nearly twenty years, but as large a role as it played, he rarely talked about it. He was a businessman more by necessity than choice, and when he came home at the end of the day he was a six o'clock sanctum where I retreated, played with his crooked tooth and listened to him read Thurber's *Fables for Our Time*, the only book (aside from Peter Arno's cartoon collection) that interested him enough to bother with.

The other ritual took place at bedtime. After the lights were out, my father would take the bear robe from the foot of my bed, leave the room and shut the door. After several moments, the door would creak open, a monstrous, evil creature would materialize in the wedge of light, and this "thing," my father with the bear robe over his head, would advance with heavy tread toward my bed. I would scream, dive under the blankets and try to protect myself. But he would continue to move forward, arms extended, until he came to a silent, frightening halt over my head. Time froze, life hung in the balance, I knew and didn't know that I would survive. Then he would swoop down, shake the bones of my rib cage and rub his scratchy beard all over my cheeks. But the rest of the time he was in Emeryville, selling puffed raisins and dried apricot slices to loony bins up and down the state.

My father's dried-fruit business has always seemed like a metaphor for the family itself. There would be rumors that the stock was due to rise. We would buy more. The stock would fall. We would then be philosophical. It was clear, and then unclear, and then clear again that General Mills was going to buy out the entire company and we would all "go national." But General Mills, which now and then sent sharp-eyed types to Emeryville for further discussion, never did. And back in the days when everybody had too much confidence, that seemed inexplicable.

Chapter
IV

There is, or ought to be, in everybody's childhood, one house which is seminal to all the other houses that come and go in our lives. It should be an exaggeration, a labyrinth, full of large rooms, small passageways, odd things and odd people which are nevertheless totally familiar because they belong to you. My own house, or rather flat, was not this place. But four blocks away, where my father's two sisters and their families lived together, was as full of sound and fury as mine was silent and full of creative boredom. Whenever I felt the clockspring of my life coiled for action, I would strike out for 36 Presidio Terrace the way one strikes out to catch up with a parade.

Presidio Terrace was an exclusive cul-de-sac full of formal houses, the families within keeping to themselves. Black wrought-iron gates fronted the Terrace entrance, technically closing out the rest of the world, but I don't think they were ever shut. The gates were simply there to remind passersby that the closing was a possibility. When I stepped beyond the gates and walked toward the Gallwey house, I inhaled the scent of grass clippings set out at intervals in burlap bags on the sidewalk, and felt more significant than I really was. I was attracted to Presidio Terrace the way one is inexorably attracted to a richer existence.

The Gallwey household didn't have much intercourse with any other household, which wasn't unusual. Within Presidio Terrace, each family minded its own affluent business and most of the other families were Jewish, which made for an additional distance. Temple Emmanu-el, a massive, orange-domed synagogue, butted right up against the south edge of the Terrace, dominating the skyline like an outsized *yarmulke*. But I was never curious about it. Nobody was. The Gallwey household was world enough.

My grandmother occupied a small, fan-cluttered upstairs bedroom next to my Aunt Dorothy and Uncle Gene's larger room. At the other end of the second floor, my Aunt Irene and Uncle Ed had what amounted to a wing—a large bedroom with sitting room and fireplace, plus a bathroom which was as full of creams, bubble bath and jars of Elizabeth Arden goop as my Aunt Dorothy's bathroom was empty of them. Down a side corridor were small servants' quarters that held children—my cousins Tim, Mary, Tony and Mimi. Johnny lived in an old linen closet. Jerry occupied the basement room next to the elevator, an old Otis cage which wheezed from one floor to the next, although not so slowly that my grandmother, who could faint standing still, was not periodically overwhelmed by its speed.

Elsewhere in the house, other semi-permanent members of the household had rooms, although thinking back, there were more people than rooms available. The house was always bursting with tenants, although from the outside of the house one could not tell anything about the activity within. It was a massive, not very interesting house, brushed stucco with leaded windows, and no real garden, except a postage-sized patio with a couple of cement vases full of petunias off the front door. Some thick privet hedges softened the lines of the house along the front. The bulk of the drama was interior to the house.

The kitchen had an enormous restaurant stove, bought at auction from Manning's Restaurant downtown after a fire. A half-dozen skillet burners and four ovens were going most of the time, and the Mixmaster on the marble slab to the left of the stove could handle three dozen mashed potatoes, with the pantry on one side holding enough plates and silver to service a wedding.

Endless rooms bloomed on every floor. There were front stairs, wide polished wood like the hallway, which all of the cousins sat upon in rows for the annual Christmas picture, candles in hand. The back stairs took you to the children's rooms, and every table downstairs held something I thought rare: a marble chess set, a Chinese lacquer box, a cluster of amber grapes in a silver bowl. The basement, which served as a kind of understage where props out of use were stored, was a maze of trunks, old photographs and boxes full of scratchy ballgowns, celluloid collars, and lemon-colored linen from various former lives. The style of the entire house was, I suppose, "contemplative materialistic." Nothing stood out. Everything worked.

Uncle Ed was a businessman with money. Uncle Gene was a baron with scrapbooks. Somehow, in my mind, this balanced out. The Gallweys were rich, but I used to pore over Uncle Gene's scrapbooks in utter amazement to think that if it hadn't been for the Nazis my Aunt Dorothy would be staggering over mountains of quail, ordering cooks around and living it up in a castle full of old retainers and children rocketing around marble halls wearing lederhosen and caps with feathers.

World War II made a wash of that possibility, and my Uncle Gene, who spoke seven languages and loved everybody, eventually joined Moral Re-Armament, an ideological movement which crested during the 1950's. For the entire time that the family occupied 36 Presidio Terrace, Moral Re-Armament (or MRA) dominated the conscience of the household, although my own mother and father tended to exist as a side-car to MRA that never quite hooked up to the main train. Because of MRA, however, I always looked upon the whole family as being caught up in a series of important ideas that involved setting up a lot of extra chairs in the Gallwey living room. It also accounted for the steady influx of visitors who trooped through the front door, adding an extra dimension to an already fully realized double family.

Moral Re-Armament was the natural receptacle for many well-born, well-meaning Americans who believed that world peace ought to be possible if everybody important would simply apologize to everybody else who was important. It was akin, on a larger scale, to my grandmother's never-followed suggestion that "if each person would just take their plate to the kitchen and wash it," then nobody would have any work to do. This simple act of apologizing would set the dominoes in motion around the world. Everybody would be friends and the Chinese Communists, just then forming up as evil incarnate, would be forced to capitulate before so much goodness in action.

Moral Re-Armament had its world headquarters in Caux-sur-Montreux, Switzerland, which I imagined as being a large, crenellated castle with grounds where nations came together in song and dance under the kindly, astute eye of "Uncle Frank," Frank Buchman, the founder of the movement. Every so often, "Uncle Frank" himself would visit the Gallwey house, which served as the local embassy for "the team," as full-time MRA workers were called, and the children would be brought to shake his hand.

He was a small balding man, who wore three-piece suits, rimless glasses, and sat like an important rubber ball, his hands resting on a cane, as he received people. He had, as I remember, a wonderful sense of humor, and it was obvious from the reverence he inspired that he was the most important person I would ever know, although he never said anything earthshaking to me, and I cannot remember a single word he said to anyone else either.

Thus, while the life of a double family ran along one level and certain rooms smelled of old socks, catcher's mitts and tangerine peelings, it was possible to walk into the kitchen and find Baroness von Gutenberg, a friend of Uncle Gene's, drinking tea in a crushed-velvet dressing gown, talking about Therese Neumann, a bleeding mystic from Europe, or walk into the living room and find a half-dozen members of the Japanese *Zengakuren* apologizing for having tipped over Jim Hagerty's press car when he visited Tokyo with Eisenhower. Presiding over all this, in semiabsentia, was my Uncle Ed.

My uncle Ed is a private man who saves his deepest emotions for his Wagner record collection, and often I would see him, stretched out after work, coat still on, in a living-room chair, fingers poked up in a tent before his face as he listened to music behind the closed glass doors. He was a solemn, dignified man who was the anchor on the ship, but I rather think he appreciated the excitement he subsidized and felt that he was part of a play that only demanded that he show up. He provided a kind of sober, responsible backdrop against which other less responsible members of the family danced.

Besides the immediate family, there was usually present a visiting MRA delegation, one or two kitchen helpers, plus various women donated by MRA who came to help out with the house in various capacities.

These MRA women remain so purely one thing in my mind that it doesn't do them justice to describe them without apologizing in advance for the depthlessness of my perspective at that time. But taken as a whole, they were a kindly, dignified, usually self-effacing group of women—neither spineless nor overbearing—and none of them seemed to have any connection with men (in the husband-taking sense) or style (if by style one means seductiveness or grace).

Connie Douglas was a florid, efficient woman who drank potato water from the icebox, wore hats even in the bathroom and lived to be at least 400. Nina Hall was widowed early but still chuckling over good memories of a good husband, and Sophie, a pink, bosomy nineteen-year-old, was an aberration from the norm, a Swiss import who didn't take Moral Re-Armament very seriously and got out altogether and married a count.

There were others, usually middle-aged, virginal and gentle women who sacrificed themselves to the family, took the photographs, fluted the pies and stood around the edges of family life, which was not without its compensations. The family was an all-encompassing production, and on countless afternoons I would head for 36 Presidio Terrace, step into the polished, Edwardian-sized hallway and wait for excitement to hit me over the head.

My grandmother was usually home. That was one option. Various cousins kicked in from various schools at the same time. My two aunts were often in the kitchen, challenging each other's integrity on who was cheating on their diets ("What do you call real butter on RyKrisp, Dot?" "Shall we just ignore the fudge sundae you had at Townsend's yesterday, Irene?"). And if the house was quiet, which was seldom, there was the Steinway, a black, glossy monster that gleamed in the bay window of the living room. I would oftentimes sit there by myself, sounding out tunes in the sea-green quiet of the afternoon.

The Steinway was a gift from Elizabeth Bates, one of the maiden MRA ladies, who lived with the family until she died. A quiet, hard-of-hearing ex-music teacher, whom we used to tease by moving our lips, which caused her to fumble in her dress for her amplifier, "E. Bates" (which is what we all called her) used to clump around the house in her perforated shoes, the butt of our mean jokes, the person who played carols on Christmas Eve and then stood silently in the background as we told the Christmas story by the crèche. When the grownups were downstairs, or out, Elizabeth was the person who read stories to the children before they went to sleep, and she was a silent, unassuming presence who stood with one hand semicurled against the side of her withered cheek in the background of every family gathering I can remember.

When E. Bates died she willed her Steinway to my cousin Mimi, and it turned out that there was a great deal else to be willed as well. Over the years, while the rest of the family was semi-ignoring Elizabeth, she had quietly parlayed her mother's egg money into a fortune by investing in the National Biscuit Company. E. Bates came from Morgan City, which is from nowhere just like Elizabeth, but when she died she was worth a bundle, which says a lot about eggs.

Some afternoons I wandered around the house from one floor to the other, exploring my Aunt Irene's darkroom, opening up the silver closet to smell the polish, or sometimes I would play Ping-Pong in the basement with a fat serving girl called Judy, who lived in a sinkhole in the basement and had terrible acne on her upper arms.

Judy was married to a skinny little sailor who used to visit her on Saturday nights. She made my aunts mad because it was so obvious what he was after, and the thought of his getting it right beneath the library and The Great Books collection gave them a giddy, helpless feeling.

"A girl that size," my Aunt Irene exclaimed.

"Well, that's my point," said my Aunt Dorothy, who said that about almost everything.

But whatever point was the point, Judy was fired on the heels of one particular game of Ping-Pong, when several rallies into the game she began to tell me just what it was about her skinny sailor husband that brought such pleasure into her life.

I was breathless with her descriptions, could hardly serve when it came my turn, and finally I set my paddle down on the table and held my breath while Judy, whose wide, lustful face grew rosy with her pornographic tale, told me about things I didn't even know existed, in places that I didn't even know I had. But she was unaware that someone in a position to act was listening through the upstairs furnace grate.

A series of after-dinner, clean-up types like Judy paraded through the Gallwey house. Some came from MRA, but most were students or, like Judy, plucked from the want ads in the *Chronicle* or *Examiner*. But there was always someone handing around the mashed potatoes with a semidisbelieving look on their faces—with reason.

Often there were two separate translations going on from different ends of the table. My Aunt Dorothy (who knew Konrad Adenauer personally, which gave her a conversational edge) might be dissecting someone's view of the Ruhr situation. My Aunt Irene (who liked to disagree with her husband just to show she was her own person) was prone to tacking her index finger across the crumbs on her placemat while she worked up steam over what Mortimer Adler had said about Thomas Aquinas. (The table could be roughly divided into those who took Mortimer Adler's Great Books course and those who didn't.) And my grandmother, who often took exception to both specific remarks and general tone of voice, sometimes pushed herself away from the table to go upstairs, leaving precisely the vacuum she intended. Various cousins, unaware of much but themselves, would be loading cap pistols under the table, zinging rubber bands at each other, and I would be hanging off my chair wondering from the drift of the conversation who or what a "Mendès-France" was.

There was one MRA houseguest, a tall, handsome Frenchman, whom everyone was scurrying around to accommodate, who struck me as particularly appealing. He didn't know any English, which triggered my compassion, and while I didn't know any French, there was a loneliness about him that caused me to disregard this minor problem and I asked if he would like to take a walk.

The Frenchman said that that would be nice, and together we roamed over the Army Presidio, picking up eucalyptus pods and speaking in hand gestures and smiles. I fell slightly in love with him, wistful old men being something of an early specialty, but I saw the differences in our ages and after the walk was over, I tried to think of a way to narrow the gap.

Just before dinner was served, I sneaked into the pantry and plucked two oranges out of the bin, slid them up beneath my T-shirt, and went into supper. Everybody was already seated, the Frenchman to the right of my uncle, when I slid into my chair and tried to look with feigned boredom into space. The Frenchman was instantly riveted upon my chest. My uncle paused, carving fork in midair, and grinned at the mantelpiece, my aunts pressed napkins against their mouths, and my grandmother looked down at me and made little clicking noises in her throat.

I deliberately decided that these reactions had nothing to do with me. In fact, I was quite intent upon only one thing— making sure that the oranges stayed even with each other. They slipped down every time I was not sitting straight, and toward the end of supper I dozed off slightly only to be jolted awake as both oranges hit my dessert plate simultaneously. The experiment was not a success. I don't know what happened to the Frenchman.

No doubt there were days when the house languished in the kind of routine quiet that, for most families, is the usual way of life. If that was so, I have mentally edited out these lapses, just as I can remember with acuteness the one triumphant moment of each year when the family gathered for

Christmas Eve, and we assembled in front of the Christmas tree on our knees to hear the story of Jesus as we stared at the crèche, an Austrian carved tableau of tiny characters that each year was set up by Aunt Irene.

That night began with my father sitting us down in our own living room to read "The Night Before Christmas" before heading toward the Gallweys'. Then, carrying my box of homemade presents, I would get into the car, and off we would roll toward the big house. All the children gave presents that evening to the grownups, although we began with a slow, singing procession down the big stairs, carrying candles, into the living room, where E. Bates played "Oh Come, All Ye Faithful," and my Uncle Ed, with his Episcopal baritone, could always be heard, richer and stronger than everyone else, singing from his place behind the children as we grouped before the crèche.

After the Christmas story, the supper was served in the dining room—turkey for the Protestants, crab for the Catholics, who went to midnight Mass later on. Uncle Ed, poised above the turkey, in his blue suit and starched cuffs, sliced up the bird. My two aunts, one on either side, dressed in silk and wool; my grandmother, in velvet; my parents; all the boy and girl cousins with wet part-lines and best clothes on—it was always a formal but hysterical supper, with the children dying to race from the table to assemble their presents to be handed out. Over those first years, when we made ashtrays out of bed coasters and telephone-book covers out of wallpaper samples, I have frozen one particular present in my mind as being the most creative.

My brother John advanced toward Uncle Ed with a coffee can covered over in red tissue paper, with a stick attached. Uncle Ed took the coffee can and asked him what he was supposed to do with it. "Take the stick and poke it through the hole," said John. His eyes brimming with amusement, my elegant, starched uncle jammed the stick through the tissue paper and suddenly there was a loud snap at the bottom of the can. My brother began to laugh uncontrollably. Uncle Ed pulled the stick from the can and there was a mousetrap clamped over the end of the stick. "That's a wonderful present," he said, waving the stick and mousetrap around. I can still see him laughing the way Uncle Ed always laughs—with tears running down his cheeks. The entire room applauded John's cleverness. His present was the hit of the evening.

At the end of Christmas Eve, my parents would sling John and me over their shoulders, since we were usually asleep, walk back out into the wet, swirling fog that often covered San Francisco at night, and take us home. But, in fact, I always felt I lived in two places, with 36 Presidio Terrace being my spiritual home. There was a richness and overblown quality in the air, a bustle and preparation for events simmering below the surface of whatever calm existed, and the combination of normality and cosmic overreach, playing Slap Jack upstairs while a chorus of Filipinos sang their national anthem in the living room, kept my imagination in a perpetual state of creative imbalance.

My Aunt Irene says that I did not spend as much time there as I claim, but I counterclaim that she simply didn't notice me, which I think was true. Then, too, time is relative to what happens in it, and during that long march across the hot, eventless plains of childhood, when I strained for circumstances and tried to surprise life into happening by being at the ready, Presidio Terrace was the one place where life was already going full tilt. My bones picked up the electricity, the excitement, the world view, and I never left that place without feeling like a battery that had just been plugged into a current which would someday empower me to go full tilt in some meaningful direction of my own.

Chapter
V

My grandmother died when I was twelve years old. She was sixty-five and in good health, which didn't preclude death coming to her anyway. For as long as I had known Grandmother, she had been battling against that possibility. Life was a virus that would kill her if she wasn't careful. Death was the unspoken reference point around which everyone, including me, revolved. And her bedside table, neatly stacked with small, meaningful religious tracts like *My Utmost for His Highest*, contained a deep drawerful of pills which Grandmother swallowed daily to diminish the odds. But the odds were stacked.

When the pills didn't work, she fainted. When the pills did work, she fainted for reasons that remained to be diagnosed. But there was no pill that could save Grandmother from the dark complexity of her own life force, and if she were still alive, I would undoubtedly come to view her for what she was, in part—a sick, domineering woman crucified by a metabolism that nobody understood.

She was, nevertheless, an electric personality, who one day might be spinning the heart of a visiting monsignor (after running through a variety of religious experiences, Grandmother finally joined the Catholic Church, which gave her enough theological acreage to run around in). The next day she might be in bed, collapsed like a Chinese fan. One never knew from one day to the next what small brush fires in her brain might go out of control. But her instability was irregular. She could never be chalked up as merely mad, and even at the age of six or seven, I had it very firmly planted in my mind that Grandmother was only safe, truly safe, in one position—sitting down. She is, in my memory, eternally seated—in a living-room chair, at the dinner table, or perched upon a padded stool in the monkey-wallpapered bathroom on the second floor of 36 Presidio Terrace, where once a month a hairdresser with the implausible name of Werner Werner came to blue her hair.

She was beautiful, even as an old woman. She had what doesn't count for much anymore, which was flair uncluttered by accomplishments. She had no close friends. In fact, the very idea of Grandmother having close friends seems ridiculous. And while she possessed no profile beyond that of her own personal definition, which even now seems more than sufficient, she dressed as if she were momentarily expecting the Nobel Prize for general excellence—pince-nez, silk blouses, long, velvet dinner robes which fell magnificently to the floor, just like Grandmother, who could crumple on cue when life overwhelmed her.

When Grandmother was well, she was brilliantly well, demonstrating a breadth of mind, scope of intuition and a sense of humor that drew people to her like shavings to a magnet. There was no one who could sweep into a room and fill it full of emotion faster or squeeze more drama from a sofa cushion in the mere act of sitting down.

But when Grandmother was not well, the entire ship of her

personality sank like a stone, leaving the whole family swimming around the vortex she created. Her intuitions turned deadly, old slights were resurrected and driven into the offender's heart, her eyes would fill with terrible, cold anger, and her face—which had the capacity to go soft or hard within two seconds—would flatten with sorrow, as if she had been hit by a blast of hot, killing air that she alone was sensitive enough to feel.

One wrist would go to her forehead, she would stagger up from whatever situation was too much for her (it could be anything—a cool look, a kitchen noise, a private thought that was intolerable) and go to her room. Then Dr. Noble (who certainly was) would be telephoned to assess the situation, which was invariably the same.

Grandmother was always sinking from or rallying back toward a life that was essentially beyond her control. Yet she saw life very clearly. No one was more triumphantly disposed toward its ultimate meaning, and when she saw a way in which life could be expanded she was ready to storm whatever fortresses stood in her way. "My Utmost for His Highest" should have been her personal crest, although she usually saw other people's possibilities more clairvoyantly than her own. The assumption I always went on was that she was already fully developed.

At one point, Grandmother saw very clearly that I was a musical prodigy. Had I not learned a Scarlatti sonata by ear? Was she not, herself, an opera singer by temperament, even though her own father had forbidden a career on the stage? There was obvious talent in my soul, and leaving all cost out of it, which was how my family usually operated, Grandmother determined that I should have the full resources of the San Francisco Conservatory of Music at my disposal—immediately.

Taking me by the hand, she marched me over to Mrs. Maud Symington's house where I was set before a piano and told to show Maud (whose connection with the Conservatory was unclear to me) what untutored but sincere talent could do. Sitting to one side of the piano, Grandmother simultaneously carried on a conversation with Maud, and when I had finally finished she said, "Well, Maud, as you can hear, the child is extraordinary."

That particular audition came to naught, but only because it turned out to be unnecessary. Grandmother landed me a scholarship at the convent school I attended the following year, but it never occurred to her that I would be denied whatever was necessary to blossom.

Sick or well, Grandmother never lost a basically vertical inclination of heart. When I walked into her room, her neuroses always lifted, and while other family members might have viewed her as a griefless widow trapped in a wing chair (in all our conversations, Grandmother never mentioned her husband, an omission which didn't seem important at the time), I saw her as a wise and accepting Delphic oracle, and the saddest thing I could muster up in my imagination was Grandmother being run over by a city bus. I would usually cry at the thought.

There was a time when it became important to learn how to cry on command. That time coincided with the sudden realization that there was a way out of my lukewarm obscurity. Hollywood. Six hundred miles down the coast. Tears would float me to stardom. Genuine, heartfelt drops of water streaming down my genuine, famous child-star face. When Hollywood exploded like a firecracker in my head, Grandmother was the only member of the family who embraced my dream with the solemnity that I prayed it deserved. Children are shrewd. If she had been putting me on, I think I would have known.

When I turned nine and it was discovered that I needed glasses, Hollywood and stardom were not in my line of vision.

I vaguely knew about Margaret O'Brien (my parents had taken me to see *Little Women* for my eighth birthday), but it was not until the day I sat waiting for my eyes to dilate in a doctor's office and listened to my mother read aloud from a book entitled something like *Margaret O'Brien's Very Own Diary*—not until that moment did I realize what stale doughnuts I had been eating all those years. My God, what a life that girl was leading! In a dark room with stinging eyes, I listened to my mother drone unwittingly on over the particulars, which I shall reconstruct as best I can:

> Today mummy and I went to the Automat in New York City. It was snowing outside and I had on a white fur coat with a matching hat and muff. You put nickels and dimes into the slots and get sandwiches and pie from behind teeny little windows.

I don't know what appealed to me the most—the all-white fur outfit in a snowstorm in New York, or simply the Automat. But my heart stretched with envy. That I should be wearing dresses from Macy's Chubette department and be 3,000 miles from an Automat. That I should be holding soggy tomato sandwiches in a hot schoolyard while Margaret was holding press conferences and getting toy Collies from unknown admirers. What kind of a God was this who would visit astigmatism and flyaway hair upon the head of one nine-year-old and bestow twenty-twenty vision and a set of shiny black braids upon another? In one moment, which extended for the next several years, I decided that Margaret O'Brien did not deserve her life. Wondering why I fixated upon Margaret O'Brien and not Shirley Temple, I think the reason was twofold: Shirley Temple was too treacly for my tastes. Secondly, Margaret O'Brien might be easier to knock off.

With freshly ground glasses on, I spent the next several weeks poring over Margaret's *Diary*. I evaluated her jokes, tried to visualize her "Story Book Doll" collection, and went up and down with her ups and downs. "It's so much fun," she wrote, "to make pictures with my new pink typewriter." Clever Margaret had made a complete face out of x's, dashes and parentheses. I found that I could do the same thing on my father's old black Remington. But that wasn't all I found.

It was abundantly clear to me that there was nothing to distinguish me from Margaret O'Brien which wasn't totally explained by one factor. She had been "discovered." Somewhere, while out buying underpants with her mother, Margaret had been seen. A talent scout had picked up on her, and now the world was her oyster.

As I saw Hollywood in my mind's eye, there were three basic classes of people living there: the stars, the orchestra behind the stars and the talent scouts. The talent scouts were responsible for finding the unknowns and elevating them to the fame they did or did not deserve. The talent scouts were deployed across the country with instructions to find future Margarets and Shirleys. They took buses, walked through crowds, looked around corners, or cruised around in unmarked cars, looking all the time. But they were lamentably anonymous. One never knew who the talent scout was or when he might pop up (there were no female talent scouts, I was nicely a part of my generation). As the dream of stardom blossomed in my head, I realized the stardom itself was not so difficult. Being discovered was the hydrant that I didn't know how to jump. Somebody had to see me.

My world was full of untrained eyes—soup-stirring mothers, hat-wearing fathers. The man next door was in plumbing supplies. Next to him was a man who distributed sausages to restaurants. The streets were full of people who weren't looking at all, although somewhere among them was a man in a brown suit who had my archetype in his mind. Where, however, was the star-crossed corner on which to jump rope?

For some time I simultaneously plotted press conferences

("I bet you all would like a little ice cream right about now, wouldn't you?" I would say generously to the reporters at my feet) and wrestled with the problem of how to be discovered so that Margaret would not continue to corner the market. But the problem seemed insoluble, at which point I went to Grandmother for advice. Then, as now, I considered her advice brilliant.

She was sitting in her room in the usual place, in a wing chair beneath her fan collection on the wall, taking little pinches of dried seaweed called agar-agar for her bowels. I drew up the footstool, which I used to sit upon for endless, dull afternoons, wrapped in the camphorated details of her past, as the present ticked away outside her door—unnoticed by both of us. But today I had present-day business to discuss, a problem that Grandmother, with all her past experience, needed to listen to, and for once we did not do what we usually did, which was to go backward in time where Grandmother came most fully alive.

She was a matchless storyteller, pulling one vignette out after the other, like the gloves she kept folded in her expanding sachet bags, or the old foxed photographs she kept in a box beneath her bed. Everyone important to Grandmother was under her bed, but I rarely asked for pictures. With Grandmother they weren't necessary, and I could just as clearly see her brother Reeves (who died suddenly when he backed into a rose thorn while reaching for a fly ball on a tennis court) as I could see the water glass in her hand. She used to punctuate her stories with pills, swallowing them dramatically at certain turns of plot. Grandmother never seemed to lead the same day twice in a row, although it seemed to me that most of the time before she was married was taken up trying to calm her heart enough to read a love letter shyly shoved across a tea table by a young man whom she was forced to reject out of hand.

But today was different. We left the groves, the gardens,

the deeply delicate courtships conducted over tea, and after announcing my ambition, I tried to explain my dilemma in some detail. Grandmother understood in a flash.

"Well," she declared, fishing for the end of her pearls in her blouse, "it has been my experience that talent scouts look for fresh faces in fresh places." The soft, unworked fingers of one hand gathered up the pearls in a figure eight and released them—kerplunk—for emphasis. "I think that our best plan" —and her eyes deepened with conspiracy—"is to have you stay right in your own hometown."

She gave a slight shift of her innards, to adjust the Baklavian layers of crepe, velvet and whalebone, and waited for me to evaluate her advice.

I let my belt out a notch and hunched up upon the footstool to think. Grandmother made good sense. Did I want to press up against the gates of MGM, part of a cast of thousands breaking their heads against the bars? I would not stand out. The idea of sitting in a large room with a lot of prettier, starchier little girls who knew how to play the accordion, tap dance, and had naturally blond, straight hair, seemed undignified. Why dilute my chances? The shrewd move, as Grandmother pointed out, was to stay where I was, let the talent scout come to me, where in a poor backwater setting, my talents would seem all the more sharply obvious.

A small scene flashed through my mind: the Blue Bird Marionette show, a man sitting in the front row thinking, "My God, there she is!" A deal in the back of the room with my parents, a phone call to Hollywood ("Hello, Mac, I've found her."), and I would be packed off to a white Beverly Hills mansion where Hattie McDaniel would be chuckling in a large kitchen, making pancakes with my name on them. And the light would shine all around.

I have always been very conscious of light. Light silvering the fog, light organizing the dust motes into columns, light filtering through the venetian blinds, playing photogenically around my curls which I tried to brush from a lying-down position onto my pillow at night just in case a talent scout happened to look through the window while I was asleep. It is difficult to be one's own makeup man, choreographer, director and lighting expert. But I had to work with what I had, myself, and hope that my small gavottes on the bedroom floor, performed before unseen cameras that whirred in dark corners, would bear results.

A latter-day thought: I find it interesting that a part of me was always teetering on humiliation and self-doubt. I found nothing to commend myself to myself except my designs on the future—sainthood, for instance, depended less upon me than circumstances which would be so sharply defined that courage would well up as naturally as Old Faithful under pressure. When it came to talent, I did a cart-before-the-horse maneuver in my head. The desire was proof of talent, which many years later, I tend to think is still proof. What we want most deeply is what, in some form, we are meant to possess. In my mind then, talent was simply a question of enough lessons. Talent scouts were interested in raw material, although the prospect of having to teach myself how to tap dance suddenly made me tired.

Outside Grandmother's window, the dull, impotent snap of my cousin Johnny's cap pistol reminded me that the day was taking its routine course without me. It seemed so nickel-dime, so horizontal, so blunt. But Grandmother had solved my dilemma. I must be ambitious but patient. I left her room in search of an orange.

Standing in my aunt's kitchen downstairs, I pulled back the rind in sections with my teeth and thought again about Margaret. Her oranges probably came peeled on a white plate held by a black maid. I wondered whether she was allowed to eat in her room. Probably not, since she wouldn't want to get her candy-striped bedspread dirty or drip juice on her thick pink carpet.

The last orange segment snaking its way down my throat, I walked outside. The afternoon was white and unpromising. My cousin Johnny—oh, crouching, dreamless nobody—flipped me half a roll of caps. I fed them into my cap pistol and dove out of target range into a mulch pile behind a wall.

Flat out upon the cool, rotting compost, I drew a bead down the tin muzzle. ("She used to play, as a little girl, in just this spot," said the tour director.) There were dots of citric acid on my glasses, and with a free arm I rubbed my sleeve across the lenses. ("Oh yes," assured the tour guide, "she was a very normal child in every respect.") I refocused but it was no use. Suspended just above the sight notch was a nine-year-old girl in a pink net tutu, dancing her heart out on a broad, waxed stage.

I don't believe that I ever had another extended conversation with my grandmother on the subject of my stardom. But one conversation was enough. She had confirmed my wildest dream as plausible while counseling me to plug on with my present life, which I was too inexperienced to know how to ditch. We should all have one person who knows how to bless us despite the evidence. Grandmother was that person to me, enabling me to straddle the twin bars of fantasy and reality with more equilibrium than Grandmother was able to do in her own life. We were equally powerless, united by our egoism and common taste for the outrageous. She never made me feel small. Opportunity was en route.

There were several instances where opportunity knocked and then ran away, and I was forced to rethink what was going on. The first chance seemed, on the surface, tailor-made. It was a wet, foggy day. I was roller-skating in front of my house when I stopped in front of a piece of newspaper which had flattened against the cement. I don't know what caused me to peel it off the pavement, but I picked up the wet newssheet and held it to the light to read. My heart jumped.

There at the top of the page was a large photograph of Margaret O'Brien. She was crying in front of what looked like an altar, between her mother and an anonymous man. The caption read, "Margaret O'Brien Disrupts Her Mother's Wedding."

The details escape me now, but the gist of the story was that Margaret's mother was remarrying, and in the middle of the ceremony Margaret had broken into tears, rushed down the aisle and pushed herself between her mother and prospective husband, sobbing "No, no," or something equally as strong.

Suddenly, I knew what I should do. It was a terrible thing for Margaret to deny her own mother (who had sacrificed so much for Margaret) this happiness. I realized that Margaret was a brat, a spoiled, noncompassionate brat, and after taking the newspaper story home and drying it over the radiator so that I could read the story once more, I sat down and wrote Margaret O'Brien a letter.

It was a beautiful, instructive letter, really much more mature than Margaret herself, written by a little girl her age, which meant that Margaret would be particularly moved by it. I mailed it off, sat back and waited for the results.

Down there in Hollywood, Margaret would open the letter, read it with wide eyes, tears would spring to her lids and she would call a press conference.

"A little girl I don't even know," she would begin in her famous squeaky voice, "has just written me a letter that makes me realize that I was wrong to prevent my mother from marrying the man she loved. If it hadn't been for this little fan . . ." Cut to San Francisco.

Margaret would not even be able to finish her sentence before the cameras would have dollied up to my front porch. I would be called out of obscurity into the klieg lights, and suddenly Margaret's press conference would be mine. Goodbye, Margaret. Hello, me.

Several months later, I received a five-by-seven glossy photograph of Margaret, with no letter attached. So much for the power of the pen.

As for the talent scout, I was only hoodwinked once. One afternoon, while jumping rope in front of my flat (whether I was jumping for the "camera" or not, I don't remember), a car pulled to a stop across the street and a man rolled down the window and gazed at me with curiosity.

I pretended not to notice. Then the car pulled away. Oh well, I thought. I was only pretending he was a talent scout. Then the car stopped, began to back up toward me again and stopped in the same place. ("The one time she was unprepared, she caught a talent scout's eye.") He turned off the ignition and opened the side door. ("Of course, my parents would have to come with me," she said.) Then he walked across the street to where I was standing.

My heart began to pound. I didn't really believe it would ever happen. I took off my glasses.

"Excuse me, little girl," he said, smiling.

What next? What next? My tongue was tied altogether.

"Could you tell me whether that flat behind you is for rent?"

"No," I said quietly, "that's just where I live."

The stranger got back into his car and drove away, taking most of my Margaret O'Brien fantasy with him as he went.

In time I was forced to relinquish my grip on that powerful square foot of real estate outside Grauman's Chinese Theater. Chances were excellent, I began to think, that my feet would never be pressed into the cement, but I didn't let go of the idea of celluloid immortality easily. I dreamed of a day when I could look Susan Figel in the eye and see nothing but envy stream back in my direction, although I planned to be totally forgiving to everyone, which included Miss Geanneacopolis, who could no longer discount me as easily as she did on the day of her wedding. I was less interested in conquering new worlds than forcing the old world to move over on the bench. I was, I suppose, intoxicated with the power I would have, and the goodness which, under new circumstances, would be so easy to dispense.

Margaret O'Brien had shown herself to be callous toward her fans. But her replacement would be heartbreakingly generous. Hollywood would be breathless over my incessant virtue. I knew I would be the most unspoiled child star anyone had ever known. My eyes would be perpetually downcast in a modesty that would win the hearts of everyone, up to and including Lionel Barrymore. All my glossies would be accompanied by personal, handwritten notes.

I don't remember when I gave up Hollywood for good. My eyes simply refocused one day, and I decided that I really didn't want to be a movie star anymore. I was, however, interested in the stars as examples of a documented life where soap, soft-drink, carpet and perfume companies begged for endorsements. Yet did the stars really use the products? I smelled a rat that I could never locate. If I knew that they did use them, then something deep inside me would be confirmed. But I was not privy to Dinah Shore's bathroom, where the Palmolive soap either did or did not rest in the dish. As I moved into my early teens, swinging the same ratio of baby fat to bone that plagued my image, the tail end of my interest in knocking off Margaret O'Brien centered around the sidebar issue of whether Hollywood stars were shills for the Colgate-Palmolive Company, or whether there were magic powers in products which, when I used them, resisted me.

I never did find out the answer absolutely, although there was one summer when my aunt and uncle invited me to their fancy tennis club in Pebble Beach, and both Dinah Shore and her dazzlingly handsome husband, George Montgomery, were on the courts. I saw Dinah Shore first, lacing up her shoes on the sidelines. She was surrounded by teenagers, and she was laughing with them, talking about her husband, and proving, in the flesh, that she was just as nice as a Hollywood star could be. I sidled up, gathered my question inside, and when there was a break in the conversation, I blurted out, "Do you really use Palmolive soap?"

Everyone laughed. I had broken the spell, asked a very stupid, irritating question. But Miss Shore was lovely about it, laughed merrily and said, "But of course."

Several minutes later George Montgomery came loping along in a pair of black socks, basketball shorts and a baseball cap. I went inwardly white with disillusionment.

When Grandmother died, I was heartbroken but not surprised. Death was inevitable, given her age. But I was wild with anger to think that she had died out of my presence. And while I was beginning to drift away from her orbit and didn't listen to her stories about who shot who back in 1912 with the same interest, she was nevertheless the one member of the family about whom I cared the most passionately, counted upon as the linchpin who would always allow me to swing by the hinges of my imagination without censure or criticism. Yet when the end came, I was not told. One day the air simply became quiet, as if a large engine that routinely operated at a distance had stopped. I mentally traced the silence to Presidio Terrace, realized that not a word about my grandmother had been spoken for at least three days, and, therefore, something was very wrong.

"Grandmother's sick, isn't she?" I accused my father when he walked in the front door.

"Somewhat," he hedged, averting his eyes.

"Not sick, dying!" I yelled. "Why won't you tell me?"

"Oh, I don't know about that," countered my father. "I don't know about that."

But I knew, and I wandered aimlessly around the neighborhood weeping with the conviction that my grandmother might be drawing her last breath at that very moment, and I was not there to tell her what, in my egocentricity, I knew she needed to hear—that I would never forget her as long as I lived.

"I want to go and see her," I begged.

"No," said my father. "She is too sick right now. The house must be kept quiet."

Then Grandmother died. Suddenly I was not only invited but commanded to appear at the house, and when I entered 36 Presidio Terrace, having never seen a dead person before, my Aunt Dorothy took me by the arm and tried to lead me gently upstairs. "All the grandchildren are there now."

"No," I screamed, surprised by the magnificence of my own rudeness. "I'm not going in there." And tearing my arm away, I backed down the stairs.

This time, my arm was taken more firmly. I wrenched away once again, turned on my heel and ran with real fear (no one in the family had ever forced me to do anything like this before) through the kitchen and out the back door.

But my aunt was surprisingly fleet. She caught me with both arms as I was halfway down the alley and pushed me back into the house upstairs until I was outside Grandmother's room. Then she quietly opened the door and led me by the shoulder blades inside.

The shades were pulled against the sun. The room smelled of candle wax, alcohol and old satin quilts. As my aunt pushed me into a kneeling position in the circle of grandchildren, my eye caught a glimpse of Grandmother—a yellow, collapsed face on the pillow—before my knees hit the floor. I didn't look at her again—out of respect.

That wasn't Grandmother. It was a betrayal of her dignity to look at what she no longer controlled, and as I plodded through the Rosary, led by my Uncle Gene who was the only other Catholic in the family, I was intent upon doing only one thing—keeping my mind shut upon my own angry thoughts.

Grandmother, the most fully realized person in my life,

had walked off the stage without my applause. The unfairness of that exit (she too weak to ask for me, I too weak to insist) was coupled with an overwhelming sense of sorrow that I no longer had anyone with whom to examine the thread of my life.

The thread was in my inexpert hands now. Grandmother was no longer available for consultation. But my deepest anger was over being denied the opportunity to set my cheek against hers and tell her of the full extent of my love. Perhaps she did not know how much I loved her. Now she would never know, and I pictured her setting out in a white nightgown with a suitcase toward God, wondering why I hadn't been there to shout good-bye across the void. I wanted to be the last voice she heard.

I wonder now, thinking of Grandmother, whether accomplishments have any real significance as the world defines them. I suppose they do, or at least we're inwardly urged to create things to prove that we were around for a few years. But beneath the books, music scores and brilliant conceptions we foist upon the world, perhaps our real accomplishments lie elsewhere—in one conversation we can't remember having, one small relationship that sets someone else believing in something more powerful than self-doubt.

For years after she died, Grandmother floated like a spirit over the bathtub I soaked in, watching me naked as I floated above the plug. She was, I believed, always watching me, even when I succumbed to my own flesh, which I tried not to do for Grandmother's sake. I was anxious to keep the connection unembarrassing, but it was a long time before she finally floated, hat and handbag, out of the bathroom to Heaven proper, where she examined me from a greater distance and my lesser acts were, hopefully, hidden from her view.

Chapter
VI

I had two grandmothers. In 1949, when I was ten years old, my East Coast grandmother died and left Mother $50,000. It was the seed money for the beginning of our affluent life.

I barely knew "Granny." She was less a relative than a mink-coated, beautiful older woman who used to fly in, usually en route to Hawaii, for several days and leave expensive traces behind her after she left. A new coat for Mother, an alligator handbag that she didn't want anymore, whipped cream. Granny didn't like to be without whipped cream or an exit, and she often hired a taxi which she kept running outside, just in case something downtown occurred to her. But she rarely stayed more than several days, which was all she could take of a flat or my father, who usually clammed up when she was around, and I had no particular feelings about her one way or the other.

Granny gave me no stories to hang my hat upon. She didn't seem to be particularly interested in grandchildren one way or the other, and while I admired her as an oddity with gold bracelets and an eccentric, trilling voice, I only remember one thing about her, the time she lost her lingerie on Stockton Street downtown. That was the ultimate shocking development in my mind, but Granny simply two-stepped out of her predicament as casually as if she were in her own boudoir. Retrieving the pile of lace from the sidewalk, she folded the article neatly into a square and dropped it neatly into her purse. "Whee, give the boys a treat," she had trilled. I never would have thought of that line, but when Granny wasn't visiting I didn't think of her, and when she died unexpectedly I wasn't moved at all.

There was a long-distance call. Mother let out a sharp cry—rather like the one she made when I walked down the aisle to be married—and pulled me onto her lap. I put my arms around her as she listened to the voice on the other end, and when she replaced the receiver on the hook and told me the news, I moved protectively into the hollow spaces of her lap, tried to fill in for the loss as adeptly as I could, feeling large and responsible, as we sat together. But the next day, as I lit a candle for Granny at Grace Cathedral, I felt absolved from any further responsibility for Granny herself. I don't remember Mother ever crying for her after that telephone call. I was too young to wonder why.

My sister Wendy, a frail blond-haired baby whom I loved, was born that same year, ending a ten-year gap between my brother John and me at the far end. The Clay Street flat was too small for three children, and with Granny's inheritance my parents moved out of San Francisco across the Golden Gate Bridge to Marin County and a brand-new model house on a man-made peninsula off Belvedere Island.

It was called a "lagoon home." We were the first family to move onto Edgewater Road while the rest of the street was a pile of lumber. The house was all plate glass, nursery seedlings, and modern ideas which sat at the end of a raw strip of landfill that looked over a lagoon destined to fill up with "El Toros" and happy affluent families skimming across the water toward nowhere.

I hated the house, longed for Clay Street, and every time I swam in the lagoon, my feet plunged down into a foot of mushy silt that revolted my toes.

My brother John acclimated a little better. He was, by nature, a more solitary child. From dawn to dusk he would jump around the flatlands of Richardson Bay, catching sand sharks by their fins which smelled, like John, who (during those days) inspired only one emotion in me, anger, as did Belvedere itself.

Belvedere was an expensive paradise with nothing to do. The local school was a chaotic, badly run place. The only potential friend who lived close enough was a sharp-faced girl who resented my efforts to copy her wardrobe and was obviously interested in keeping me at arm's length in case a boy she liked happened to bicycle by. The whole place was a no-man's-land that mirrored the adolescence I entered into at that same period of time.

Adolescence didn't strike, it accumulated, like my own fat, which had been building up under the counter of Bath-old's Drug Store on Sacramento Street, where I used to crouch eating ice cream cones and reading comics I could not afford to buy.

"Puppy fat," protested my mother, who tried to make me understand that one day my metabolism would dissolve the fat into a memory and I would be free of plumpness forever. But I didn't believe my mother. A neighbor in Belvedere had once told me that I had ballerina legs, meaning muscular, and my father called me "fat fairy," an endearment that was not dear to me. The mirror gave back every ice cream cone I had ever consumed, and on all sides fat hung like the solid charge of my own ungracefulness.

I lapsed out of cheerfulness and spent most of my time

locked behind my bedroom door, angrily filling up coloring books and thinking of new ways to wreak my rage upon the household. That household within the next several years expanded to include another sister, Cindy—a solid, doe-eyed baby—and a series of domestics who never did make up the difference. They complained all day about "piles" or husbands or both, and none of them really looked like the maids I used to dream of. They never wore uniforms and never made a dent.

There were several fat black ladies from Marin City who would slap around the kitchen in raveled bedroom slippers and got the ironing done after a fashion, and one rather terrifying professional housekeeper who made anyone who misbehaved sit in a chair while she read her latest *Watchtower* tract. But they were better than nothing, and when the diapers started piling up, my mother was entirely preoccupied, my father began to dream of Chris Crafts and I was left to my own fat, preteen devices. They were not very effective.

An enormous amount of unspent energy was whipping around my rib cage. It had no place to go except against myself, and my only recourse was to channel that energy into a series of mean-minded plots, which pivoted upon such self-defeating moves that I was always forced to undo the plots and capitulate to my own incapacity to sustain the action.

I staged a series of hunger strikes—days locked away in my room followed by nights in a dark kitchen silently eating through a loaf of Wonder Bread. One afternoon in the pouring rain, I broke my hunger strike to walk to the drugstore two miles away in a new dress that was too small for me. I hoped that the exercise would shrink me. I got to the drugstore and bought three Milky Ways. There was no exit. Every plate-glass window in that horrible house gave back a reflection of a squint-eyed, fat-cheeked malcontent, and there were very few days when I was fit company for anyone, a realization that I would not admit to myself or only rarely.

One evening, in a burst of good humor, I walked out in the yard to say hello to my father, who was smoking a cigarette at the end of the lawn. I was glad to see him. I called out, "Hi." But as I drew closer and saw him turn his face toward me, I saw a look in his eyes that slowed my steps. His eyes were full of plain dislike. I had never seen that expression before, but in one brief moment of clarity as I stared back at him, I thought, "I don't blame you. I don't blame you at all." I was impossible to like at the precise time that I would have given everything to be adored, but when I think back to that terrible, ribless time, there was a moment within it that was, in a way I will never forget, my father's finest hour.

In the middle of the sixth grade, invitations were sent out countywide to all the students who attended private schools (I only lasted one year at a public school in Belvedere) to attend a formal Christmas dance in San Rafael. It was a Father-Daughter dance. Long dresses for the girls, blue suits for the boys. Months before, I began to think of the dress.

For some reason a new dress was out of the question. In my parents' sudden flirtation with a new life-style, all the cash had gone into other things. But my mother was very positive about an alternative. "Your cousin Mimi's dress is just perfect. She only wore it twice, and it's really better than anything you could find right away now anyway. It came from Magnin's." Everything Mimi got seemed to come from Magnin's. Everything I got came from Mimi. That's just the way it was.

The dress was sent over from San Francisco—a limp, scoop-necked formal that hung like a faded blue day lily on the hanger, its silver circles embroidered on the skirt as dull as rain clouds. I burst into tears. "It looks awful," I said.

"We'll have it cleaned," said my mother, who honestly believed it was possible to snatch the bacon from the fire. "It will look brand new. The cleaners can do wonders these days."

I wasn't convinced, but Mother was plucking at the skirt,

fluffing it optimistically with her fingers, and seeing possibilities that I had to take on faith. Faith was all that was left.

The day before the dance the dress came back from Vogue Cleaners. I ripped the plastic off the hanger and my worst fears were confirmed. The silver circles were as dull as ever. The skirt was not puffy. It looked just like what it was—an expensive, secondhand dress without sparkle or hope. I stared at it with tears pricking my eyes. "It doesn't stick out," I said quietly. Mother sighed. "No, not quite as I had hoped," she conceded. I stood silently before the dress and made an uncharacteristic decision. I would be noble.

That evening I announced in as even a voice as I could command, "I've been thinking it over. I'm not sure I really want to go to that dance tomorrow night at all."

"Is it the dress?" asked my mother.

"No," I lied. "It doesn't have anything to do with the dress. I just don't particularly want to go. I don't have to, do I?"

"Of course not," said my mother.

My father didn't say anything at all.

The next day I stayed in my room artfully shading in Walt Disney characters in my coloring book. I was, to the best of my recollection, unusually pleasant to everyone, hoping to simply get through supper without giving way to my real feelings.

At six o'clock there was a knock on my bedroom door.

"Come in," I mumbled.

The door was kicked open. My father was standing in the hall, almost hidden behind two shiny long boxes, with a small white box balanced on top. He strode into the bedroom, dumped the boxes on the bed and threw his hat into a corner.

"All right," he began, "don't say anything until I've finished. It's up to you, of course. I mean, what do I know about these things? But I got to thinking about this Father-Daughter dance and about you not wanting to go, and I figured this morning as I was driving to work that maybe you'd reconsider the whole thing if you had something to wear that set your mind racing a little. If it's just a matter of the dress, I'll be damned if you're not going to go to that dance tonight, and so I took the day off from work and called up your Aunt Irene, and the two of us traipsed around San Francisco looking for the perfect thing. . . ."

He paused to catch his breath and went over to the boxes, which he started to open, and then stopped.

"I don't know what young girls like to wear, but I got you two to choose from, plus one of those little flowers from Podesta's that your Aunt Irene says girls wear on their wrists. Now, you've only got about an hour before we have to be there, so you'd better take a look and tell me what you think."

I cannot think about what those boxes contained without feeling the same disbelief that overcame me then. I opened the first, and out sprang a pink net dress covered with tiny stars. Out of the second box came a pale blue net dress with white daisies embroidered all over the skirt. The box from Podesta's held a white gardenia with a pearl pin stuck through the ribbon. Suddenly the room was full of white tissue and hope.

"Oh, Daddy," I breathed.

"Oh, Daddy, nothing," he shot back. "No fat fairy as pretty as you should be without a new dress to her first dance. Now you get yourself ready, and I'm going to go and make myself as presentable as I can."

That night my father made every other father look like Dagwood Bumstead. He twinkled, he grinned, he never left my side. I thought he looked like Fred MacMurray. I slid my eyes around the floor to see whether any of the other girls were envying me. But it didn't make any difference if they envied me or not. I knew I was enviable. My father was the handsomest man in the room, and when the band struck up its hyenic notes and a hundred feet in new satin shoes fought for balance on the basketball floor, I hung on my father's shoulder, held his hand, and we waltzed beyond all fear. Only once did he threaten to undo my dignity.

When the Charleston struck up, he threw out his legs at an angle, stuck his fingers behind his head like an Indian and began to wiggle his fingers with a grin.

"Oh please, Daddy. Don't do that!" I begged.

"What's the matter," he grinned, "don't you think the old geezer knows how to cut a rug?"

But after a few knee-weaving gestures, he straightened up and led me to the punch table. Together we stood against the table and looked out at the crowd.

"I don't see any competition for you out there," he said, pinching my net-covered arm. "Never seen such a bunch of Bozos in one room in my life."

Together we went back out on the floor. "Watch out, buster," he said, as a sweating boy in a blue suit crunched on my heel.

"Just you wait," he said. "When you get a little older, I'm not going to be able to get within ten feet of you." I stared at my gardenia wristlet self-consciously, my plumpness obscured under fourteen separate tiers of net. "You look so pretty," he added.

I looked up at him and said something I had never said to him before. "You are the most handsome father I know."

He was, of course, the handsomest without doubt and the first prince in my life to come through, unwittingly setting me up for every other prince who was delayed in transit later on. But that is another story and to make dry, sociological references robs the story of its merit. One night does not melt away an adolescence, but I'm glad I have it to refer back to. It confirms my deepest feelings about my father, who confirmed my deepest hopes for myself. The night was full of light, contentment and store-bought stars, and I don't know how to repay my father for it except to tell the story and let it stand on its own—like a new dress.

My adolescence never came to full term. I was jolted off that train and put onto another train going down a parallel track at a faster speed. I credit and debit Moral Re-Armament with that fact, although I was looking for a way out of adolescence and MRA provided it. Seek and ye shall find.

My Aunt Dorothy invited me to spend two weeks with her at 833 South Flower Street, the Moral Re-Armament Center in Los Angeles. Whatever her motivation—and undoubtedly she saw a chance to shape me up as nobody else had done so far—I leaped at the chance to get out of Belvedere and see the world. Two weeks later I returned so full of virtue that it took everyone's breath away.

Los Angeles was not entirely strange territory. In the middle of my Margaret O'Brien phase, my father had driven me all the way down the coast for a two-day orgy of star-watching, an expensive weekend of living at the Beverly Wilshire, lunch at the Brown Derby, dinner at Chasen's and driving around Beverly Hills with a map of which stars lived where so that I could get it all out of my system once and for all. I don't know where he got the money. When my brother John was born, he had to sell the car to get him out of the hospital. But my father has never thought about money as an obstacle.

I saw no stars, with the exception of Tony Curtis, who arrived in a swirl of luggage and microphones at the Beverly Wilshire on the afternoon that I spent skulking around the lobby looking for autographs. I wasn't interested in Tony Curtis. He looked too stuck on himself, too greasy, too uncharismatic. But I incorrectly identified the star of "The Fat Man" radio show, who was not pleased about being called someone he wasn't, and ultimately I forged a movie-star signature myself and brought it upstairs to my parents, who hadn't believed I would find anyone. In those days I was a terrific liar. They believed I had proven them wrong. I can't remember whose name I forged. We left Hollywood on a Sunday morning, and all I had in my memory was the backside of Clifton Webb, who was just getting into his car in a parking lot. Clifton Webb in a parking lot was, in the end, how I characterized Hollywood—something of a disappointment.

In browsing through a paperback book called *What Is Moral Re-Armament?* (the authors don't really know themselves, or at least they give you fourteen different answers which don't sum it up), there is a picture taken from an airplane of Hollywood Bowl, presumably filled with MRA boosters, who were present at its inception in the Hollywood area.

Perhaps the MRA people originally envisioned Hollywood being bowled over by its message, but the film world held onto its decadence quite nicely; only a few of its more thoughtful or guilty citizens gave MRA the time of day. And 833 South Flower Street, the MRA headquarters in downtown Los Angeles, attracted builders from Pasadena, clubwomen from Santa Monica, and entirely normal-looking, upper-class people who, with few exceptions, had no connection with the movie industry at all.

An old residence hotel, with a large dining room, an outdoor walled garden, and plenty of places to sit and read periodicals under parchment reading lamps on library tables, "The Club," as everyone called it, would have made a good Harvard Club.

It was not a child's place, although there were a half-dozen other children there, on the coattails of parents who were staying for several weeks, and we formed a kind of bothersome, short-sheeting subculture that ran around the periphery of the main action, which revolved around the morning and evening meetings in the upstairs meeting room. I was familiar with the format.

Ever since I had been old enough to keep a piece of paper still on my knees, I had been an irregular part of a family ritual called "quiet times." My own parents never had these sessions, but the Gallwey house featured them in a regular way. The quiet times were usually held in the Gallwey living room, and all of the children would be told to sit silently and listen to what God was saying to us in our hearts.

I don't remember God ever telling me anything, at least not in the cavernous, stentorian voice that I assumed He had to speak with if He were going to say something significant. But God dealt with trivia; at least that was what usually came out of these guidance sessions, as we went around the circle sharing what we had written down. God didn't want Jerry to listen to the radio when he did his homework, He was displeased with all the teasing of E. Bates that went on, and one day my cousin Tony, who always did have a pronounced materialistic side, looked up from his lap and said, "I got it that I should have a present."

That bit of "guidance" was immediately made part of the family lore. Everyone thought Tony was a riot, and perhaps the reason why I never felt brainwashed in the slightest by these sessions was because I knew you could always bail yourself out by being funny. In the eyes of the adults, who supervised the quiet times, they were probably viewed as gentle disciplinary devices to bring fresh order into our ranks, and I knew, as I sat with my stub pencil and doodled in the margins, that we were imitating, in a minor way, the adult sessions that took place behind glass doors in the evening at 36 Presidio Terrace. During the adult quiet times, men and women wrote with gold fountain pens in leather books, and most of their thoughts were very high-minded and intercontinental, dealing with how France could be reunited with Algeria if only men on both sides were "more God-guided."

At 833 South Flower Street the meetings were more confessional, more off-the-street dramatic, and I would sit in the
back of the room and watch a succession of people get up on
the stage and relate personal stories about how MRA had
radically transformed their lives.

The stories were all of a piece, although the details varied,
case by case:

> I was leading a dissolute, selfish life (as a high-paid
> executive, frivolous socialite, labor leader on the
> take), but deep down, I was very unhappy. My family
> life was a mess. I had bad relationships at the office.
> Then, when I met MRA, I realized that if I wanted
> to change I would have to give up certain things (ex-
> cess profits, makeup, kickbacks). I didn't want to do
> this, but I realized that if we were to have a world in
> which all nations were to be reunited under God, I
> would have to start with myself. So I began to put
> things right with my life (my wife, my business, etc.),
> and I am here to commit myself entirely to the work
> of Moral Re-Armament and the force behind it.

Some stories were better than others, but all of them were
proof of the MRA pudding, ballast for the already committed
and inspiration for the not-entirely-won-over people in the
room, which I suppose included me. But unlike fresh recruits
off the street who had never heard of it before, MRA was
already interred in my bones. My family had been in it forever. How could one decide for something that was already
a fact, like the Steinway in the Gallweys' living room, of one's
existence? Yet I wondered, as I listened to the various life
stories, whether I was too young to donate my own. Could
I scrape up the courage to stand up on the platform and make
a clean break with my past? There wasn't a great deal of past

to break with, but I was interested in getting rid of my bad personality, and I was also, in retrospect, bored—with my life, with 833 South Flower Street and the magazine racks full of MRA periodicals, all of which said the same beautifully photographed thing, rather like *China Today*. It occurred to me, however, that if I confessed myself sincerely, I might be given a part in one of the MRA plays. I loved their plays.

Moral Re-Armament always had at least two or three revues traveling around the world—fast, boot-stomping, colorful musicals full of hundreds of cast members who would hit the stage like paratroopers, singing at the top of their voices about cowboys making friends with farmers, management making friends with labor, or communists making friends with the rest of the world. The plays were the wedges that got MRA into countries and into the papers. They "sang" for their supper this way, inspired leaders, got people clapping to the rhythm and sometimes got the audience, individually, later on.

The plots were entirely predictable, although the music was so excellent that the propaganda was lifted slightly off the ground, and the closing scene always featured a full lineup of international singers who belted out the final number and then immediately descended into the audience to reap the harvest before any of the inspiration leaked out into the lobby.

As the years went on, I grew more perceptive. There was always, I noted, a clique of MRA people strategically placed in the front row who would jump to their feet to give a standing ovation when the curtain fell. Usually, people behind them automatically followed suit, which was the whole idea, and then, in subsequent MRA periodicals, it could be written that *The Good Road* had played to a cheering, on-their-feet crowd. Men with cameras would photograph everyone beaming. The photos were testimony to MRA's force, which was a lot of claptrap. It put on fairly good plays, but if you had seen one you had really seen them all.

All that being admitted, the thought of being in an MRA play greatly appealed to me then. But I knew that you couldn't be in one unless you were committed to the work, and I believed that the commitment effected an internal cosmetic change that would turn me into a clear-eyed, clear-thinking, exuberant girl—like Jenny Austin, a sanguine, pink-cheeked girl whose guidance always flowed effortlessly from her pen every morning in Los Angeles and who was, in my eyes, the "top preteen" there. I was not Jenny Austin, but had only myself to blame for that. One morning I got up from the audience, stood before the microphone and said, "I don't come from anyplace exotic." A few people giggled. The text of my capitulation is lost to my memory, but I sat down afterwards and was, in my mind, a brand-new person.

That same week I was invited to be in the back row of a hastily thrown-together revue scheduled to be performed for some people in Culver City, a back-lot city behind Los Angeles. I sang "Everything's Up To Date in Culver City," mingled with the audience, some forty or fifty housewives who didn't seem particularly overwhelmed, and felt slightly let down. But I felt closer to Jenny Austin in archetype and a great distance from the wrathful, destructive person I had left behind in Belvedere two weeks before.

When I returned home, I was so outrageously kind, generous and forebearing that my parents had a hard time adjusting. The simple request to "pass the butter" became a call to excellence. If the butter was at the other end of the table, I walked across everybody's head to get it.

I don't remember ever being overtly angry again. I ceased rebelling against my parents—perhaps because it was no longer necessary—and the one time I ran away, I left a note saying I would be back the following morning.

I didn't turn into a dream child, but I did leapfrog over the dark forces that had been rocking the small craft of my personality. Once again, I was in love with goodness, although I did not love myself. The two were separate in my mind. The point was to strain away from one toward the other, to keep one jump ahead of my own shadow. If I were always directly beneath the sun, I would always be safe.

Chapter
VII

Grandmother's last act of generosity toward me was to throw herself upon the generosity of others. Whether she subconsciously realized that a transfer of power was going to be necessary or not, I don't know. But one afternoon the year before she died, she clamped on her best velvet hat, swung an extra rope of pearls around her neck and traveled across the Golden Gate Bridge to Marin County to have a little chat with the sisters at Dominican Convent in San Rafael on my behalf. The year was 1950.

I will never know exactly what transpired between the nuns and my grandmother that afternoon, but by the end of it the nuns had been fleeced out of a scholarship which enabled me to attend their school for the next seven years. Had I wanted to, I could have stayed longer, continuing on with college and the novitiate as well. But I never wanted to be a nun. I might add that I was never seriously asked to be one either.

Grandmother was perfectly capable of selling coals in Newcastle if she were convinced of her end of a transaction, and

I believe that she obliquely hinted to the nuns that she was actually doing them a favor by informing them of my existence. Of course, the nuns didn't even have a snapshot to go by, which was probably a good thing, since I was a rather run-of-the-mill eleven-year-old, who tended toward plumpness and rumpled expressions, but my grandmother refreshed the nuns' memories as to the larger family involved.

My great-grandmother, they would remember, was one of the school's first graduates back in the days when it was still an academy. My cousin Mimi, who won the "I Speak for Democracy" contest, was a recent graduate, and I was a very talented, albeit unlessoned pianist who had taught herself "Für Elise" by ear. Granted, I was not a Catholic but that should not dissuade the nuns. The convent was hardly off limits to Episcopalians (in fact, it was a source of pride that so many attended), and there were certain prominent Jewish families in San Francisco who regularly fed their daughters into the school for want of an alternative.

As for my grandmother's religion, she had converted to Catholicism ten years previous, after Christian Science had flopped in her mind. Whether she played up my own conversion possibilities, I don't know. My guess is that she played up everything she could think of, including herself. Grandmother could make Ethel Barrymore look like a short-order cook if she wanted to, and on that day she did.

Actually, Grandmother pulled off two scholarships—one academic and one musical—in a single afternoon. Mission accomplished, she got back into the car, was driven by my father back across the Golden Gate Bridge, and the nuns went back to do the paperwork, having been conned into believing that they had just rescued a Hapsburg from the gutter.

This wasn't exactly true, although Grandmother was on as firm a piece of ground, genealogically speaking, as California provided. The Spaniards were the first aristocrats in the state, and when the Bear Flag Republic became a part of the continental United States, its borders were overrun with gold prospectors, saloon keepers, merchants and Americans of wild inclination who saw a chance to make something of their lives. The state was full of people who had made desperation moves, although California was not exactly full of bums. One historical chronicle detailing the history of the Dominican Sisters in California reports that ". . . it must not be supposed that in the sweeping majority of the motley aboriginal and foreign population that overran the Coast at this time, there was an utter absence of order and culture."

My father's family was part of a third wave, or wavelet, that broke across the state in the 1890's. The gold was gone, the golf courses were just being laid out, and people were beginning to filter across the state line for ancillary reasons. Doctors, lawyers, entrepreneurs—actually, it's a little vague as to what any of my ancestors did for a living. We're related to Howard Hughes, but the last time anyone saw him was in 1931, when he bumped into my Aunt Irene at a dance in the Fairmont Hotel; he looked at her angrily and said, "Irene, what are you doing at a party like this?" My aunt shot back, "I have every bit as much of a right to be here as you do, Howard," at which point he huffed off never to be seen again except in the newspapers. I doubt that Grandmother mentioned our Howard Hughes connection, although the nuns could count. I was a fourth-generation Californian. "That means," said my father when I asked him what a fourth-generation Californian was, "that if you were here before that you'd be a Digger Indian."

Never mind that this fourth-generation Californian was currently languishing in a public school, drawing pictures of what her ideal bedroom would look like, jamming Milk Duds into her mouth at the Saturday matinees. Connections were there that ought to be made, and it was high time, my grandmother declared, that I received an education that would bring out my potential.

As for the particulars of that potential, I imagine that Grandmother did a little artful trailing of scarves over that part of my resumé, but she was a genius with the pregnant pause, and she managed to convince the nuns that they would get back their investment in a hundred different ways.

Several months later, standing in front of the mirror with my new green Dominican uniform on, I was relieved to be shedding my old, unworkable individuality in favor of a group definition. The pleats of the plaid skirt were sharp, the cuffs of my sweater springy with new elastic, and soon I would be sitting in a long, high-ceilinged study hall, beneath a series of wooden plaques which bore the names of past students who had carried off the prizes for excellence in one subject or more. A quiet feeling of snobbery welled up inside of me at the prospect of being so exclusively defined. I felt like I was signing up for *The Bells of Saint Mary*, a feeling that the convent physically underscored.

The mother house, built in 1899, must have used up half the trees in northern California. A large, cream-colored extravaganza, which sat like a Victorian birthday cake behind a fringe of palm trees, its red tile roofs could be seen from all the surrounding hills of San Rafael, an area which was discovered by Father Serra's monks, who were looking for a sanitarium site for Indians, and was named after Saint Raphael, "the angel of healing."

The architect had left nothing out. There were cupolas, bell towers and turrets. Various other buildings behind the mother house were rigged, one to the other, with delicate, spindled walkways. A gymnasium, a pool and a pair of tennis courts flanked the backside of St. Thomas Hall where we had classes. And there was a separate parcel of land, called Forest Meadows, where we clashed our hockey sticks against each other on hot afternoons that smelled of eucalyptus oil.

A formal garden ran along one side of the academic building, and various pieces of statuary—angels, virgins, small children in the state of grace—gazed with stone eyes through the shrubbery. There was also a grotto. It wasn't used much, except on the Feast of the Assumption, when the sodality president placed a wreath of flowers on Mary's head and the school sang, "Oh Mary, we crown thee with blossoms today." I was sodality president the year I graduated, but I never got much out of the honor. If I had been student-body president, the whole upper school would have eaten cake in Hawthorne Court on my birthday.

Hawthorne Court was the Saint Peter's Square of the complex, and in the spring the hawthorne trees sent pink blossoms sifting across the courtyard into piles against the brick retaining walls, where we sat with our mail and laundry bags in the sun. It was the centerpiece of the convent, although there were dozens of small, interesting cul-de-sacs elsewhere, like behind the soup kitchen, where every morning we were doled out broth by a grumpy-faced Chinese cook, who undoubtedly plotted the overthrow of the capitalist order in his bed at night.

It was an entirely privileged existence, and if some of the girls rebelled against the sisters' exquisitely codified plan of life, I embraced it all—the uniforms, teams, rules, songs and roll calls—from the very first day. Ritual filled me with significance. I yearned for a fascism to order my untidy life.

For the first two and a half years, I was part of the grammar school, an interlude that doesn't bear going into except to say that I was marking time until I could graduate into the high school and real life. The nearest I came to real life in the grammar school was an eccentric old Scotswoman called Kate Rennie Archer, who taught poetry nobody understood. She would lean against the radiator while we all intoned, "For God, our God is a jealous foe, who playeth behind a veil," and get a faraway look in her eye. Mrs. Archer often digressed into her former life, when she drove a three-wheeled ambulance during the London blitz, and several times she said, "Goddamn," just before Sister Kathleen walked back into class.

Sister Kathleen was a small, thin woman who had immense dignity and a disregard for all children who were not faultlessly polite. "Of all the gall," was her favorite expression, and I was quite frightened of her. The other nun who routinely filled me with dread was Sister James, an extremely fat, choleric woman who ate chocolate all the time. She surprised me, however, by weeping quietly in class as we all sat and listened to Douglas MacArthur on the radio say, "Old soldiers never die, they only fade away." Large tears streamed down her chocolate-fed cheeks, and I did not understand at the time why. When I graduated to the upper school, scholarship intact, I breathed a sigh of relief.

During the day, we all wore green cotton aprons. I used to let the ties of my apron hang, to deemphasize my waistlessness and demonstrate a certain flyaway independence of the rules. But I was a small-time crook. An egg-throw behind the soup kitchen was the nearest I came to flirting with disaster, because deep down I loved the rules and regarded the nuns who enforced them with affection and respect.

Every noon, the Angelus tolled in soft, sorrowful triads over Hawthorne Court. The entire school would pause in its tracks, and the sisters would obediently fold their hands under their scapulars and murmur, "Behold the handmaid of the Lord. Be it done unto me according to Thy will." The nuns were exemplars of the grace that, one way or another, we were all meant to acquire under their direction. The Bishop of San Francisco called them "my happy order." He loved to visit.

There are orders of nuns, and then there are other orders of nuns. I was lucky. We were not subjected to the ham-handed parochial-school viragos who yelled about the evils of sex and instructed girls to bring telephone books on dates in case they had to sit on a boy's lap in a car. Of course, we weren't exposed to boys either, so perhaps there was no need to yell, but certainly the nuns liked men in general. And while we didn't see any except on Sundays, and these men were our fathers, the nuns used to flutter about them, obviously enjoying their presence, swapping baseball scores as knowledgeably as Saint Theresa swapped political insights with Ignatius of Loyola. The sisters were flirts, and the fathers would go away shaking their heads and thanking God that women like the Dominican nuns existed. Their daughters were in good hands.

In the 1950's the world was in tolerably good order, but the nuns improved upon that order by distilling it further within the confines of the convent. What was excellent was welcome, what was not excellent was worked upon, and what was unacceptable was simply not allowed in.

There was one inadvertent exception. One year a young, shiny-haired drama teacher was hired to produce the Christmas tableau. She had porcelain skin, high cheek bones, was witty and thoroughly bewitched the nuns, who wanted to believe it was possible to have theater connections and still be clean-cut. But she turned out to be sneaking boarders off to San Francisco to Finnochio's, a transvestite hangout on North Beach, and after rehearsals she held a mock Christmas tableau at one of the day students' houses, complete with that year's "Blessed Mother" swinging a gin bottle and singing dirty songs.

The nuns were sickened when all this came out, and she was fired within the hour. But by and large, the world was effectively "frisked" coming and going. The nuns spent long hours in adoration before the Blessed Sacrament exposed, but the incense did not addle their understanding. On the one hand, everything was in God's hands. On the other hand, they censored our mail.

The slit envelope was a routine part of life, and if it violated our civil rights, it never occurred to any of us to object. The nuns weren't stupid. Every year there were several instances of hormonal overflow, and if a girl made the mistake of slipping down a knotted bedsheet for a rendezvous after dark, she would be packed up by the next morning and, with one phone call to tie up the details, gone by lunch.

The nuns genuinely sorrowed over these wayward girls, but in every instance they were expelled. Mischief was tolerated but evil was not, and if the convent hadn't been such a deceptively large "plantation," I might have come to view it as a kind of high-priced penitentiary, like some of the wealthy South American girls who never got off campus did.

One Sunday afternoon when my mother brought me back to school from a weekend, she sighed under her breath and said, "I wish I could check into a place like this and lead the kind of life you do." But I wasn't sufficiently mature to appreciate her point at the time. For despite "The Bells of Saint Mary's" atmosphere, I was inwardly unhappy much of the time. But it had less to do with the convent than the fact that I was an adolescent Christian trying to make spiritual and emotional ends meet. It was hard work. I staggered against my own stomach—which registered the pains of unpopularity, pride and self-doubt—toward virtues which even now, just enumerating them in my head, fill me with peace: wisdom, patience, fortitude, love.

I see in an old school binder (dated 1955) that I had divided up the virtues on a piece of paper into two categories. "Easy: (justice, fair play, good-fellowship, almsgiving, kindness and hospitality); and Difficult: (prudence, perseverance, self-denial, temperance and chastity)."

These same difficult virtues are still giving me trouble today, although where "chastity" cranked into my schedule back in 1955, I can't imagine. It must have had something to do with "bad thoughts." Looking back, they must have been as pornographic as shadows on a cave wall. I had so little material to work with.

Popularity with boys was not the lead card in my deck. I didn't even know any outside the circle of the family, and at the few dances I attended—horrible, punch-cooled purgatories run by ladies in harlequin glasses who looked like they were trying to direct World War II—I usually made the mistake of talking too much in a desperate attempt to keep the relationship going on the floor. The few dates I had were all disasters, primarily because I used to laugh at the wrong time. Once, when I was deeply involved in a romantic dialogue on the screen, my movie date leaned over in the dark and said earnestly, "Excuse me, but would you care for a fresh stick of gum?"

I wasn't the only one who led with the left foot, but I usually made matters worse by pointing out theirs, under the assumption that we would have something in common to laugh over. My father was an insidious influence. He used to think my stories about the boys I went out with were hilarious when he should have been telling me to keep my mouth shut or talk about cars. I had no sense of the fragile male ego and very little sense of my own.

When I was fifteen, I had a deep but silent crush upon a wonderfully unobtainable boy called Gary Scales, which I am sure would be absolutely news to him. A handsome, snaggled-toothed boy who was away at school all winter, he used to be an altar boy at the local parish church near our house during the vacations, and after I became a Catholic, I used to hop on my bike and peddle down to St. Anselm's, hoping that the early bird would get the worm.

As I figured it, I thought Gary Scales would be impressed with my piety, particularly since only old ladies went to the 6:30 A.M. Mass and he couldn't help but see me in the near-empty church. But the experiment backfired.

In order to be pious, I had to keep my head bowed. All I ever saw were Gary Scales' loafers as they squeaked down the aisle under his surplice behind Monsignor McGarr. During the unbowed parts of Mass, his back was to the congregation, and at communion time, when he held the paten under my chin and was presumably looking at me, I had my eyes closed and my mouth open—which wasn't a very attractive close-up on which to form an opinion. It was a doomed relationship.

I did not smoke or smolder during my high-school years, and at the few living-room dances, when we all coiled around each other and danced to records in a dark room, I remember two sensations: the smell of shirt-collar starch and sweaty palms—theirs, not mine. I was glad that, with the exception of holidays, I didn't have to face my own raving unpopularity.

Something lost but something gained: Had I routinely mixed with boys in a normal high school, a hay ride with an Eagle Scout would not have caused me to sit bolt upright in the wagon, pointing out the Big Dipper, perspiring profusely with fear that I might be yanked back into the hay if I stopped my lecture on astronomy. But I continue to be glad, in an ambivalent way, that I was given a stretch of segregated time when I was able to wander through the labyrinth of my mind, testing ideas, making resolves, and being myself without having to worry about my cash value at the "Sock Hop."

During my adolescence, most of my sexuality was channeled into painting backdrops for school plays and dealing with the internal realities of my own redemption. The outer realities were fairly tame. On Sundays the nuns wore fresh scapulars, the creases where they had been folded still sharp in the cloth. By Friday the creases would have disappeared.

The creaseless scapular was just about as close as you could get to the humanity of the nuns behind the habit. They ate out of sight, slept behind closed doors, could not even be photographed, they rarely referred to themselves in the first person singular, and their past was an absolutely closed book. Some of them, we knew, drank coffee—you could smell it on their breath after breakfast. But their separateness gave them stature, although we were all bound together in a kind of cloistered innocence that one could spend an entire lifetime rowing back upstream to recapture.

I am thinking just now of Sister Francis Xavier, who was responsible for all the musical education on the campus. Three times a week, I would go to Angelico Hall and sit before a piano in a small practice room on the second floor. Sometimes I actually practiced, but often I ate oranges, looked out the window and made up team cheers in my head. But when I heard Sister Francis Xavier coming down the hall, her rosary beads clicking against each other as she opened and closed doors, I would jam the orange peels into my apron pocket, flip open the music to a familiar piece, and when she burst into my room, there I would be busily practicing, the model fraud.

I pulled that same trick on Sister Francis Xavier for seven years and she never caught on, although I was too shortsighted to realize that the larger trick was on me. I still avoid any piece with over three sharps. I will be playing "The Moonlight Sonata" wrong for the rest of my life.

Four afternoons a week, excluding the Sunday morning Mass warmup, Sister Francis Xavier would come pounding into the study hall, wrench the bench out from beneath the piano, sit down and mash the music book against the stand. A large, magenta-cheeked woman with bright blue eyes and a congenital whistle in her voice, Sister Francis Xavier moved like a Mack truck, and it was her responsibility to bring the student body together under one liturgical tent, teach us the Gregorian chant, divide and conquer the part music, and pull our donkey brains behind her so that the Latin was pronounced correctly.

As our stomachs grumbled and the afternoon breeze brought the smell of fried fish through the open transom, we followed the chunky black notes up and down in our books—

the "Kyrie," "Credo," "Sanctus" and "Agnus Dei"—our eyes following the cramped, atonal music as Sister Francis Xavier pounded away penitentially up front.

Sometimes the most extraordinary sounds were produced. The study hall would fill with music to make a pagan weep, and I would wonder, as I sang, whether the Chinese cook bent over the kitchen grill wasn't ineluctably being persuaded by the "Panis Angelicus" to convert to Catholicism, as eventually I did.

But other days the music was full of rocks, and when it seemed as if our minds would split and notes were passing like dots of blood before our eyes, Sister Francis Xavier would stop, push the chant book to one side and then pounce back upon the keyboard, dash off a wild medley of Irish jigs, run her fingers to the end of the keyboard and dash from the room. We would stamp, clap and go out of our minds with appreciation. "Encore, encore," we would shout, but she never acceded. It was that kind of orchestration between discipline and relief that kept us all well.

Sister Francis Xavier died, or so I heard, several years ago, and I thought about that strong, forceful woman whose chalk-grooved fingers used to jab at my Czerny exercise book, knocking her gold ring against the piano wood to straighten out my timing. I doubt that she had any deathbed regrets about her vocation. She had reached full stature at a stable time, her eccentricities did not violate the larger context— they only spiced them up. I was sad to hear that this large, innocent Irishwoman had whistled her last. She was so purely one thing. Other nuns, in retrospect, were not.

At the beginning of my sophomore year, I began to take instruction to become a Catholic. The nuns wouldn't have allowed it had my parents not made a companion decision to join the Church. Their decision was partly due to a promise my father made to my grandmother on her deathbed, and partly due to a certain inexorability that both my parents felt about making such a choice. "We look Catholic," said my father. "We might as well be Catholic." They now had five children. The more support the better. My parents saw the Church as an external source of comfort, and with Grandmother having already paved the way, the whole thing seemed somewhat inevitable. I didn't see it quite that way.

For years I had been taking instruction one way or the other—dogging Julieanne to catechism classes, reading religious comic books, planning my own martyrdom and working out my spiritual convictions in an intuitive, nonsyllogistic way. The convent ratified a body of belief that I already subscribed to, but when I sat across a table from Sister Dolores and listened to her drone on about the Mystical Body of Christ, I endured her with a politeness that didn't quite mask my contempt.

She was a misfit, a mistake, one of the few nuns who did not command our respect, and when she walked into her classes, her thin, small face twitching like a rabbit with advanced nervousness, none of us were even inspired to pull out our best tricks to thwart her further. There was no reward, no thrill in sideswiping Sister Dolores in the various small, note-passing ways we had to prove to the other nuns that we were clever.

Sister Dolores seemed to vacillate between a fear she could not name and an anger that she could not use effectively, and I would sit with the catechism book splayed across my knees and rarely even look up into her eyes, which skidded nervously back and forth in her head, pleading for a respect that I would not give her.

Yet Sister Dolores did prove one thing that might not have been so obvious otherwise. Had I been given a winning, charismatic nun like Sister Thomasine, who one time yelled, "Do you want to get raped?" when she discovered my best friend and me raiding the nuns' laundry baskets for clues as to their undergarments after dark behind the gym, I might have doubted the validity of my own conversion. Sister Thomasine was the brains and creativity of the school. She could convince you of anything. No, I knew my conversion had to be due to the "gift of faith." Sister Dolores couldn't convince a dog to chase a cat. May God have mercy on my arrogant soul.

In the semifeudal division of labor and responsibility, each nun was assigned a certain plot of land, and it was her duty to make it bear fruit. But Sister Maurice, the principal, was something more. The other nuns were personalities. We loved or did not love them in exact proportion to their loveableness. But Sister Maurice did not inspire love. She transcended it. And our adolescent hearts, which might otherwise have laid themselves down like dogs at her feet, kept their distance.

It was widely rumored that she had migraine headaches, the tipoff being the small flesh-colored mole in the middle of her forehead which would turn dead white in the middle of an attack. Sometimes she proceeded despite the pain. But when the attacks were too severe, she vanished into her room, a room which no one ever saw and was, naturally, an object of prurient speculation.

Did she sleep in a nightgown, use a mirror to comb her hair; what hair, what mirror? The small comings and goings behind that door, out of which she emerged every morning at 6:15, crisp and scapular-centered, were gone over in our minds, although perhaps I should only speak for myself. We didn't share these kinds of fantasies with each other. But I used to wonder whether Sister Maurice, when she divested herself of the fourteen separate parts of her habit, became a palpable, flesh-colored, even weeping human being. I never took my imagination so far as to imagine that Sister Maurice actually cried, but on various rain-soaked days I used to conjure up scenes where I would be sobbing miserably in an empty recreation room only to have the door quietly open, Sister Maurice rush to my side and, with one cool flick of her index finger, wipe away the tears of my terrible loneliness.

This is the embarrassing but true fantasy that has tempted me, in one way or another for most of my life—the person or Pentecost that would redeem me in lieu of being able to redeem myself. And in various ways, the convent fostered that fantasy, filling the day with prayers full of entreaty, supplication and mindfulness that, without the intercession of God, Mary and a lineup of saints, we were doomed to wallow in the mediocrity of our not very original sins.

"Hail, Holy Queen, Mother of Mercy, our life, our sweetness, and our hope. To thee do we cry up, poor banished children of Eve! To thee do we send up our sighs, mourning and weeping in this vale of tears! Turn then, most gracious advocate, thine eyes of mercy toward us . . ."

Reviewing those old prayers today, the sentiments hold up. Life is suffering, redemption can't be purchased by the proud and we are dependent upon a charity that surpasses our capacity to claim it. But the prayers have a distinctly adolescent fittingness about them, and for all Catholic girls in the 50's, Mary was the source of all answers on everything, including the hottest issue of our times, "going steady."

At interschool Catholic federation meetings, we were always being handed purple mimeographed sheets full of rhetorical questions like, "Do you think that most teenagers are particularly well advanced in the practice of Prudence? Specifically, does Mary play a part in our development of that virtue as regards the problems of Purity?"

The nuns tried to be relevant, although we were breathtakingly pure by any standard, and there were other ways of monitoring our excellence, various punishment-reward systems that were both elaborate and incentive strewn.

Each week we received conduct cards—small, white, printed cards divided into five categories: Neatness, Deportment, Punctuality, Conduct and Attitude. Each girl was called individually to the front of the study hall, where Sister Maurice, flanked by two lower-ranking nuns, sat on a podium. If we had fallen below standards in one or more categories, we would be detained for a lecture, which the entire student body could hear. It was a masterful method of crime prevention.

Once a month we received report cards. The scene was the same, although if we had earned a B average, Sister Maurice slipped a white cord with a medal around your neck as you knelt before her. All A's earned a gold cord and applause from the student body. And the highest average in the class merited the pink cord, which Sister Maurice would announce at the very end of the ceremony. The little bookworm whose name was called would rush to the front of the room, receive the pink cord and know that she could get into Stanford when she graduated.

For such a thoroughly Catholic school, the girls routinely went to "Cal-Berkeley," Stanford and other secular colleges. The nuns seemed to encourage it, which says something about human snobbery but more about the caliber of most Catholic colleges at that time. I tended to view most Catholic schools as places where slow students with funny-looking clothes went. Dominican was different.

The education was scholastically demanding, pivoting upon a great deal of memorization, defining of terms, essay writing and analysis. Vocabulary was very important—"apples of gold in frames of silver," said Sister Samuel, who taught English. Our school plays were always boring but artistically done. We listened to two hours of the Griller String Quartet twice a month, and at one time I knew enough about Catholic theology to have made a canon lawyer.

I could tick off the seven fruits of the Holy Ghost, the eight gifts of the Holy Ghost, the twelve beatitudes, the various kinds of virtue (natural, supernatural, acquired, infused), and in my junior year, I confidently analyzed the bombing of

Hiroshima according to the Principle of Double Effect.

"I do not think that the good effect was great enough to compensate for the evil," I wrote succinctly, in neat, strong, manuscript letters which flowed from the nib of my Esterbrook pen. "Therefore, the bombing of Hiroshima was not justified. No time to explain—the bell just rang." "Good comment!" wrote Sister Gregory on the bottom of the paper. So much for the bombing of Hiroshima.

One of the joys of a Catholic education in the 50's was that everything was very clear, at least to me. Every so often my spiritual clarity would get on my father's nerves, and he would rear back from his place at the supper table and say, "Oh, she's a deep one!" or "Pass the bread, Mary!" But these were weekend insults. I knew that my parents weren't very advanced theologically. How could they be? It was a question of time and teachers.

As students go, I was not quite at the top of the class, although the nuns were wise enough to realize that a consistently sanguine girl was worth a dozen sad-sack brains, and they regularly accepted girls whose best feature was "peppiness." Peppy girls provided the school with the kind of yeast that made everyone's spirits rise, and the nuns were also smart enough to throw bright patches of paint upon our schedule, which might otherwise have been unendurable. In a closed-circuit environment, entertainment was crucial.

We held bazaars, gymkhanas, class parties and song festivals. There were ring teas, plays, skits and games. Once a month we sat in the gym and watched movies like *Sally and Saint Anne*, and stuffed our mouths with popcorn. Then, too, there were those unrehearsed dramatic moments between festivals, when Sister Maurice would storm into the study hall and confront us with a crime that she had uncovered, some breach of conduct for which she would then excoriate us in hot, sarcastic words, sometimes singling out a particular girl to stand up and take a verbal assault if she was responsible for whatever crime it was. Oddly I only remember one of those occasions. It was not representative.

One evening before supper, Sister Maurice walked rapidly into the study hall, excused the sister at the desk and stood before us, her hands clasped beneath her scapular, her face a study of sternness. Something awful had happened.

"I have just discovered," she began quietly, "the evidence that was lacking to me heretofore, which proves to me . . ." —she paused to look several girls directly in the eye—"that certain girls have not been . . . cleaning out . . . the bathtubs . . . just as I suspected."

Whipping out a bathbrush from beneath her scapular, she held it at arm's length and passed it slowly before our eyes. "Mushrooms, my friends," she whispered sarcastically. "Garden-variety mushrooms." At this announcement, her face relaxed, a smile broke across her features, and we broke into loud, relieved laughter. The bathbrush was a marvelous joke, and our tension liquefied under the absolution of her gaze.

Sister Maurice was a powerful, potent woman, and during the entire time I was at Dominican, I only felt her judgment to be wrong once. Ironically, it fell upon the one girl at Dominican who disliked me intensely.

I could not have imagined then that there would ever come a day when I would find myself writing kindly about Reagan. The entire thrust of her life seemed to be directed against me. And while I came to terms with that, even before I had left Dominican, I understood that her reason for existence was perhaps broader and more complex than the simple desire to sabotage my ego. Reagan was a dark, scowling presence who was perpetually ready to swipe whatever self-confidence I had managed to build up for myself on the previous day.

That she was able to do this so effectively was not because Reagan was a model student, an ideal girl, or even particularly well liked. There was a kind of abrasive, impatient rebelliousness about her that she dragged like a sword in reserve behind her back, which gave her a power base from which to operate, a kind of fearful respect that made other girls take her into account. Objectively, I had more friends, although they tended to come from the lame, the halt and the blind segments of the school. (I always had a small coterie of rejects following me through the halls—dark, bad-complexioned girls from valley towns who wanted me to sit in their rooms with them while they had nervous breakdowns.) My other friends, drawn from the popular ranks of the class, were more independent of my charity, less secure in my life. Reagan was on the fringes of the popular group, without exactly being popular herself. As for the nuns, they didn't like her at all.

Reagan was intelligent but would not study, wordlessly insolent when being corrected, and everything about her—the way she slumped her shoulders, laughed heartlessly over other people's clumsiness and influenced other girls for the worse— were daily reminders to the nuns that their effectiveness was not necessarily universal, their prayers could be in vain.

My troubles with Reagan were reflected elsewhere in Reagan's troubles with the school, and I suppose I should have felt some satisfaction when she stood frozen-faced before Sister Maurice on the podium while she was dressed down for her various sins in front of the school. Yet I don't remember being flooded with vindication at these moments. Reagan's battles with the nuns were an entirely separate action in a different theater of war. The fact that she could, and did, call up Sister Maurice's wrath so continually only underscored how potent my enemy was.

Reagan had several advantages over me. She was rich and knew the difference between the "haves" and the "have-nots." And while I can now only intellectually summon up those dead passions, which revolved around wanting a Brooks Brothers shirt, a Lanz dress, shoes by Capezio, I remember being inwardly devastated by Reagan's astute observations as to how pitifully I tried to approximate the "look" that only real money could buy.

It was difficult enough being on a scholarship without having to cope with Reagan's charm-bracelet consumerism, although where she drove the knife deepest was in her ability to let me know that the friends I wanted were actually hers, that the swimming pool at her house was not, unfortunately, open to the public. Reagan found my school loyalty oppressive, my charity off-putting and my family neither fish nor fowl.

A part of me knew that she was a flash in the pan, understood that her tactics were not only cruel but cheap, but that part of me was usually inoperative in her presence. I was too vulnerable to my own deep-seated desire to be well liked. I had begun Dominican vowing that I would never do or say an unkind thing to any girl in the school. It was not an entirely pure vow. Part of me believed that faith without good works was dead. But another part of me hoped that this Lutheran approach to popularity would win more votes when it came to elect the class president. But time after time I lost the presidency by a hair, and quiet, inoffensive girls like Tappy De Carle, who had sweet smiles, clean fingernails and metabolisms that never boiled over from one year to the next, were elected instead. I have come to think that most successful leaders resemble Tappy De Carle—unthreatening, reliable and not prone to flaunting their enjoyment of power. She was an archetype within the school that was particularly admired, less for anything in particular than for simply being an aggregate of qualities which taken together were endearing. Methodical but feminine, excelling without being noticeably ambitious, no rough edges, a cool to cold personality. Looking back, I was none of these things and probably would not have voted for myself either. On the other hand, Reagan was never even nominated for an office. She was so blatantly running in the opposite direction.

All this being said, there was a period of time toward the middle of our junior year when Reagan showed sudden signs of reforming. For one solid month, Reagan's papers were letter-perfect, she never missed a homework assignment, and she ostentatiously stayed in during class breaks, studying for tests. Her handwriting, which usually resembled a plateful of collapsed noodles, was noticeably clearer, and during this time, she made a concerted effort to wipe the smirk from her face, the discourtesy from her eyes, and she was never late for class.

Against all the tides of rebelliousness she ordinarily rode upon, Reagan pulled hard in the other direction, and I rather cheered her on, respected her for what she was trying to do, and hoped, if she won the white cord at the end of the month, that she would have less taste for killing me off.

At report card time Reagan stood in the class circle, having already tallied up her grades beforehand and found that she had at least a B average in every subject. Her face was nervous but smiling as she watched the cards as they came up, alphabetically, in Sister Maurice's lap. Reagan's last name was Zeidel. There was something fitting about her card being the last to surface.

"Reagan Zeidel," said Sister Maurice quietly, holding the report card in her fingers. "All B's," she read out, her eyes still looking at the card.

Reagan mounted the platform, the smile now breaking into a grin of triumph. But then there ensued several terrible minutes while Sister Maurice spoke, in unhearable tones, with Reagan, and to our amazement she did not extend her hand toward the rack of white cords once during the conversation.

Reagan's shoulders began to twitch. Her feet started to sneak back into their usual foot-tapping impoliteness, and finally she jerked away—angry, red-faced and with tears in her eyes—and walked down the other side of the platform. Without a white cord. All alongside one wall of the study hall, the rest of the nuns sat in a white row, eyes on their laps.

Reagan's reformation had put the nuns in an intolerable position. The gadfly, the curse, the girl least anxious to bear the moral standards of the school had beaten them at their own game. Reagan technically deserved to kneel and be blessed by the nun whose choler she most regularly called forth. Yet by exhibiting excellence, Reagan had inadvertently insulted the powers that confirmed it. She was told that afternoon that the white cord was being withheld because she "did not represent the spirit that was supposed to be part of a Dominican girl."

Reagan never capitulated again. She relaxed with a vengeance into her old ways, and while I lost track of her soon after graduation and have had very little cause to think of her since, I have often wanted to right that wrong, acknowledge to her that I thought an enormous miscarriage of mercy had taken place. There was a nose-thumbing insolence about Reagan that was undeniably irritating, but that she was capable of displaying her insolence in a school so entirely weighted in the direction of conformity and acquiescence to authority is a feat that I now respect her for. My sense of outrage, which was usually directed toward myself, has never quite forgiven Sister Maurice for interpreting Reagan's brief shot at excellence as an insult to excellence itself. In that one instance, Reagan was asking for approval and it was not granted. She never asked for it again.

I am far enough away from that one period in my life so that if I had been so inclined, I could have found reasons to reject it by now. But it is not rejectable, any more than one can walk through a field of California poppies, emerge upon the road and claim that the poppies behind do not exist.

Certain aspects of it seem invalid or open to great criticism. We were, after all, steered toward sainthood, which did not preclude the Junior League. We were taught values in an experimental vacuum and I was given a scholarship, but there was never any particular push to expand that program to include the black girls who lived in Marin City, or other minority groups who probably lived within the shadow of the convent itself. The nuns regularly subsidized down-and-out girls who deserved better than they could afford, but they tended to come from genteel families and there were, in fact, several Hapsburg princesses on the campus for a period of time. Over and above that, we were the usual middle-class mix of car dealers' daughters, debutantes and girls who weren't one thing or another, a category, I suppose, that I fell into. There is much to be criticized, but I don't have the taste for it. The snake in my basket is peculiarly my own.

For seven years I lived in an environment which answered my strong desire for a total plan. I was anxious for answers, greatly in need of external order, and for a person who was interested in defining things, it was the right place to be. Everything was defined, categorized, compared, contrasted and set upon its proper rung on Jacob's ladder. Including me.

"What should be our first concern in life?" reads an old question on a religion test.

"The desire to know, love and serve God should be our first concern," I answered.

That answer still holds up in my mind. I can find no fault with my original response, although it was probably lifted in its entirety from a book with *nihil obstat* written all over it.

Some of these answers, so sharply specific in their newness when I discovered them, have been worn as smooth as stones, and they are all mixed up together—part ballast, part reproach—in my pocket, sorting themselves around, losing their edge, and one stone looks very much like all the others.

No, the devastating effect of that convent time was not that we were taught lies but that we were taught truths. Although if I am to believe the alumnae bulletins, truth has not produced any revolutionaries or soup kitchens for the poor. Only children, gratitude and enthusiastic class reunions.

Sometime during the 60's, Dominican relocated. The plaques were unhooked from the long, amber wood study hall and attached to the interior walls of a new building, and the Angelus now rings electronically over a low-slung, adobe-style complex in the foothills of San Anselmo. The bells fall upon the ears of a generation of girls almost old enough to be daughters of mine, or of the hostess of a recent alumnae reunion I attended in honor of Sister Maurice. She is no longer principal of the school, but travels around the country as a fund raiser and projects director.

I had been several years behind the hostess in school. She was an avid horsewoman whom I never knew except by name, since the group of girls who rode horses was a separate clique which revolved around the paddock, horse shows and a schedule that kept it somewhat separate from the rest of the school.

Sandy had married a military man, who stood at the front door, the objective fulfillment of an old dream that made me smile. Handsome, deep-voiced, paternal and indulgent, he was the perfect man for a Dominican girl, and Sandy, who could still be a stand-in for her own yearbook picture, with the same bright eyes, pink cheeks and blond curly hair, was a good exchange for him.

The house was bright, well tended, and full of polished silver, the smell of hors d'oeuvres and a Saint Bernard, which lolled expensively before the fireplace and undoubtedly filled up the annual Christmas photograph. "A Happy and Holy Christmas from Brad, Sandy, Annette, Sidney and 'Brandy'." It was a comfortable, entirely noneccentric house, an expensive brick in a cul-de-sac of expensive bricks, each one painted with Williamsburg colors, with this year's station wagon, a gas eater that hauled peat moss and hockey players, parked in every driveway.

I could hear Sister Maurice's voice, which hadn't aged a decibel, in the middle of a crowd of women at the buffet table. She caught me with her eye as I came through the door and broke from the table—her arms extended, her face as rosy and full of intelligent light as it had ever been. The mask of authoritarianism was no longer necessary, and her features looked softer and more pliant than I remembered, which was a good sign.

We embraced in the doorway and moved into the room.

She knew from letters that my life had altered. I was one of many graduates who, against all predictions, had become a statistic. Carolan had gotten divorced. Cressey as well. And now me. The peppiest girls in the class of 1957 had not been bailed out by their enthusiasm for life. I had heard that, ironically, Reagan was a settled, married woman, or at least married. I didn't mention Reagan to Sister Maurice. There would be no point.

We settled down in a corner with some food, apart from the chatter, although various graduates, some of whom I knew, dipped in and out of the conversation, anxious to refresh their memory or share an old scrap of their Dominican days, one of the prime reasons for an alumnae reunion, a reason Sister Maurice understood.

"I can remember the conduct cards," I said, "but I can't remember the five ways in which our lives were categorized as being good or bad—there was neatness, punctuality, conduct, deportment and . . ."

"Attitude," supplied Sister Maurice. "You would never have gotten demerits in attitude."

I felt a rush of gratitude. One is never too old to be blessed by an old mother superior.

"Tell me," she said, leaning forward with a sober look on

her face. "Why have so many marriages failed? Was it something that I had not said or was not done when you were at school?"

The question was a sign of continuing grace. I had no desire to blame anyone but myself. Yet it gentled the issue, coming from Sister Maurice. I searched for an answer which she could take back to Dominican and apply against the next group of graduates now studying for examinations.

"I never thought of myself as an individual," I answered.

"What do you mean by that?" she asked.

"Somehow, I saw myself in relation to other people, marriage, children, even God, as a kind of receptacle that would benefit from all those relationships. But it never seriously occurred to me," I added, "to take myself seriously without them."

Sister Maurice was silent and then reflected, "I think I see what you are saying. We did not stress the importance of coming to yourself before coming to anything else. Somehow, we assumed that without ever saying it."

"I guess I thought of myself as more of a catalyst than a person," I said. "You know, if I tried to be a good person that good things would happen to me and with those around me. But a catalyst is a catalyst—I tended to disappear in the process . . . and I have to say that some very bad things happened because I had that idea."

Enough was enough. I was more anxious to repay my scholarship, in words, to Sister Maurice than dissect my life. "I wonder if you have any idea how privileged I still feel to have gone to Dominican."

"You were at the right place at the right time," said Sister Maurice, and I had the distinct feeling that she actually had a clear recollection of my specific time there, even though it overlapped with a hundred others, and our particular graduating class was not the sum total of her life when we left the school.

The conversation widened to include the rest of the room. The hostess, perched on the edge of a sofa, addressed Sister Maurice.

"You know, Sister, when I was in school I used to hate all those festivals, parties and pageants that we were always giving. But since I have become a wife, mother and part of the community, I'm so grateful that you made us take part in all those events that I used to think were so silly."

"Why?" I asked.

"Because," she continued, "I look back and realize how they helped me to organize and be efficient in my life now."

That analysis knocked me out. I, who had been transported with creative power over the sight of four dust mops moving in synchronized precision to the tune of "H.M.S. Pinafore," had never thought of those festivals in terms of how they taught anyone to be organized.

"I'll say two things for my wife," said Sandy's husband, "she is practical and she has good bodily hygiene."

The room laughed, while Sandy, whose cheeks flushed and eyes brightened, laughed as well—the quick, innocent reaction to a multidimensional comment that could be malicious if one didn't know that her husband couldn't possibly have meant to say what he had just said. On the other hand, perhaps these were legitimate values that held them together. But I prayed to God that nobody I cared about would ever sum me up before a group of people in that way.

The evening drew to a close. One by one, Sister Maurice embraced the alumnae, each of whom felt it necessary to donate their favorite piece of school lore.

"We used to smoke in the shower with open windows."

"I hated the curtsying."

"We didn't curtsy in the high school."

"Yes, we did."

"No, we didn't."

The men who were married to the women at the reunion

began to shift uncomfortably against the walls, waiting for their wives to finish up talking about the time of their lives. What were they thinking? I did not know, but as I examined the faces of the graduates, they seemed to become more girlish with each reminiscence. Was that a lisp I heard? a dormitory giggle? a cry for help? Every face was surface bright, but some of the eyes pleaded a different story. It may have been my imagination but, as they part confessed, part reminisced and refreshed Sister Maurice's memory with pranks that she must have heard a thousand times before, they seemed to be asking Sister Maurice to tell them what to do now. But it wasn't that kind of an evening. Sister Maurice was no longer in a position to advise, only bless.

"What ever happened to Sister Dolores?" I asked, as the two of us walked outside toward my car.

"Oh dear," she sighed. "She died of a brain tumor. It was something she had had all the time, but nobody knew it. She left the convent and died at home . . . with her father, I think."

An old, prideful chicken came home to roost. So that was why Sister Dolores had been the way she was.

"And Sister Thomasine?" I asked, knowing that she had been Sister Maurice's unacknowledged closest companion.

"Not well," said Sister Maurice, whose face took on a pained, ambivalent look. "She left the order too. She's teaching at a private girls' school in Piedmont."

"Do you ever see her?" I asked.

"Not often," she answered. "She has a very hard life now. And she is not physically well."

"I wonder why she left," I said, not expecting to get an answer.

"I don't know," she answered, "but she told me it was just something she had to try. But it seems to me that she is doing the same things she always did, only now she is without all of the supports around her that she had when she was a nun."

"You must miss her," I sympathized.

Sister Maurice nodded, as if to terminate the conversation. I embraced her and drove away.

The entire way home I thought of Sister Thomasine. I had no assurance, adding it up, that she was happy in her new life. But I admired her courage and hoped that it would not let her down. Six months later I heard, via a black-bordered announcement in the Dominican alumnae bulletin, that Sister Thomasine had died. Someone had found an old poem of hers and printed it alongside the obituary. It was a very good poem, about the sea and being true to one's compass. I hadn't known she was a poet. When I was at Dominican, I hadn't known her at all.

Chapter
VIII

In 1956, to circle one of the last years in which the family was still sharply, self-confidently defined, my cousin Mimi got married. Mimi's wedding was the first in the family, and the circle joyfully expanded to take in a new member, since everyone shared exactly the same opinion of Mimi's future husband. He was wonderful.

I confess that I was jealous of her luck. Mimi had found a man so perfect that all hopes of my duplicating her performance were dashed to the ground. He was handsome, Harvard-educated, played competitive tennis, had a well-honed sense of humor, wore heartbreakingly Eastern clothes, and was interested in Russia. The mere mention of Russia always caused the family to stop what they were doing and draw their chairs into a circle.

When Hank was introduced to the family, he must have been overwhelmed with positive response, a trait which has always characterized the family, although I wonder whether the burden of so much good will has tended to weigh on the stranger's mind. Can this really be me? Am I, in fact, who I'm told I am? Both within and without the family, the largest burdens have been burdens of good opinion that cannot be substantiated over the long haul. But in 1956, when Mimi introduced her future husband to the rest of us, optimism had always served the family well. And while I was jealous of Mimi, I couldn't help but think that she was eminently deserving of her good fortune. She, too, was wonderful, a family opinion that Mimi struggled against in later years.

I did not worship Mimi. She was far too self-deprecating to inspire that emotion. But I admired her from afar, as a sharp-eyed acolyte who took notes on her life, although sometimes I think that in those days I tended to look upon her less as a person than a wardrobe—a collection of piqué collars, cinch belts and circular felt skirts that would revert to me, along with her life, once I was old enough to take possession.

Our temperaments were vastly different. Mimi was of a more logical turn of mind, and I would sit beside her on the piano bench at 36 Presidio Terrace, where she would sit in her blue-and-white Burke's uniform and play rippling arpeggios across the keyboard, one blond arm leapfrogging over the other with practiced grace. I would beg her to show me where to place my own fingers so I could duplicate her performance. Mimi was not overwhelmed by music as was I. She was, therefore, able to concentrate upon the music itself. But I did not care about reading notes. I already knew how they should sound. Mimi would always comply, and several weeks later I, too, would be playing Scarlatti, badly and with the wrong timing, but the music would be mine and I didn't care whether it was technically accurate or not.

This impatience for perfection, without deference to method or time, separated Mimi from me. I would eye the contents of her purse, a model of fragrant organization, her unopened pack of Wrigley's gum tucked neatly beside her wallet, and be full of admiration. I never came into a pack of gum that

I didn't immediately consume all five sticks immediately. But Mimi could carry around an unopened pack for weeks on end, which I found very mature. Her appetites were in control. On a practical level, that meant that most of her hand-me-downs didn't fit.

Yet we were linked, like circles that Mimi kept adding onto just ahead of me, and her life, in my eyes, was an expanding series of successes that layered themselves, like crinolines, one on top of the other.

When Mimi got engaged, I was still in the convent, thinking about marriage in the most abstract terms, and Mimi had just completed her freshman year at the University of California. But love cut her education short, and suddenly she was splashed all over the social pages in the *Chronicle*, the latest girl to relinquish her place in "The Spinsters," a non-philanthropic organization in San Francisco where girls from good families traditionally idled before they got married and joined the Junior League.

Ever since Mimi had come of age, she had sporadically appeared in the social pages for no other reason than the fact that she existed—along with a select crowd of boys and girls who also existed—on the tennis courts, skiing, dancing, or, the ultimate place of non-news—at Monday lunch at the Saint Francis Hotel. One would think, to read the social pages, that all of San Francisco was caught up in the doings of about fifty people—healthy, seersuckered bons vivants who skied at Squaw, sent their children to "La Jeunesse" dancing classes, and then sat back to watch their tuxedoed sons escort their white-gloved daughters at the Cotillion at Christmas. That was what I thought, and, as the cousin who sat across the bay in Marin County reading the *Chronicle,* I lived vicariously through the reportage and wondered what the impact on my life would be if I found myself smiling over a tennis racket in the middle of the page.

I don't think the *Chronicle* carries on about nothing in

quite the same way anymore. "People are worried about kidnappers," said my Aunt Irene, and the last few times I was in San Francisco and picked up the papers to see who was drinking wine in the Napa Valley, the *Chronicle* had been reduced to printing pictures of old dowagers eating hot dogs at Candlestick Park—a far cry from the old days when a good party rated a triptych of photos, a page of copy, and it was quite possible to follow the suitcase of anybody who was anybody from one year to the next.

I was an early fan of the social pages for a number of mostly bad reasons. I liked to project myself into the lives of people, most of whom I didn't know, and float around the periphery of the action, which I did in reality as well.

A half-dozen times a year, I would commute across the Golden Gate Bridge with a dress squashed into a suitcase, soak in my Aunt Irene's tub and be part of the photographed scene. But I never quite got my footing. I had no backup ranch to secure it, and I was in awe of the bright, well-heeled, spoiled girls who whirled around the dance floor in ginger leis, their razor-cut hair swinging like cornsilk over their shoulders. Their names matched their hair.

It seemed to me that one's name laid out one's life. Thus, a Pauline Pezzollo was doomed to eat garlic sandwiches and be excluded forever, while a Wendy Burnham automatically woke up to the sound of a maid sorting silver in the kitchen downstairs. I saw connections between names and lives, and it was my fate to be surrounded with names like "Page Demming" and "Diana Grey," while my own name had no signature and fell between the cracks in a city where names were crucial to success.

San Francisco has more cooked-up phony names than any other city I've been in since, and I used to pick up the *Chronicle* and look for my favorites, which I divided up into romantic, Blue Chip and ridiculous. "Kate Kirkham"—romantic; "Averill Crimmins"—Blue Chip; and "Poom de

Ralguine"—ridiculous. I never met Poom de Ralguine. I imagine him chinless. For the duration of the time that I dabbled in San Francisco society, I kept mental files, although the only time I ever got my own name into the *Chronicle* before I was married was on a ski weekend when I broke my leg right after the picture was snapped, and at a waltzing party where I am dancing in a pair of "popette" pearls with a boy who later committed suicide. When I got engaged to be married, there was a bordered picture, the border indicating that you weren't from the Marine District. Unless you are very social, they don't print your picture when you get divorced, although one of my second cousins, who was part of a distant branch of the family, qualified for that dubious honor when she ran off with a walnut picker from her husband's ranch.

By the time Mimi got engaged, she already had a thick scrapbook of clippings, which interested me far more than they interested her. Mimi was not a socialite at heart. She participated in the ritual of growing up correctly in San Francisco with more obedience than fervor, and my favorite picture of her never appeared in the papers at all. Around sixteen years old, she is seated in a side chair, her hair in soft curls with a gardenia bobby-pinned behind one ear. She is wearing a long taffeta dress with a scoop neck and puffed sleeves. Last summer's bathing-suit strap marks show on her shoulders. Her mouth is self-consciously parted in a half-smile. Her freckles are unpowdered, and she is entirely oblivious of how lovely she is, which was Mimi's best asset. She never did know, unlike some of the other jut-jawed socialites who were part of the larger circle, until she broke from it altogether.

Mimi was part of the San Francisco context, as were her bridesmaids with whom I sat before the mirror in 36 Presidio Terrace the day of the wedding adjusting our turquoise dresses that matched the tablecloths while the photographer took our pictures. They were smart, laughing, popular girls with wide smiles and every expectation before them. I watched them in the mirror and wondered whether one day I too would go out with men who hunted wild boar and ultimately marry a plastic surgeon.

Yet Mimi transcended her own context. She was never truly one with the social environment, and I always saw her as ineffably special, not for any one thing but for all things which worked in complete harmony together: the girl in a white Dominican uniform who read her "I Speak for Democracy" speech while Uncle Ed beamed with tears, the debutante who wore a white beaded dress and Grandmother's red quilted bed jacket, spruced up by my Aunt Irene with new wine-colored ribbons, to the Cotillion when she came out.

Every year a small number of girls made their debut at Christmas time, and I was never terribly sure what the ground rules were as to who qualified for the honor. One year an ex-classmate of mine, a girl whose father was so rich he could have repainted the Golden Gate Bridge with gold, was refused a place in the class.

Everyone buzzed about it, the more so because Fiona was beautiful, lived in an enormous house in Hillsborough, and her father was reputedly one of the richest men from Scotland, constantly shuttling horses back and forth, via air freight, from one continent to another. The details of why he was rich slip my mind, but he was determined that his daughter, who had violet eyes, blue-black hair and a place on the United States Equestrienne Team, would "come out" like everyone else.

But Fiona did not get an invitation, and her father, who was Goddamned if San Francisco was going to thumb its parochial nose at him, retaliated with a vengeance. Renting out the entire ground floor of the Mark Hopkins Hotel, he banked it with gardenias, ordered filet mignon for five hundred at midnight, hired Ernie Hecksher's orchestra, and sent out white leather wristwatches along with each invitation.

Fiona stood against a tapestry of flowers and violins in the lobby, where all of San Francisco lined up to shake her undoubtedly petrified hand.

I felt sorry for Fiona, even though I didn't come out either, for lack of funds. It was a joke in our kitchen. My father would yell, "Come out!" and I would spring from the broom closet and go, "Ta dah!" But Fiona was a pawn in a game that I could have played if I wanted. She was invited around to other parties, just like everybody else. But as she stood at one of the teas, I remembered her back in the sixth grade, the only girl who had two sets of books so she wouldn't have to carry any home. I had admired her for her English accent, her unconventionality and a certain "Little Princess" quality that I found odd and romantic. Yet the next time I saw her, grown up, she had turned into a doll, a quiet, inward, correct little doll with a wardrobe full of Dior dresses and black kid gloves that she wore without enjoyment. I don't know what happened to her, but she didn't hang around San Francisco very long after her own party. There was no point.

I have never known a city more materialistic without being gross about it than San Francisco. Money counted for a great deal, and there was a great deal of it to count. Girls who were debutantes, at least in the late 50's, tended to have parties on the Grace Line at anchor or dance around pools chock-full of gardenias, which I find wonderfully up front. But to qualify for the Cotillion you had to be born and bred in San Francisco, which is where Fiona fell off the horse. She wasn't real, just like the Jews, who practically supported San Francisco philanthropically; but there was a psychic dividing line as wide as Van Ness Avenue that separated the Jews out.

The morning of the wedding found my Aunt Irene flitting about the round tables, covered in turquoise organdy cloths, with bouquets of flowers in the center. Mimi was sequestered in Grandmother's old room, packing her trousseau. I wandered around the ground floor of 36 Presidio Terrace, listening to Tim and Johnny complaining about the studs in their shirts, watching the maids who had been imported for the day laying out buffet silver, and keeping my two little sisters, then aged four and five, from ruining their dresses, which had been especially bought for their flower-girl roles. E. Bates kept tapping her hearing aid to make sure it was working. Everyone was in a state of advanced hysteria. But the sun was bright, the groom was nervous, and as I watched him polish his shoes in the back room, I wondered for the umpteenth time whether I would find anyone who read Yeats, listened to Gregorian chant and had sandy eyebrows that curled at the outsides.

I hated myself for feeling so acquisitive at Mimi's most triumphant moment, but as I stood at the back of St. Mary's Church in Chinatown, I had the despairing feeling that by cooperating in Mimi's wedding I was participating in the only wedding that would ever come up to my own expectations of what a wedding should be. Then the music started and I set my foot down on the white-sheet carpet that led to the altar. Once again, Mimi was ahead of me, although this time she had stepped entirely out of my orbit and would be, until I got married, in a separate, secretive world. The couple left in a hail of rice, for an unknown destination. I impatiently marked time until she returned.

Mimi would be changed. In what outward way I did not know, but I knew why. Whatever else I was ignorant of, I knew what honeymoons were for although one didn't speak of it, sex being too special and reverent and wonderful to refer to. In lieu of knowing anything more than the basic maneuver, my imagination supplied me with several metaphors; golden chalices, cruets of wine, symbols of the Mass, transubstantiation and passionate commitment, which was what purity, when relinquished, was replaced with. I was entirely prepared to give purity up, although I was equally sure of what constituted right circumstances. Only my father, who wasn't so chalice-oriented, leavened my attitude. "I'm not sure sex is what it's cracked up to be," I had once said. "Don't knock what you haven't tried," he shot back.

Two weeks later the new couple arrived back in San Francisco. The night that Mimi and her husband came over to Marin County, I plunged downstairs in eagerness to look into her face. But Mimi did not appear very transubstantiated. If she had experienced the most significant moment in a woman's life, it didn't show up. She was happy. She was full of life. She was as lovely as before. But somehow I had expected her to be standing in a pool of gold, instead of a wool coat and a paisley scarf. I was disappointed. But in this instance, I couldn't quiz her on the details. She had secrets that would never be mine until I learned them myself.

There were other weddings and other divorces after 1956. Indian reverends, vegetarian receptions and second chances brought the family together, but never in such full and splendid force. Some of the family had died, some had moved to Los Angeles, still others felt disinclined to participate in weddings (when weddings were actually deemed necessary) because the thread of the family had lost its tensile strength. Then, too, there were those of us who no longer defined themselves as part of a flesh-and-blood unit which took precedence over their own spiritual growth pattern.

But 1956 was a particularly innocent year. There were no shadows on the back wall. My sisters scattered rose petals down the aisle, looking combed and wide-eyed and bound in blue satin sashes, which is how we all were, give or take a few wisecracks from the back row. Nobody knew about joss sticks, or alternative life-styles, or swallowing gauze to purify your intestinal tract. We danced to "Echoes of Broadway," listened to Tom Lehrer records, and as I stood in the reception line and gazed up at Vincent Butler's handsome beach-browned face, I wondered whether that particular hand-me-down of Mimi's was regarding me in a new way.

I looked down at my dress and realized that all of those years of jumping up and down before the mirror to see if anything moved were over.

Chapter
IX

From earliest memory, Moral Re-Armament had swirled quietly around the periphery of my existence, less a force than an extra pair of arms that encircled my life and gave it partial definition—like Liz Sumner, the gentle, serving soul who took every good picture the family possesses, turned out a pie a day in the kitchen at 36 Presidio Terrace and moved unobtrusively around the outskirts of all the MRA meetings, picking up cups, listening to conversation and simply being there in case one of my two aunts came unraveled by any of life's details.

I regarded Liz Sumner with affection, although she was like a favorite picture on a wall that I only appreciated in passing—one of many MRA "pictures" in my mind, along with "Uncle Frank," handsome women in good wool dresses, and the annual Easter egg hunt at "Aunt Kitty's" large estate in Burlingame.

Aunt Kitty was one of many wealthy women who, at MRA's zenith, donated their houses and money to Moral Re-Armament, which repaid them with a deference that they might not have received any other way.

She was almost a member of the family, although her husband was reputed to be a dreadful man who thought MRA was for the birds, and Aunt Kitty looked rather like a bird herself—an expensive, small-boned bird, who peered out from beneath a puff of white hair with a pair of pale blue eyes which didn't reflect any marital tension whatsoever.

Aunt Kitty's husband was powerless to subvert his wife's hobby, but from the snatches of conversation I wove together in the back seat of the car en route to these Easter parties, he was continually consulting with his lawyer and ne'er-do-well son to make sure that when he died his money wouldn't revert to MRA or any of the "Buchmanites" who tromped through his house and left their hyperbolic, self-serving literature all over the house.

"Uncle Francis" was the villain, and the one time I laid eyes on him, glowering powerlessly at us from a back patio as we dashed through his tulips looking for eggs, he reminded me of Little Lord Fauntleroy's grandfather, although I couldn't imagine what he had against MRA. From what I knew, it was not one thing or another.

"It isn't a religion, it's not a point of view, it's a world wide revolution, and it STARTS WITH YOU!" That is a stanza from one of MRA's many songs, which were rhythmic, catchy, tune-quick things that could have been written by Gilbert and Sullivan on an off day. Whenever one of the MRA plays came to San Francisco, I would sit in the audience and hum along with the chorus as they belted out songs, many of which I already knew from records at the Gallwey house, scores from the road shows that MRA used to attract new customers to itself. In the bathtub I would shout along with nobody, "The whole world is your neighbor, when you and I get together." How could Uncle Francis dispute that message, given the times?

In those Eisenhower years, when McCarthy was ferreting out communists in Washington and the mainland Chinese were rising every morning to do T'ai Chi exercises in preparation for taking over the world, Moral Re-Armament was an insistent, well-bred voice warning the Western world that it was going to be blitzed out of its complacency if it didn't marshal its God-given energies and stand militantly firm against the powers of evil.

How one stood firm was unclear in my mind, but there were certain rules. One had to be morally straight, in tune with God's plan, adhere to the "Four Standards" of honesty, purity, love and unselfishness, and the adherence had to be absolute. Moral Re-Armament was an absolutist ideology. But living in the midst of a comfortable, upper-middle-class family where the closest I came to World War II were the black mines that bobbed ominously above submarine nets under the Golden Gate Bridge, I didn't have the impetus to run absolutely scared.

I associated a world crisis with my Aunt Irene dusting off the glass-grape centerpiece in the middle of the dining-room table, E. Bates nagging after my cousin Tony to pick up his socks off the guest-bathroom floor, and a lot of extra running around with linen to accommodate a new Japanese delegation of political leaders passing through town. World tension did not translate into personal peril in my mind, only a fresh stream of people coming through the front door of 36 Presidio Terrace, which was the San Francisco "situation room" for whatever was going on in MRA worldwide.

Not living at 36 Presidio Terrace, I missed out on being thoroughly indoctrinated, and my own parents who never did grasp the MRA torch with any real enthusiasm were often accused of laughing themselves above the point—which was true. Thus, I was a bastard member of the movement, neither taken into account nor totally ignored, and I formed my own judgment as to what MRA was all about, a judgment that expanded as I learned to distinguish myself from the world around me, which at one point was entirely filled with MRA, at least on the periphery. Oddly, I discovered that MRA was born in California, over crossed spotlights, in the Hollywood Bowl at a rally in 1939—the same year I was born. Its founder, Frank Buchman, died the same year I graduated into the world from college, 1961. The 60's were not good years for MRA. Buchman's philosophy was not flourishing in that permissive liberal period. When he died, you might say he died just in time.

It has been whispered that Buchman openly admired Adolf Hitler, although there is no particular proof that I have ever seen, and he obviously changed his mind at the onset of the war. But Buchman appealed to a group of people who, not unlike the Nazis at their most innocent, if they even had an innocent phase, embraced his vision of a cleaned-up race of spiritually guided men who coincidentally happened to be primarily Anglo-Saxon, intelligent and upper-class. Moral Re-Armament plays were militant, the beat was martial, and to take the comparison any further might be unjust, but I cannot help but think that MRA was a pale reflection of a kind of nazism—conformist, obedient and basically elite.

My father, who was none of these things, had once carried the American flag in an early MRA rally in Stockbridge, Massachusetts, and we still have the old newspaper photo of him. He looks like the quintessence of American manhood—curly-haired, clear-eyed, patriotic, looking into the distance. But to hear my father explain that picture, he was actually scanning the crowd for Mother so he could ditch the flag and run off to a coffee shop for a cigarette. He was not good MRA material.

My father often poked fun at MRA, a nervous habit he tends to revert to whenever he can't grasp the bottom line of an argument or is bored with it. He wasn't a bridge player for roughly the same reason he didn't like MRA—both were too solemn. "Three no-Goren" he would say halfway into a rubber, which would make my two aunts slam down their cards and exclaim, "Shall we deal with Jack now or later?" But they never dealt with my father at all, except as their adorable younger brother, who was beyond rehabilitation by MRA or themselves. My father aside, it did take a certain kind of person to keep a straight face in a room full of world-minded people listening intently to each other's clichés.

My father couldn't stomach the clichés, my mother tended to melt among high-minded people who made silent connections between the cigarette in your hand and the mess in the world, and to converse with a group of people who had nothing but Red China was not my idea of a good time either.

In the 1950's, my teenage years, Red China was the dark terror sharpening its bayonets across the Pacific Ocean, while the rest of the world went to cocktail parties, slept late and led lives that were woozy with self-gratification. If you followed the Four Standards, you didn't do any of these things—unless you were "off the ball."

Anyone who was "off the ball" had temporarily lost sight of one or more of the Four Standards, which, as I saw them, were the parallel beacons that were supposed to converge at the center of your life, like spotlights over the Hollywood Bowl. And anyone who case-queried this paradox (and later on I did) was accused of trying to cover up a sin, which was true, I suppose, if you squinted your eyes.

My Uncle Ed, for instance, was "off the ball" on cigarettes for the entire time that MRA occupied his own house, but he had the good sense to smoke when he was walking the dog, so nobody knew he smoked until the house reverted back to his moral possession. But certain vices were not possible to hide, and if a girl or woman wore lipstick, she wasn't just "off the ball," she was "off the team." It was easy to spot at a glance which women attending an MRA function were allied with the movement; the guests wore lipstick and looked nervous, the MRA women wore their own lips and looked fashionable ahead of their time—by about fifteen years. Lipstick was a real sticking point. In the 50's a normal female simply wore it, but as Frank Buchman stressed, these were not normal times.

"If we all pull together," went one MRA song, "we will all pull through." Through what? I sometimes wondered. Through moral filth, I guess. If you "clean up the nation from bottom to top, start with yourself in the home and the shop." Whenever I heard that song, I had images of whole countries washing windows, shaking out sheets and waving from balconies to clean-minded teenagers who were marching toward their high school to buttonhole the student-body president, who was powerful but morally confused.

Moral Re-Armament had a youth program, or emphasis. Their films and periodicals were not all aimed at labor and management "getting straight with themselves" before going to the bargaining table. In 1957, the summer after I graduated from the convent, I spent three months at the MRA headquarters in Mackinac Island, Michigan. One of the youth films I saw was a grainy, black-and-white production called *The Drug Store Revolution*. The plot escapes me at this point, but the best part of the film was when the anti-hero, "Mr. Cool" high-school student walks into the drugstore, and the song "Here's the handsome hunk of heaven" was voiced-over. He looked wonderfully human, although by the end of the film he no longer used grease on his hair.

I had always kept Moral Re-Armament at arm's length, particularly during my teenage years, but just prior to leaving Dominican, I was introduced to Anne Howard, the twenty-two-year-old daughter of MRA's second most important member, Peter Howard. Locked-in at the receiving end of her quiet, steady gaze, all prejudices and past impressions dissolved. I thought she was the most impressive girl I had ever met, in or out of MRA. Anne was her father's child.

Peter Howard was a towering, electrically charged Englishman, an ex-championship soccer player for Great Britain, a former rising star in Lord Beaverbrook's newspaper empire on Fleet Street, and—as Frank Buchman's closest aide-de-camp—the Malcolm Muggeridge of the movement, who wrote with a laser beam, pinning down the enemies of our time. Peter was a handsome, gaunt man with high cheekbones, snapping black eyes and a voice that could lift an entire room of partially committed people to their feet with words I cannot at this point recapture. But Peter could fling the whole tapestry of MRA's intent on a back wall, nail it down with shining brads, and the next thing anyone knew, Sophie Wellington, a retired teacher who only had a pension to tide her to the grave, was quietly unclasping her mother's seventeen-jewel Bulova watch and offering it from the floor.

Peter was no watch-snatcher, but he inspired that kind of commitment, simultaneously offering great hope and filling you with apocalyptic dread that "it was late, but not *too* late" to join the greatest tide of people fully committed to bringing about change in the world.

I never listened to Peter that summer I was on Mackinac Island without feeling terribly small-minded, a Lilliputian taking Gulliver's word for things, but incapable of grasping the high beam because the height wasn't there. I admired him rather the way one would admire John the Baptist—from a distance. Peter was at the hub of a chariot that was much too swift, with too few seats inside to squander on the uncommitted.

The Howard family was, from the biographical information on the jackets of several books scattered about 36 Presidio Terrace which Peter had written, special in my eyes. They exuded a kind of heroic normalcy, had a working farm in

169

Surrey, and produced three arresting-looking children, including Anne. But until I met her, Anne had been frozen in my mind as a dark-eyed, pigtailed little girl sitting on her father's lap on the back flap of one of Peter's earliest books, *Ideas Have Legs.*

Anne was tall like her father, with an olive complexion, dark, registering eyes, and a broad smile that revealed a set of perfectly polished teeth. Anne was perfectly polished in every way, slim, with cherry-colored cheeks, a definite voice and a natural intensity of being that made her stand out like a Greek princess in a sea of pastel dresses. There were a lot of pastel people in MRA, or so it seemed to me, and I had always thought that, with very few exceptions, most of the people in MRA were well-dressed, didactic duds.

The men impressed me as being elegant, well-bred and snapping with a kind of canned enthusiasm for their convictions, which were interchangeable as the clichés changed into new clichés. This is not to say that I wasn't attracted to them. As I grew older and I focused upon them as individuals, I could not help but react positively to their power, but there was a kind of repelling coldness at their cores, which contradicted their passionate convictions, and while a disproportionate number of the MRA men were exceedingly handsome and intelligent, witty and urbane, I felt inferior in their presence; there was a kind of high-speed urgency about them as they burst through doorways, moved briskly across carpets, like businessmen en route to important board meetings—all high purpose and agenda—that made me shrink against the wall.

The MRA women were their limp adjuncts, who conformed to a stereotype that, in retrospect, makes me think that they were, in some crucial way, robbed of their own natural vitality by the men. Perhaps there was a poor sexual exchange between them. It was often said by MRA women instructing younger girls on how to act, that to wear certain kinds of clothes "was not fair to the men." In other words, women must not tempt the men. There was an abnegation of selfhood which was particularly noticeable among the women, who seemed to try for dullness and had personalities that beamed out thin messages of sacrifice, containment and quiet self-scrutiny. I found MRA men dazzling but cold, MRA women approachable but noncommunicative. And among the leadership there was a conformity and genetic sameness that would have enabled many of them to blend unnoticed into Anne Morrow Lindbergh's personal family scrapbook.

Moral Re-Armament was heavily bankrolled by old pedigreed families trying to wash their hands constructively with the money that had been handed down by less ethereal ancestors.

Anne was none of the above. As Peter's daughter she received a certain deference that was hers by association, but Anne was perfectly capable of creating her own place wherever she went. She was fully herself, full of passion, and fully, self-consciously beautiful. That, in a way, was her final, humanizing charm. She knew she was beautiful. Beauty informed her as effortlessly as her English accent, and when I once teased her about what her wedding dress would look like when she got married, I said that she would never wear anything prim or Quakerish. "It wouldn't be dramatic enough," I said. Anne looked at me with consternation in her eyes and said, "Oh dear, I think you're right about that." When Anne was accused of not being dull enough, she would blush and look more beautiful than before. I admired her from the first moment I met her, and when she walked across the Gallwey living room, grasped my hand and introduced herself, Red China did not dance in her eyes. I was, I felt, important to her for nonideological reasons. When she asked me that same evening to come to an all-expenses-paid summer at Mackinac Island, I couldn't think why not to accept.

"We are having many student leaders from all over the

world this summer," she said. "I would so like for you to be there too."

A student leader? At that moment, with high-school graduation only a month or so away, I didn't even know which college I would be going to, much less whether I would be a student leader once I got there.

"Perhaps we can room together," she added. "It would be great fun."

I accepted.

Six weeks later I held a diploma in my hand. The last seven years at Dominican came to a swift, lachrymose climax as the convent expanded and contracted in a series of meaningful ceremonies, each ritual inching the graduating class a little closer to the front-parlor door.

Then I was an alumna. Within the week I was on a plane flying toward Mackinac Island and a fragrant, car-less experience full of new friends (student leaders) from Korea and Connecticut, two places which were equally as romantic in my mind. Whatever second thoughts I may have entertained were blotted out by Anne, who would serve as a powerful protection if I needed it. But rolling around the bottom of my purse was one small article of rebellion—a tube of Tangee lipstick. I didn't plan on using it, but something Lilliputian inside insisted that I bring it along.

Mackinac Island is a postcard heaven—a small, quaint outcropping of pine trees, wildflowers and white clapboard cottages where wealthy Michigan sailors vacation during the summer months after the ice has broken, the winds grow warm and the Grand Hotel—a large, white mausoleum with a red-carpeted entrance flanked with orange geraniums in pots up the stairs—is open to the public for the season. But when MRA had its national headquarters there, it must have been one of the most schizophrenic islands in the Western Hemisphere.

The ferry boat took me from the mainland to the island. When the ferry docked, everyone piled out in one of two directions. "Not left, not right, but straight ahead," said an MRA song, which had nothing to do with geography. But on Mackinac Island there were only two ways to go.

To the left was a cheap good time—postcard racks, rayon pennants, popcorn machines and souvenirs that the islanders dutifully set before the tourists on the main street of the village.

But if you turned right, and I did, you were in a different world altogether. There were no popcorn machines on the MRA-dominated half of the island, and if a stray tourist made a wrong turn and went right instead of left, he would feel, as he straddled his bicycle, that he had stumbled into a time warp or a summer colony for the United Nations, which is how I felt as the horse and buggy sent to pick me up rattled up the path toward the Great Hall, where all newcomers were greeted and processed.

Swedes, Japanese, Koreans, Africans, American Indians— a collage of kimonos, dashikis, saris and business suits filed past me as they walked from one building to the other. Here and there I saw a familiar face, some old visitor to the Gallwey house who was present for the conference. But as the horse and buggy drew up to the entrance of the Great Hall, I felt a slight chill come over me. This place meant business. I could tell by the taut, intent expression on everyone's face.

I was assigned to the breakfast shift on the second day. Technically, everyone was given some kind of manual labor, although I don't remember Peter Howard slinging hash or carrying suitcases, but the theory was that in MRA there were no classes, except moral ones, and I do remember one afternoon in the wet, sloppy bowels of the basement scaling twenty-pound fish next to a Polish count, who wore gold-rimmed glasses and striped pants hung by suspenders.

It was my job to get up at 6 A.M., meet with the rest of the shift for a short "guidance" session (one was supposed to have already risen an hour earlier for a solitary session on your own) and then make breakfast for the delegates.

I was in charge of the oatmeal, which I made for 500, by pouring boiling water into a large, stainless-steel mixing bowl riveted to the floor of the kitchen, stirring in the oatmeal and then ladling it into serving bowls that we set out on stainless-steel serving counters for the hostesses who carried them into the dining room.

At first I loved the assignment. Walking toward the kitchen in the semidarkness, donning a white oversized apron and unfreezing my fingers over the boiling water in a large, gleaming kitchen seemed spartan and true—rather like Janie Powell swabbing the decks in the movie *Luxury Liner*. But the shift was dominated by a small, Swiss-German woman who had raspberry-colored cheeks, a broad, involuntary smile, and a step-scrubbing, window-polishing mentality that made me think her idea of heaven was to be perpetually poised with a white napkin ready to catch a slop of oatmeal before it dribbled down the side of the bowl.

"Ve must not make a poor appearance with ze oatmeal," she would grin cheerlessly. "Ze bowls must not haf any little messy sings on ze sides."

One did not sling oatmeal in Moral Re-Armament. Oatmeal must be an island of brown perfection resting dead center in the middle of a gleaming dish. The same standards of perfection applied to setting out spoons, always aligned like soldiers, just so, on the sideboard, or folding the napkins, which had to be perfect birds of paradise, each corner saluting God straight up. To be less than perfect was to be less than "absolutely caring," and it was directly implied that if you left a fork crooked you were "letting down the nation," a stock MRA phrase that was imprinted in my mind along with all the others.

But the cold center of the breakfast shift was the guidance center before making the oatmeal, where the shift sat around on stools with notebooks in our laps and went around sharing what we had been struggling with that morning—jealousy, vanity, pride, dishonesty.

Everyone's guidance was always directed toward improvement—either your own or somebody else's in the circle. But compassion always played second fiddle to truth, and there were many times when someone would level a criticism at somebody else, and, like the Red Chinese or the Trappists, the person under fire would have to sit there and take it without complaining.

Around the circle we would go—each girl reading from her notebook what God had "guided" her to say. Usually God spoke in clichés. As the circle closed in on me, I would begin to feel a noose tightening around my throat. My thoughts would scramble. My mind would seize. When it came my turn to "share," I would yield, like the dummy in the bridge game, to the next person. "I don't have anything," I would say, blushing with embarrassment.

Eyes would lower. A short silence would ensue. People would recross their legs, tap their pencils, look at me with a mixture of resignation and irritation. The pause, well-nigh unbearable, would then, after several moments, break, and the next person would pick up the slack in the circle I had just thrown out of shape. Every morning I broke the circle with a dash, and it was not long before I became terribly unbalanced, wondered what was wrong with me and why was I not grasping the impact of what was going on? All around were choruses singing national anthems, people in native costumes, speakers testifying to their moral renewal, and Peter Howard striding on his impossibly long legs through the hallways, on fire with conviction, his hair always perfectly parted, with a fresh shirt on whenever I saw him.

I had not been at the conference a full week before I realized that the spirit of the conference was eluding me. I did not, as the days progressed, fit in.

The Great Hall, which dominated the MRA complex, was a massive, teepee-like structure surrounded by glassed-in translators' booths in the back and a stage in front. To one side of the stage was a large mural—a collage of familiar MRA faces: Frank Buchman, Rajmohan Gandhi, a Burmese woman politician whose grinning importance escapes my mind, and other people, all of them smiling in a kind of nonverbal advertisement for MRA which was supposed to overwhelm you, like a Coca Cola ad. It did but not for the right reasons.

Moral Re-Armament was a familiar object in my life; the faces made me homesick. I didn't understand why I was having such trouble being a "student leader." Yet I could not seem to find my way onto the same emotionally thrilling path on which everyone else was moving in such lockstep joy, and I would sit in the Great Hall for the assemblies, which were held twice a day, listen to the speakers from various delegations and feel the thrill of their conversions pass right over my head without ruffling a hair on it.

There were, at the conference, other teenagers—girls like Jenny Austin and Trisha Twitchell, who were far too austere and committed to confide in. The twins, Mako and Takay Kabayama, daughters of a rich Japanese industrialist, who were on vacation from The Shipley School near Philadelphia where they were being polished before reentry into Japan, were bouncy, exuberant girls. But I did not dare confess to them my ambivalences about what was going on. I did not dare confess to anyone, even Anne whom I valued too much to let down. I kept my lack of true revolutionary fervor to myself, hoped for a breakthrough and took what little comfort I could from a spare five minutes with my cousin Johnny, who every so often would waltz up from behind, give me a hug and beat it.

176

With every chance for inspiration to strike, I was entirely unmoved. I would take my bicycle and I would pedal around the island, so lovely and so fragrant with wildflowers that I did not have the impetus to appreciate, and try to stay away from the conference long enough so that I would miss the meals I didn't have a plan for.

Time hung heavily on my hands. I often rode down to the docks to watch the tourists roll off the boat, their winter flesh rippling underneath halter tops as they herded down the main street, a riot of bad taste and bad bodies in search of a bottle of Orange Crush or a few snapshots to take back home.

One load would disembark from the ferry, which then opened its jaws to another load waiting to return. They would clatter onto the boat, throw their overexposed film into the water and chug mindlessly back to the mainland.

I would watch them with snobbish horror. The tourists seemed so pig-eyed and beery, such a marked contrast to the stripped-down, disciplined delegates back at the Great Hall, the men pan-flat and aquiline, the women crisp, laundered and directed—like Grete Holmquist, a pale blonde from Sweden who washed her hair with cornmeal, wore hand-knitted sweaters, and was one of the girls on my breakfast shift who always shared her guidance in a thin, steady voice which I thought was detached and contemplative, just as I thought she was the perfect model of contained femininity and effortless personal hygiene.

The tourists were as good an advertisement for Moral Re-Armament as MRA itself, and I often watched them, straddling my bicycle, killing time to avoid going back to the conference. The greatest torture to me were the meals.

Anne had made a concerted effort during the first few days to introduce me to all the people she could. But after that she effectively dropped out of my life, and I spent a great deal of time searching for my Aunt Dorothy or Johnny, neither of whom could ever be found. The word about my lack of "guidance" had leaked out. Mealtime invitations dropped to zero, and each day dragged by, a paler repetition of the day before, although mealtimes were the worst times of all.

Three times a day the entire conference milled around the entrance to the dining room, which was partitioned off into three sections, two main halls and "Frank's Dining Room," a closed-off portion where only the very top people ate—by invitation. It was there in the lobby that everyone chose who they wanted to eat with, although eating was hardly the point of the meals. Little cadres of delegates quickly formed. You were in demand if you were new, famous, or had what, for want of a more accurate description, could be called "conviction."

I was new only for a few days. I was not famous, like the president of a student body, or related to someone who was famous, like Rajmohan Gandhi (always referred to on the stage as "Rajmohan-Gandhi-grandson-of-the-Mahatma"), and after a half-dozen meals when I sat at various tables and couldn't seem to come up with the kind of "conviction" to impress anyone in lieu of anything else, I was seized with a kind of terrible panic.

Perhaps the jokes I made were inappropriate. Perhaps I tried to change the subject too much. But suddenly I wasn't being asked to eat with anyone, and people I asked always had another plan when I asked them. I must be, I thought, "off the ball." The punishment for being "off the ball" was isolation, silence, a lack of mealtime invitations, and I would turn up at lunchtime, walk around the lobby with a frozen grin on my face as everybody else pointedly rushed around me asking others, "Do you have a plan?" "Oh, no, I don't have a plan." "Ah, well then, perhaps we can join up?" The lobby would empty into the dining room, and I would try to make an exit toward my room before it was any more obvious than it already was that I didn't "have a plan" at all.

I don't think that this isolation was premeditated on anyone's part. But it was very real and, in my instance, almost total. And while I was asked to be part of the breakfast crew—which turned out to be my only continual source of social interaction—I was not asked to do anything else—sing in the chorus, be on a stage crew, act in a play or greet new delegations as they came off the ferry.

I plucked at my imperfections, developed silent, one-way crushes on several perfect older girls, who were perfect Moral Re-Armament women—chaste, popular and untroubled—and watched Anne from a distance, her busyness in inverse proportion to my idleness, and realized that I had caused her terrible grief. Anne had miscalculated. I was not a student leader. And while Anne would sit, with shining eyes dressed in her Greek national costume (her mother was a Metaxa), listening to speakers who carried her away with interest, I would sit like the nobody I was in the back of the Great Hall, my seat growing harder and harder with each recycled slogan that came from the stage.

The meetings were fairly predictable, only the speakers changed—one morning a Douglas Aircraft executive would be featured, the next morning the son of Mendès-France. Sitting behind the speakers were the MRA big-timers, men like Peter Howard and Basil Entwhistle, sometimes a woman, although there were no important women at the top of the movement. And while the Broadway lead in *Pajama Game* came to Mackinac that summer with a ton of makeup on her face, which was gone by the time she left, you had to be a stage actress or an aristocrat like Dame Flora McCloud, who always showed up with her own bagpiper, to make a dent.

Moral Re-Armament was controlled by men who treated women with a respect that bordered on contempt, and even twelve-year-old girls were told to wear girdles when they served as hostesses in the dining room. There was a tremendous emphasis on plainness, detachment and appropriate clothes. The female uniform in Moral Re-Armament was a light-colored cotton dress with a full skirt, a high neck and three-quarter-length sleeves. Stockings were required. Hair was to be clean but not flyaway. You could wear pearls and earrings. You could look middle-aged. We did.

Boys and girls at Mackinac Island were forbidden to mix, the unspoken message being that any solution other than separation would threaten the integrity of the movement. The goal was to be single-minded, chaste and active in order to keep sexuality from swamping the boat.

There was one conference meeting which defied the planners. The head of the Filipino delegation, which had arrived a week before, rose to speak at the microphone. I settled in to be bored.

But he was obviously very agitated, although I didn't know what he was saying because he was speaking in Tagalo, and the translator at his side gave a start after the third sentence, which seemed to be saying something dramatic or out of the ordinary. The Filipino finally paused, and his translator began to convert his speech into English. "He says that he has not been leading a pure life . . ." The Filipino could not wait. He went on more rapidly, with great arm gestures and tears running down his cheeks. His wife—a small lady with high eyebrows and butterfly sleeves—suddenly plunged her face into her hands and began to weep. Then her husband strode off the stage, and the ashen-faced translator started again.

"Uh, he says that, uh, he has not been leading a pure life, that he feels very bad about this, that he has a mistress in Baguio, for maybe fifteen years now, and a child by that woman . . . and since he comes to Moral Re-Armament he feels very bad, very sorry for this and wants to confess and not do it anymore."

"Bunny" Austin, an ex-tennis star from Wimbledon, who had been in charge of the delegation, leaped off the stage, his wife Phyllis, who used to be a famous star on the London stage, right behind him. Their faces were genuinely stricken. A terrible, inhuman thing had just happened, and it was perhaps the only time that the veil of self-righteousness was lifted from their faces, revealing their human side in a way that I could understand. Together they left the Great Hall in search of the Filipino. From that time on, delegates' speeches were very closely checked before they got to the microphone.

By and large, the meetings were not spontaneous, although I loved the beginnings and endings—which usually featured some kind of talent. Ivan Menzies, a former singer with the D'Oyly Carte Opera Company, would bound like an aging leprechaun onto the stage, singing in his perfect, silvery voice some wonderfully funny but didactic song. Every once in a while the Coldwell Brothers, an American trio of cowboy singers, would jump onto the stage with their guitars with some down-home country music. Or the chorus would sing "Take It to the World."

My heart was swept away by the chord changes, but it sank with the clichés, and I began to wonder whether the stubborn gray cloud that I walked under was my own life. It was never overtly suggested that my life was my problem, but there were other ways of making the same point.

Sporadically someone would materialize in my room after supper to talk about his life. Fay Thompkins, a large, healthy-looking girl from Alberta, Canada, spent an entire evening recounting how she used to fall down drunk at parties, make free of herself with men she didn't even know, and, until she met Moral Re-Armament, had been living an entirely impure life, "if you know what I mean."

I didn't know quite what she meant, and Canada seemed like such an odd, furniture-free country in which to be dissolute, but I was fascinated by her story and slightly embarrassed that I had nothing to offer of that kind from my own life. In fact, it never occurred to me until later that the whole point of her performance was to get me to perform myself.

Fay Thompkins was simply laying out obvious themes that were supposed to trick my memory or give me the courage to talk about what I knew very well.

Another girl, without prompting, told me about what she used to do with her dog when she was ten years old. Again, I had nothing to add, although I will never forget her story, which is as unprintable now as it was then.

Even Anne, who never resorted to lurid tales in order to convert, once gazed meaningfully in my direction and said, "I wonder if there will have to be bombs and blood in your streets before you realize that there is not much time before your way of life will be ended."

I took that "blood in the streets" remark very seriously. Anne had survived the bombing of Britain. She used to tell me about how she used to crouch in the root cellar as the Germans flew over the countryside, tearing it up at random. But it was clear that my "way of life" was, in summation, a life apart from Moral Re-Armament, whether I drank myself under the table or not. Anne was a heroine in my eyes. It occurred to me and occurred to me again until finally I saw no way out that I must "go over the Four Standards," which in Moral Re-Armament meant going over the coals, fishing up the garbage, cleaning up my shop and—in the end—confessing every impure, dishonest, unkind, selfish act in my life.

I bought a guidance book, sat out on a grassy bank behind the Great Hall and made four columns: Honesty, Purity, Love, and Unselfishness. All afternoon I tried to fill them up, capitulating to my scruples, Anne's image and a craving desire to "have a plan" for all three meals. I wonder how many other delegates to the conference could tell roughly the same story? How many of us were making four columns and searching their souls for want of an option? I don't know; nobody was that honest. But after I had written down my sins, I looked at them and scored them for the embarrassment factor. Most of them I could tell without blushing. A few would be almost impossible to report. But the very impossibility was the key to redemption. If I didn't suffer, I wouldn't be released from my past altogether.

The next day I caught Anne by the sleeve and whispered to her that I thought I was ready to "go over the Four Standards." Anne looked at me with a mixture of gratitude and concern. Did I want anyone else to be there as well? Out of the blue I plucked another person—Anne's mother, Doe. I did not know Doe, except to watch her across the conference hall, a small, white-faced woman that Peter had to bend over double in order to speak with. I wanted Doe to be there as well. I sensed power, humor and magnanimity in her heart, and I found her wry, rabbity face with its mouthful of teeth, which she didn't feel the need to straighten, a distant comfort. She was eccentric in a conformist atmosphere. Also if I was going to confess my sins, I wanted to confess them to ranking members of the priesthood. Two Howards were better than one. My forgiveness was more assured.

Those redemptive scraps of paper, scribbled over with sins that I orally handed over page by page like tickets to the dining room that refused me admission, are gone. I tossed them away, like the outline for an exam that I passed, the afternoon I sat with Anne and Doe on a back lawn, examining myself flaw by flaw. Each admission was a cloud gone from the sky. Every forced understanding was a new section of highway laid down into the future, and my sins—as I heaved them off my shoulders—were planks that slid into Lake Michigan to be carried away from the center of my life. Or so I hoped. I did not know quite how one proceeded through the Four Standards. I had to create my own form. But I sat in my lawn chair and tried to be ruthless with myself, pulling away the rotten timber that surrounded my ego, all the better to raze the building to the ground.

The wind blew up against my hot face in cold absolution

for my life as I revealed it—bad friendships, devious motives, selfish acts—all the garbage of my scrupulous, fearful mind. Doe leaned against the back of her lawn chair and said nothing. Anne's sharp, perfect Greek nose tilted toward the sun in silence. My voice was the only voice—halting, uneasy, dogged—and, as I consciously worked backward toward the most unspeakable and therefore most important sin to confess, I could feel my throat constricting, gagging, unable to cough up the worst memory of all—Tommy Chiesa's penis, which had lodged itself in the back of my throat ever since I was four years old, meaning that I had felt its presence for fourteen guilt-ridden years since.

There was silence as I told the story. Both Anne and Doe looked at me, their faces blank and unopinionated. I hated myself for the pollution of my own words, could hardly pull them out of my mouth. But I knew that I had to do it, even though it meant being forever associated in their minds with the worst thing I had ever done.

Did they know other stories as terrible as this one? Would Anne be somehow changed in substance and form from this moment forward as she sat, in her velvet national costume under the floodlights? How does one carry oneself with old dignity when there is a new obscene story in the forefront of one's brain? As I recited the story of Tommy's backyard fellatio, I realized that I was doing the very thing I did not want to do—reducing myself to an obscene connection in the eyes of the one girl whose respect I most coveted. But it was too late.

I finished the story, slumped back against my lawn chair and waited—for an opinion, a feeling of lightness, some kind of an internal or external sign that now I was on the side of the angels.

The wind did not die down. Nor did it pick up. The sky took on no new colors, there was no particular feeling of spiritual lightness in my heart. And as I sat, head lowered with self-consciousness over my "guidance" book, Anne and her mother simply looked at me, or so I assumed. I was too embarrassed to confirm their eyes with my own. The meeting dwindled into small talk—was I going to write to the girl in high school whose friendship I had wanted because she was "social"? Yes, I thought I would do that this evening, apologizing to her for having sought her out for the wrong reasons. Other than that, I had no easy means of making retribution for what had gone before. Tommy Chiesa was not mentioned. What I did not realize until years later was that the bulk of the Howards' silence was probably due to the fact that they had nothing to say. My life, next to Fay Thompkins', was a blank page.

It was an unremarkable conversion, without bells. As I gathered up my scraps of paper, I uncapped my pen and wrote "Wheew!" across the top of the confession. Anne caught the word out of the corner of her eye. We walked back toward the Great Hall. "I saw what you wrote," she said, plucking my elbow with new friendship, her face wreathed in the broad, merry smile that was her hallmark. I smiled back, but inwardly I was very disappointed in the results of the afternoon. For confessing to Tommy Chiesa's penis, I expected to feel a significant change of heart. But I felt nothing at all. The summer at Mackinac ground to a nonconclusion, each meeting an increasingly intolerable repetition of its predecessor the day before. Koreans, Douglas Aircraft executives, Swiss-Germans, Indians—the delegations came and went, sari-clad, slant-eyed, self-righteous and out of reach.

Finally, it was over. I was accompanied to the ferry by one of the Swedish girls, who helped me carry my suitcase and spoke significantly of "what will lie ahead" for me in the coming year.

"It won't be easy for you, in some ways," she said, under the assumption that the summer had been a success.

"What do you mean?" I asked, since I had every belief

that the minute I put my foot down upon nonideological soil, life would immediately improve.

"Well, you know, not going out with boys," she explained, "not wearing lipstick."

I looked at her and said firmly, "But I *am* going to go out with boys, and I *am* going to wear lipstick."

There was nothing she could say to that. I was one foot on the ferry. But she managed to smile—a small, wafer-thin crescent of politeness that was full of understandings which I had not earned the right to share.

I never did say good-bye to Anne. But years later I heard she had married a member of Parliament. He was all right on the subject of MRA, I assume. I cannot imagine Anne marrying entirely away from the movement. I was in college when Frank Buchman died. Moral Re-Armament fell into the hands of a troika of assistants, with Peter as the unacknowledged leader. But Peter died of a heart attack in South America several years later. The MRA conference center was first a college and then was sold, as were most of the other townhouses, estates and reception centers around the world.

People who had been full-time in Moral Re-Armament were forced to reenter the actual world, although fortunately my Uncle Gene died of a heart attack while giving a eulogy at Peter Howard's memorial service at Aunt Kitty's estate. I cannot imagine Uncle Gene working in a bank or any other place of commercial profit. He was too large for that kind of life. But, in another way, Moral Re-Armament was too large for its own britches. When Peter Howard died, the movement split and some of the top leaders retrenched. The MRA name still exists, along with its reduced cadre of believers. But the bulk of the American leadership either got out or incorporated as a piece of slick entertainment, a road show renamed *Sing-Out* and then *Up With People*. But I seriously doubt whether any of the teenagers who sing "What Color Is God's Skin?" and hit the stage with their feet running in a way that is a dead ringer for the old choreography of *The Good Road* have any idea of the origins of their performance.

The last time I went to an *Up With People* performance, I sat in the top balcony of a large sports arena, holding an empty aluminum Coke can, which vibrated in my hand. I was unmoved, as usual, but the decibel level was dangerous. In Moral Re-Armament, people always thought that you had to shout in order to be heard.

Chapter
X

I cannot remember a time when I did not want to leave California. It wearied my eye, like the profile of Mount Tamalpais which stretched across the backside of Marin County, an Indian princess (according to the legend I never bothered to pursue) in perpetual sleep.

Indians, real or imagined, did not interest me. Arrowheads, stories about the Gold Rush, the stuff of state-issued textbooks that told the tale of California bored me, just as the Spanish missions bored me, although I wound up being married in one ("Mission Impossible," cracked my father), and by that time I was not insensitive to their charm.

But even the missions were something to joke about and when, the day after my wedding, the local papers reported the wedding under the caption "Tourists Applaud Bride," there was something déclassé about being married in a tourist attraction, just as I always felt that there was something déclassé about California itself.

Within the state there still exists a natural antagonism between the northern and southern halves, and until my cousins and I were grown, nobody lived in Los Angeles, which somebody in the family described as roughly comparable to "floating down a sewer in a glass-bottom boat." But San Francisco began to get on my nerves as well. I feared that I would wind up marrying a summer house in Lake Tahoe instead of marrying life, and the only bit of California history which never failed to rivet me was the story of the Donner Party, which had crawled on bleeding feet through the Sierras to the other side of the mountain. As far as I was concerned, that was the most interesting thing that had ever happened in California, although the other side of the mountain was Sacramento, a dusty low-slung town that my father used to travel to on business trips, the backseat of the car loaded with plastic bags full of dehydrated fruit samples that he took to show state dietitians. The capital city seemed full of fat men in dark suits sweating over fruit salads in hotel restaurants. Sacramento did not trick my mind, although other parts of California did.

The fog filling up "pneumonia gulch," a deep cleft of mountain that fed the highway onto Golden Gate Bridge from Sausalito, was a moody swirl of wind and wetness that made the Golden Gate Bridge seem even more miraculous, shining like a harp, than it was. A grove of eucalyptus trees slicing up the sun on a warm day in the Presidio filled my head with poetry. San Francisco on a sharp blue day can catch your heart from a distance and up close—running down Montgomery Street, the city's financial district, where everyone in Pacific Heights had an insurance file, I felt full of ticker-tape importance, even though I was only running toward a yogurt stand.

Montgomery Street was the closest I could get to Wall Street and still be in California. But leaving California, like going to college, was an assumption that I counted on, and I had always hoped that the two assumptions would materialize at the same time, making each other true.

The summer before my freshman year, when I had spent three months on Mackinac Island being molded unsuccessfully into a student leader, the college question was still undecided. I returned to California unshriven, a disappointment, the all-expenses-paid trip which MRA was obliged to honor yielding up no new member of their international chorus. It was plain that I was not going to be a charismatic student leader who would magnetize a campus or hold the door open for a phalanx of MRA recruiters to enter and revolutionize the campus for me. But it was beginning to look as if there would be no campus to revolutionize, unless it was the University of California in Berkeley.

The thought of attending the University of California depressed me. Judging from the few times I had visited my cousin Mimi there, it seemed like a large, sorority-dominated institution which revolved around The Big Game, taking notes in halls that were so large you couldn't hear the professor, and worrying a great deal about "the drinking problem."

"They won't ask you out if you don't drink," Mimi had warned. I imagined hot evenings backed up against the mantel of the Deke house while a muscle-bound quarterback in a sawed-off sweat shirt tried to pour beer down my throat as the room filled up with cigarette smoke and my eyes crossed with fear and hopelessness—my dream of getting out of California shot.

From the beginning of my junior year in high school, I began to pore over college catalogs as I gained confidence that my grade average would merit a scholarship somewhere other than "Cal." Smith seemed ideal, Barnard was a possibility, although the girls looked a little intense, but the half-dozen Catholic colleges I considered looked as if they might be hiding oil tanks behind the tree line, and the student bodies were full of coeds who seemed badly dressed and probably hung around telephones which rarely rang. I made up my mind to go to Smith, and then I was snagged by an article, handed out in senior religion class, called "Should Catholic Lambs Eat Ivy?"

I was probably the only senior who wasn't going to be a nun who took the article seriously, but I followed the reasoning of the Jesuit who wrote it and suddenly realized that the next four years would be the last time that I could study my religion in a mature way. I took Catholicism seriously. I saw it as the only weapon I had for the rest of my life. I dug further into the catalogs and unearthed a Sacred Heart college which wasn't too far from New York and looked collegiate enough to satisfy my aesthetic side, which wanted to be Catholic and look Protestant and have the best of both worlds.

I left for Mackinac Island in June with two acceptance letters—from Smith and Manhattanville College of the Sacred Heart. Both acceptances were useless because of the small scholarship attached. My grandmother's philosophy of life being full of corners that obscured gift horses champing at the bit was momentarily threatened. Yet while I doled out oatmeal, listened to the Korean national anthem and was being ignored at mealtimes for lack of ideological conviction, letters were criss-crossing the country on my behalf. Problems were being resolved without my knowledge, and I arrived home at the end of the summer to find that the waves had been parted in a last-minute way.

Nobody in my family had ever heard of Manhattanville. The nuns at Dominican thought Sacred Heart nuns were a bit precious and didn't encourage me to apply there, preferring Stanford or their own Dominican College on the same convent campus as a better place to go. But a friend of my mother's, a transplanted Philadelphian, had not only heard of Manhattanville but had been student-body president, and she took pen to paper and wrote Mother O'Byrne, who was president of the college, and informed her of my dilemma.

Did Mother O'Byrne realize that this applicant had actually been accepted with a scholarship to that great secular institution in Massachusetts, Smith College? She thought that this fact might have escaped Mother O'Byrne's attention, but if the situation did not alter at Manhattanville's end, this applicant would be forced to consider Smith seriously. A Catholic lamb might, in fact, be forced to eat ivy and that, she gently lied, would be that.

Back came a letter. No, conceded Mother O'Byrne, the college had not known all the details. There were additional funds that could be freed up, given the glowing recommendation of her dear friend. Money should not be an obstacle. In a cliff-hanger that was to repeat itself in an equally miraculous way the following year, I was granted a reprieve.

My grandmother's philosophy was still intact, and the next four years spread themselves before me as rich and promising as the '57 college issue of *Mademoiselle* magazine, which was full of creamy-complected girls chewing delicately on Number Two pencils as they read Plato in skirt and sweater sets which could be purchased at Lord & Taylor. Lord & Taylor didn't even have an outlet in California, confirming my feeling that California was a backwater that I wanted to row out of.

"Lord & Taylor" had a Dickensian ring to it. I scoured Macy's for knee socks and anticipated being part of a student body of kilt-bound girls who came from Connecticut—a Revolutionary state which filled me with a sense of cobblestones and antiquity.

There was more than one reason for wanting to leave California. It occurred to me, for instance, that I might not be invited to be a Kappa, which would have forced me into a dormitory full of Pakistanis and drips if I had been forced to study at Cal. But I had a strong urge to connect with a tradition that was more rockbound than my own. Brick houses, stone walls, men in earmuffs shoveling out driveways banked with snow I had never seen—even now when I return from California to the East, my eye is comforted by these things. Brick houses still appeal. They seem safer places to have a nervous breakdown than inside one of those Malibu Beach houses that hang, half-hitched, to a cliff. If I went out of my mind, a man in earmuffs would know how to get me to a padded room faster than a man in an Indian caftan. Then, as now, what has always appealed to me about the East Coast is the protective coloration of the environment. Logic, like the sharp division of the seasons, was a sling that would support me if blind intuition—which my family tends to gravitate toward—didn't work.

I packed my suitcase, my head full of wide-planked rooms furnished with Quaker quilts, hooked rugs and squash rackets—articles of a solid civilization that my mother had left behind her when she came West, trading all of it for the relentlessly blue Pacific Ocean, which hurt my eyes with its brilliant, seasonless brightness. The only hitch in the plan was my father. On the night before my departure he suddenly, inexplicably, tried to tell me I didn't deserve to go.

"It is a very expensive school," he said, with a pained look in his eyes.

What could I say? "I know," I answered, unsure of his meaning.

"The scholarship doesn't exactly pay for even half of the cost," he added. "And I'm also paying for John at St. George's."

I felt mousetrapped. What he said was true.

"There's no reason why you couldn't go to Cal," he persisted. "It's a damn good school, and even that would be expensive, with all the fees."

"But I've already accepted Manhattanville," I began to

plead. "I'm supposed to leave tomorrow morning. What are you trying to say?"

"What I'm trying to say," he said in a cold, reasonable voice, "is that I don't think you appreciate how expensive this is, and I don't know why you should even be going, since you don't appreciate it and you are not, after all, the only child in the family. There are five others. I've got to think about college for all of them, and there's only so much money."

My thoughts jammed. Why was he saying this now? I had not known or thought about these things. I didn't know how to act, what to say to relieve his irritation, or whether I should sacrifice college itself. I could not read his mind.

"You mean," I whispered, "I'm not going to get to go?"

My father was silent, his face tight with a hostility I did not understand. He was looking at me as if he wanted something but he wouldn't tell me what it was. Before he could answer and ruin everything, I slid off the sofa arm and ran upstairs.

Through a crack in my bedroom door, I heard an unnaturally loud cry from my mother—a sharp, sobbing "How could you!" I did not hear the rest of the conversation.

The next day I flew to New York, a Donner Party of one, in reverse.

The college was surrounded by a wall. I had not expected that. A wall implied limits, and college was supposed to be free of external restrictions. But I changed my mind about restrictions. For the next four years I spent most of my time making small, heart-pounding forays into the world. But with very few exceptions, I failed to get my footing, and it was only when I drove back through the college gates that my heart would relax into a more rhythmic, regular beat. Off campus I broke into cold sweats. Within the confines I was relatively safe—part of a snack-bar culture with a resident priest ready to hear my confession if I didn't die before it was my turn at bat.

The first day on campus, I had been seized with terror. I knew no one. The bright-eyed junior in a kilt skirt who carried my suitcase to my room left me in it without instructions as to how to get out. The room was a gray cinder-block cell with only a bed and a desk. I had counted upon having a room-mate, someone who would steady me as I walked toward the dining hall, sat in assemblies, found out where everything was. But I was a late admission. Everyone else in the class had been paired up, and I stood inside my room, listening to the thumps and shouts of the other girls as they ran up and down the halls. I realized that in my excitement over going East I had neglected to be scared.

Suddenly I was very scared. I felt tears rising in my throat. There was no one on the entire Eastern seaboard that I knew, much less could ask to help me through this rite of passage. Instinctively I fell to my knees, buried my head in hands on the bed and offered up my fear. "I don't know what is going to happen," I prayed, "but all I ask is that I am myself, no matter what."

It was the right prayer. I walked out of my room and found friends. The campus was a smorgasbord of friends. Odd, funny, elegant, interesting girls who came from Winnetka, Brooklyn Heights, Rochester and Grosse Pointe. I was intoxicated with the thought that I had expanded my horizons so effortlessly. Each girl had a story to tell, a family to be introduced and a tradition that was strange and enviable to me. It was several months before I realized that everybody was Catholic.

It had never occurred to me that I had chosen a college which was utterly devoid of Protestants or Jews. I had made an incorrect assumption that any college on the East Coast would, ipso facto, be a melting pot. But almost everybody in the pot was named Shannon, Bridget and Michael Mary. It was a school for upper-class Irish and Italian girls, whose fathers had earned the right to send their daughters to a carefully chaperoned, academically excellent school—far enough from New York to keep them safe, near enough to White Plains so they could use their parents' charge cards at B. Altman's and never miss a Sunday Mass. I had inadvertently flown from California, which I considered parochial, and landed in an environment that was parochial in the extreme. But the extremes fascinated me.

A Grosse Pointe girl who had her hair streaked once a week and wore mantillas that had been personally blessed by Pope Pius XII was a new experience. The large, freckled Irish families, with fathers who got tears in their eyes, spoke with a lilt about "the wind always being at the back of you, darlin'," and had sons who went to Holy Cross and were altar boys, were perhaps the most warming families of them all. Behind every girl there seemed to be a misty-eyed father and a mother who squeezed real orange juice for everybody's breakfast on weekends at home. These were picture-book Catholic families, although as time went on I learned to see beyond first appearances and read some of the pain behind the eyes of the women who never missed 6:30 Mass.

All the Kennedy women or in-laws had gone to Manhattanville. It was almost a breeder station of beautiful, appropriate Catholic women who would presumably lead beautiful, appropriate Catholic lives. I was continually struck by the photogenic perfection of these women: the Gilbane girls, each more arresting than the last, with their wide eyes, high coloring and solid, healthy bodies; Chantal de Cannard, a lithe Belgian girl with translucent skin and a soft laugh, who married Rita Cannon's brother—a good match, light and dark, silk and tweed; Marty Bergeron, who hopped like a sparrow around the campus, her hand-knit ski caps with pom-poms framing an innocent, merry face. They were genuinely nice girls and then, as now, I saw a natural virtue and generosity of spirit about them that was more the rule than the exception.

In the beginning I dove enthusiastically into college life, yet my internal reaction to this crisp, brand-new environment was mysteriously at odds with how happy I thought I was at the outset. My subconscious must have been lying coiled all these years, waiting to strike, and one evening I walked back into my room after monitoring the halls after lights were supposed to be out, and my subconscious struck—fast, hard and without warning.

As I was walking toward my window to get a final breath of night air, my heart gave a loud thump. It was followed by a tattoo of small beats which I had never experienced before. Then another thump, followed by another tattoo. I clutched the windowsill, tried to focus upon a street light and saw black circles telescoping in from the void. "I'm dying," I thought. I turned and ran out of my room.

Next door were two girls—Kewie Waters and Eileen Leach. I knocked on their door, and when Kewie opened it I said, "I think I'm having a heart attack."

Kewie immediately burst into tears, threw me onto her bed and began to say an Act of Contrition. "Oh my God," she said, "I am heartily sorry for having offended thee . . ." Eileen simply said, "Oh my God," and ran to find a nun. Over and over again, Kewie repeated the prayer through her tears, while I lay on the bed and tried, in vain, to calm my heart. Mother Whelan came into the room, took me to the infirmary, and within an hour I was back in my own room.

The attack had suddenly ceased. I was told it was tachycardia—a harmless phenomenon brought on by anxiety. But I could not think what I was anxious about, except my heart.

The thought became the mother of new attacks. I never knew when the sudden thump-tattoo syndrome would begin. Each new whirring of my heart convinced me that I would die if I didn't get control of myself. Yet I could not confess this fear, since it was medically without grounds, and in keeping the fear to myself, the fear increased.

Sitting in a classroom, listening to Mother Clark slice

through Augustine's *De libero arbitrio,* my heart would suddenly start up.

". . . and so," said Mother Clark enthusiastically, "as Augustine rightly said, thus correcting Plotinus, 'freedom comes not from separation of mind and body, but from seeking only those goods which a man cannot lose against his will.' "

I would rub my hands against the side of my skirt, as I felt my head become a cap of electric snakes.

"Again we see Augustine's moral trend as he views the problem: For him, wrong-mindedness is nothing other than wrong will. Truth is all about us for the taking; another's possession of truth does not leave less for us."

Mother Clark never flagged in her admiration of Saint Augustine, and if love were helium she would have had to teach in a windowless room, since she seemed perpetually on the verge of flying out the window with her conclusions, even as I was sweating in my chair and wondering whether I would be alive for the next class period.

The bell would ring and I would jump up from my seat to go nowhere in particular. My fears beat me about the halls, although I swung through them ostensibly as cheerful as the next person. But sometimes the fear would ambush me, particularly if I were off campus in Manhattan. I would lose my breath, as if punched. Gulping, frightened and barely able to count out the change for the fare back to college, I would board the train to White Plains, shut my eyes as we passed Spanish Harlem, and somehow arrive back on the safe side of the stone walls. But I did not feel entirely safe anywhere, and sitting in my room reading Kierkegaard, I would be overwhelmed by an insight (his), feel floods of anxiety (I cannot live up to that truth) rush from the room into the chattering snack bar, and wait until the last light was out before I made my way back to my room.

With the lights out, I would lie in the dark and do battle with my heart, pulse and electrical system. It was then that I feared blind lunges for razors. The breach between my mind and heart was unendurable. I did not know why the breach existed, and at times I would sit up and switch on the lamp by my bed to search through the bible of my symptoms, a small paperback given to me by Mother Cavanagh entitled *Achieving Peace of Heart.*

I don't know who Narcisca Irala, S.J., was, but he wrote a book full of charts, graphs, complex ABC progressions, and in the outline diagram under "Mental Fatigue or Weakness," I found myself.

Bodily symptoms: "Quite varied," he wrote. "A sensation of a band of heat or pressure around the head or forehead, incipient dizziness, trouble with respiration, etc. . . . In short: a bothersome duality and uncontrolled activity, loss of control and dominion over oneself."

The graphs comforted me somewhat, although the graph showing how to cure the symptoms was too abstract.

> Catharsis or ventilation or interpretation of conscious or unconscious problems. Auto-suggestion and the re-education of mental control. Since the illness is above all a psychic or psychosomatic one, the cure must begin with the patient himself, with the self-conquest and re-education through personal relationship with the counselor.

I would turn the light off and beg for sleep, only to be afraid that I would die—my wish in spades.

I don't know how many other girls were going through the same or similar nights of dread. I assumed, in my egocentricity, that I was the only victim, although late in my senior year I overheard Anne Stokes talking about how she had wanted to commit suicide once, and I was overjoyed to realize that someone as brilliant, accomplished and truly Sacred Heart as

Anne could suffer from my old disease (I went back and forth between mental breakdowns, physical destruction and self-destruction). The school seemed full of clear-eyed, bridge-playing girls who hung their lace slips up to dry every night, made hair appointments downtown, blocked their sweaters and kept on top of their lives in an ordered, anxiety-free way. I envied them their mental health more than anything else. They knew who they were.

It had never occurred to me to think about who I was. Despite a loneliness I never articulated, I had always been well defined by a series of concentric circles—family, friends, religion—which exerted an external pressure upon me and enabled me to stand in the center, suffering at times but within a context that made sense. One day that cosmos cracked.

Standing in the middle of the dormitory's center hallway, I watched students rush past on their way to class across the mall. I saw them in a new way—each girl operating from the middle of a circle, in a separate orbit, which only included me as a minor planet. I was a minor planet in everybody's universe. Positioned here on one circumference, there on another. Each girl rushing by snagged a part of me, like a piece of lint, and took me along out the door. I stood rooted to the floor, powerless to prevent my own diminution. Watching everybody push through the glass doors to walk across the campus, I was attacked with a new, virulent thought. I was not the center of the universe.

For the next four years, I tried to figure out what was at the center, and I lost all reference points, including myself, and became a person who simultaneously doubted the existence of God and prayed that I was not in a state of mortal sin. I came to hate confession, but I used to pace around the chapel door-way waiting for Father Ziccharelli to slip into the box. What if he were detained? Suppose my contrition was inadequate to my sins? Ahead and behind me were other girls, kneeling in monogrammed sweaters, regulars like myself, who viewed confession as a duty, like washing your hair, that made you feel better afterward. I was no different in that regard, although I would emerge from the confessional in a state of euphoria that did not match the caliber of my crimes. I did not feel better, I felt ecstatic, strong and full of bleached intentions. But by the end of the week, I would be circling the chapel hall again, as anxious as the week before, to unload my stones in the grill-obscured presence of a tall, thin priest who had lived through the bombing of Nagasaki and now, as a kind of perverse reward, had to endure the sins of college girls whose feelings were spliced fine by scrupulosity and too many stories of Saint Thérèse of Lisieux.

College was supposed to be the time of my life. "On one level," as my Aunt Dorothy was fond of saying about everything, it was. I was elected the class's first president, sat on development fund boards, ate pizza at The Cobblestone's Restaurant on Friday night, joined a singing group, went sledding on cafeteria trays, and spent every spare dollar I had buying cheap new clothes at Alexander's, a large emporium in nearby White Plains, where you could snatch something off the rack for practically nothing and wear it until it melted in the rain.

I had expected everything from college, and everything was what I got—including death—and I swayed like an unweighted metronome between the joy of contemplating an ice-coated tree in the moonlight and the terror of losing all psychic control and moving blindly toward the medicine chest where I would take a razor blade from the shelf and slash my own wrists.

Until college I had never thought about death except to assume that I would die young. The good always do, a private thought that was at variance with my own low opinion of myself. Death was something I mulled over in my preadolescence. Twelve-year-olds are strangely warmed by cold lips. But death, like sorrow, was an intuition that filled my binder full of bad poetry, which I wrote as if I were practicing to meet the real thing. When my heart first skipped a beat, I was not prepared.

I think if I had gone to Smith, I might have died. It was a more pragmatic, agnostic environment, and if Manhattanville served any prime purpose, it was to act as a womb which expelled me and took me back as many times as I needed to retreat. God knows I didn't have time to study with death so continually on my mind. No sooner had I focused upon death than I got my nose rubbed in it. There were two ways to react, and if I were to survive I had to laugh—which I did.

The first Yale-Harvard game in October of my freshman year, my cousin Tim, who was at Harvard, telephoned to say that he was coming down from Cambridge with a friend, and if I would find a date for him he would sign me up with his friend.

I immediately picked the most beautiful friend I had—a tall, blond cheerful girl from Erie, Pennsylvania, called Denise. Having secured Tim's date, we then had to find a place to stay in or near New Haven, since it was a strict rule that Manhattanville girls could not stay at hotels paid for by their escorts, the theory being that boys got what they paid for, and the nuns didn't like to compromise their girls in advance.

Not being able to afford to pay for our own hotel rooms and with New Haven loaded to the gills with visiting dates on that weekend, I scoured the campus for someone who lived there and might let us stay with their parents for the weekend. It seemed hopeless. I could find nobody who had a place, but at the eleventh hour the night before Denise and I were supposed to leave, a sophomore overheard our predicament and said that her parents lived in Naugatuck, which wasn't too far from New Haven, and she was sure they would be happy to take us in for a few nights.

We accepted on the spot and then asked for directions. The

sophomore, a girl called Nina Patowska, drew us a map and then, almost as an afterthought, said, "You can't miss the house. It has an awning."

What kind of a house has an awning? I wondered. "It's a funeral home," she explained. "O'Donnell's Funeral Home— you'll see it printed on the outside part of the awning."

It was too late to back down. I looked at Denise, who tucked her lips together and looked away, and then said, "Oh, I get it. Uh, sure."

It was too late to renege.

Both Denise and I were mortified (all weekend long, words like "mortified" sprang like toads from our lips) to have to tell our dates that we were staying above stiffs, and I needed a funeral home like a heart attack, but Denise was an outwardly steady girl and as we drove up toward New Haven, I counted on borrowing her vibes. We found our way to Naugatuck and the awning, parked our car and walked to the front door.

Denise rang the bell. The first stanza of "Rock of Ages" sounded from inside. Above the bell there was a small printed sign, "Ring Bell for Emergency Service." I wondered what constituted an emergency. Finding one's grandmother dead in her room, two weeks after everyone had thought she had gone to Philadelphia? But wasn't that a problem for the Health Department?

The door opened, and Mr. and Mrs. Patowska (I don't know why it was called O'Donnell's Funeral Home—I was too nervous to ask irrelevant questions) welcomed us inside. Clutching our bags, we filed past Parlors A, B and C—empty, I assumed, although empty could be full in a funeral home— and mounted the stairs.

The walls leading up to the living quarters (see what I mean?) were hung with dozens of photographs of Nina, their only child. Nina in tap shoes, Nina in a tutu, Nina in a majorette's uniform. They were sharp, hectic little snapshots which, given the fact that they hung in a funeral home, seemed to confirm life in an overactive way, although the fact that they were tinted seemed appropriate.

We settled down at the kitchen table, and Mrs. Patowska brought out some chocolate éclairs on a white plate. My cousin and his friend wouldn't be arriving for some time, and to make conversation I hesitantly asked the Patowskas "what was involved" in running a funeral parlor.

"Oh, it's more than a parlor," said Mrs. Patowska, a short, competent woman with gray hair and flesh-colored (sorry) glasses. "My husband and I are both licensed embalmers and morticians."

"You mean you fix up the bodies too?" I asked, taking a new look at her hands and trying to remember how they had felt when she shook ours at the door.

"That's right. We have certain responsibilities, just like doctors. Why, when Connecticut was hit by that big flood several years back, we were required by state law to stay until the all clear."

"That was some storm," reminisced Mr. Patowska, a pale man with a brilliant scalp. "We lost an awful lot of valuable equipment."

". . . and several remains," reminded his wife.

Denise rolled her eyes and fell to examining the contents of her purse.

"Tell me," I asked, feeling a heart attack pushing against the shafts of my Merry Widow, "do you ever have to, uh, prepare someone who has been a good friend?" The thought of Mrs. Patowska draining an old bridge partner was ghastly.

Mrs. Patowska smiled. "Of course, that sometimes happens, but frankly—here, don't be shy"—she pushed the plate of éclairs toward us and took one for herself—"we've been in this business for so long now that it's just like opening up a can of beans and throwing out the contents." She bit down into her éclair with a quick chomp, and a jet of yellow custard oozed suddenly from the far end.

That night I slept in fits. I don't remember the Yale-Harvard game the next afternoon at all, and my date, a young intern who couldn't quite believe the "Rock of Ages" doorbell, was drunk for most of the weekend, which was one way to deal with the situation. I never remember weather from one day to the next, but I know it rained for the football game. Mr. Patowska insisted that all four of us take raincoats—gray pallbearer coats that he had plenty of, so not to worry.

The Patowskas were generous, even to the point of giving us a tour. We inspected the casket room, the vestment room, and passed by the embalming room which Mrs. Patowska thought "might be a little shocking," which was right. Through the open door I saw a white porcelain table, slightly tilted, with a hook and bucket attached at the lower end. My imagination ran wild at the ramifications, and by the time we got to the garage to inspect the hearse, I was almost ready to lie down in the back and get it over with. Mr. Patowska pushed a button, and both Denise and I shrieked at the same time. It wasn't the hearse that frightened us but the roar of the electric garage door that went flying over our heads. We might have shrieked at less, but by that time we were so fine-tuned that we were fainting at dog whistles, or at least I was.

All the same, it was such an awful experience that I found a certain artistic merit in it. I called home to tell my parents what had happened.

"Well," said my father, who had been too far away to do me any good, "you must have saved the boys a bundle on flowers."

Every so often I took the train to New York. I learned to be afraid of these trips, although never so afraid that I didn't go again. New York intoxicated me. The thought of standing under the clock at the Plaza Hotel, the drama of the streets, the sharpness of the skyscrapers, the one time I met a real nephew of Adlai Stevenson in the middle of a snowstorm outside of Schrafft's. Mine was a deep and empty cup.

I could not get enough of New York as I ran down the sidewalks with Gershwin on my mind. One time I actually walked past an empty ballroom in the Waldorf-Astoria Hotel and looked through the door to find a man in a tuxedo behind a grand piano playing "Manhattan Towers" to an empty room full of gold chairs. New York wasn't possible, except in my imagination, yet I did not make up the man in a tuxedo. He existed. The problem with New York was that I always feared that I would die, just on the edge of life.

Standing on the corner of Forty-second and Park, I would begin to feel dizzy with insignificance. I feared that I might die unconfessed on a sidewalk, stared at by strangers who would have to rifle through my purse to find out who I had been. Waves of anticipation broke against waves of fear. I wished I were Clare Boothe Luce, who always had Fulton Sheen, the ultimate confessor, behind her in tow.

I never went anywhere that I didn't have in my pocket the name and address of someone who was supposed to be waiting for me behind a door, with a lamp lit and magazines on a coffee table. It was usually enough to have the name and address. I would push the elevator button, ride to the apartment of the person whose name was in my pocket and stand —cheerfulness incarnate—waiting for the door to be opened.

Only I knew that I was incapable of being alone, that inside I was empty of all solidity. To tell anyone of my fears would only exacerbate them, give them a flesh they didn't have. I operated on the belief that what I did not say did not exist. To tell anyone that I was afraid of nervous breakdowns, suicide or heart attacks was to guarantee that one or more of them might happen. People would be on the lookout for symptoms. I pushed against my own fears and told very few people that I had anything more important than cheerleading on my mind. During this time, I combed my hair all the time. Whenever I felt panic coming over me, I would reach for a comb and dig it into my head, try to comb my nerves into a straight line. Nobody but I knew that was what I was trying to do, but as I gazed out the train window at Spanish Harlem, I would comb and recomb my hair until the dirt and the poverty were past.

I couldn't integrate Spanish Harlem with my life. The poverty and misery were too large to fix. Worse, I wanted to get away from them, a feeling that flew in the face of myself the heroine, who only needed a leper in order to prove her love of mankind. Full of conflict, I would hyperventilate. Spanish Harlem was a sweat-stained paradox that burdened my straight-line, catechetical mind.

Back at Manhattanville—with the nuns, the lawn, the 5:30 Benediction, the peace—I relaxed somewhat. Within the walls I recuperated, hyperventilated less and filled up the bathtub with lavender salts, which made clouds of steam on the bathroom ceiling. I would stare at the clouds overhead and try to see the face in my future. I wasn't wise, but I was marriageable. All of us were, although I felt more marriageable in my freshman year and not at all marriageable by graduation. There was one dining-room ritual which confirmed my feeling that college was the last dash before all things were resolved, nuptially speaking, for better or worse.

Every so often after supper, one of the class presidents would rise from her seat, stand on her chair, and the entire room would fill with excitement. Another girl had been chosen for the altar.

"The Class of 195–," she would begin, "takes great pride and pleasure in announcing the engagement of Mr. John Michael Moriarity to . . . Miss Sylvia Anne Keller."

The class of 195– would rise like a rush of doves from a

piazza to where Sylvia Anne Keller sat, the engagement ring she had been hiding under her napkin now out and flashing on the dining-room table for everyone to see.

It was a wonderful, moving ritual. One couldn't help but hope that it would happen to you before graduation day.

My notions of the man I would marry were vague but stubborn. He would be Catholic. He would, if possible, have gone to Harvard. He would, in small, Protestant ways, be extraordinarily attractive in an aquiline, tortoise-shell-glasses way. I had, in my mind, an archetype that other girls had already gotten themselves engaged to—a Moriarity with fine feelings, a fine family and a sacred sense of theater that would inspire him to slip an engagement ring over my finger at the communion rail at Christmas Eve Mass, as Mary Helen Cronin's fiancé had done. Mary Helen Cronin, in many ways, was my ideal of the perfect Catholic woman—girlish, sincere, beautiful in a pug-nosed, wide-eyed way, fun loving, devout, slender and self-sacrificing.

There were other girls at Manhattanville I admired who didn't fit the stereotype I most emulated from afar. Savvy, busty girls who had heavy relationships with Yale boys who drove Aston-Martins. They were out of my league. My idea of a large weekend was to kiss two different boys on two different evenings and wonder how I could justify both, given the fact that I didn't like either of them.

Other girls, who seemed born to the telephone, were effortlessly popular, as befitted their blond pageboys, leggy figures and wide, aquamarine eyes. They were clean-cut, conversational, feminine girls who snared clean-cut, conversational, masculine boys.

I fell, for want of a real category, into a third class, attracting quiet boys who spent all day in library carrels digging up Perelman jokes for my amusement, shy boys who were too frightened to ask out girls that smoldered, boys who had their own death wishes. There were very few boys encountered during my four years at college I could imagine marrying, although I pushed at the limits of my imagination with each one of them and prayed that I would fall in love with Toby Shanley, who weighed 115 pounds and only had one thing to recommend him—an uncle who used to compose songs for Walt Disney productions.

I was neither popular nor unpopular. It was my impression that the boys from Princeton, Yale and other Ivy League schools tended to omit Manhattanville from their calculations, unless they were Catholic and had a specifically Catholic girl on their minds. But there were weekends that fit the description rendered in *Mademoiselle* magazine, invitations to New Haven and Princeton Junction that I always anticipated as being wicked and wound up being quite the reverse, which I chalk up to several factors: I didn't want to be wicked, I wasn't sure how one would be wicked anyway, and I got very little instruction in the fine art of having an immoral good time. Then, too, I was nearsighted, and while I had a prurient interest in watching other people misbehave on a grand scale, I didn't know what I was looking at most of the time. Dark rooms hid shapes that I could not decipher. I was on the lookout for copulation, but I couldn't see it even when it was happening right in front of me.

Weekends at Yale were distinguished by a great deal of Frisbee throwing and riding sidesaddle on the back of bicycles to hockey matches. One of my roommates, an entirely artless girl called Anne McGrail, was semiengaged to a law student. I regularly traveled north to New Haven in a Volkswagen loaded with Anne's roommates, who were parceled out to Joe's roommates at Corby Court. We lurched around through the swill of their untidy rooms, ate hamburgers, went to movies and—with the exception of Anne and Joe, who loved each other with the passion of puppies who hardly knew where one left off and the other began—no romantic fires were kindled.

The several times I went to Princeton, I was accompanied by high-minded boys who trembled on the front steps when they said goodnight, and while Princeton was an uncorked whiskey bottle from Friday night to Sunday afternoon, I didn't drink and would find myself in conversations that only I took seriously, although at the time I thought that they were two-way exchanges.

Scotty Stuart, a compact, blond superachiever whom I had known from California, slammed his hand against the wall of the Charter House, took a swig from his highball glass and said, "What is all this crap about papal infallibility, anyway?"

Pinned against the wall, I began to marshal my arguments. "Oh well, it just means that in matters of faith and morals . . ."

But he didn't seem interested in pursuing the question beyond itself. I was left with my arguments and my gin-clear head while Scotty released his hand from its suction position on the wall and wandered off.

I was a theologian without an audience, a member of the Church Militant who could never find the battlefield I assumed existed in everybody's life. The nuns had prepared me for atheists but not agnostics, and when I ran up against the deadweight of a world which didn't care one way or the other whether God existed, it shook my faith in God Himself. I was an expensive, well-honed jackknife, full of cutting gadgets to use on cause and effect, substance and accident, the Five Proofs for the Existence of God, and a full explanation of the pivotal nature of the Resurrection as proof of Christ's divinity. It came over me gradually that a lot of people, perhaps most people, didn't care whether they were in a state of grace or not.

My heart pounded with irregularity, matching my inability to find a sustaining rhythm in my life. On the one hand, I knew everything. On the other hand, I had not experienced anything at all. I had yet to know what I knew in the deep, time-tested way that comes after being forced to relinquish everything and wait in the dark. The strain of trying to hold on to everything took its toll, and I was saved from spiraling completely to the bottom by a chance remark by my theology teacher, a clever although orthodox nun called Mother Hargrove, who was probably to the right of Fulton Sheen but had the capacity to sound avant garde and in this instance she saved my mind.

"It is my conviction," she said in class one morning, "that every human being is certifiably crazy for twenty minutes every day of their lives."

Having said this, she popped her blue eyes open, shut them again and moved on to something else. But I pounced upon her conviction like a life raft. I began to allow myself twenty minutes every day to be insane. Some days I didn't use them. That gave me forty minutes for tomorrow. I began to think that I might be at least half as normal as Mother Hargrove, who floated like an astute angel into class every morning. It was Mother Hargrove who equated despair with having to make one's bed every day. "The futility of it," she moaned. "The absolute knowledge that it will have to be done again! It is difficult to live without the Sacraments and knowledge of an afterlife, is it not?"

The Sacred Heart nuns varied from one to the other, despite the fact that they all wore black habits and had little cupcake-pleated wimples that framed their faces like pale almond slivers between the pleats. It was an old French order. The customs of the ancien régime still applied—the Child of Mary society, the white-handkerchief-waving ceremonies as the Reverend Mother took off for other parts of the vicariate for visits. But they were a strong-minded group of women, and while I was a very poor student, due to my fear of dying in between classes, I observed their eccentricities and appreciated them. Classes were intellectually demanding. Entertainment from the front of the room was not rare.

"Which of us," moaned Mother O'Gorman dramatically, "has the courage, when the end comes, to keep from clawing the bedsheet in abject terror over the arrival of death!" She gazed out of the window, *The Death of Ivan Ilyich* held in one hand. It was some time before I realized that Mother O'Gorman got most of her best jokes out of the *New Yorker* magazine.

"The question is," said Mother Dowd, the head of the philosophy department, in which I was the least-stellar pupil, "was Augustine a saint or a psycho?" She would then proceed to read a paper, written by an extraordinarily brilliant girl from St. Louis, who wrote all her papers in one sitting in the typing room, her hands folded quietly between thoughts. My question was, who was smart enough even to formulate the question? Mother Dowd was a small, sharp-eyed woman who had no use for second-class minds. My own mind was third-class and unstable. I staggered through philosophy, impaled on insights I was not large enough to incorporate, and it was only when I was in the presence of some of the friendlier thinkers, like William James or Pascal, that I could relax my muscles enough to absorb the printed page.

I had entered Manhattanville with English literature as the field I wanted to specialize in—for no particular reason. I certainly didn't have any career ideas, and it never occurred to me that I would ever be a writer in a professional sense. But I had won the English prize in high school. I loved words. The other branches of knowledge seemed sterile in comparison with the poetry of literature, where one didn't have to spend frustrating hours achieving perfect titrations between acids and bases. But I ran up against a brick wall after several months of that major at college. The head of the department was an ancient, white-haired woman, who rarely deviated from lecture notes which had been written twenty-five years before. Miss Cave was a reputedly brilliant perfectionist of a scholar, who happened to believe that the written word after Juliana of Norwich's contribution suffered with each passing year.

There was no room for creativity or interesting sentence structures. My papers were routinely returned with the same comments and grades, alluding to my incapacity to incorporate Miss Cave's most important insights. Miss Cave made me angry. She was fiddling with the one talent I had. I was not a serious enough student to challenge her directly, but at the end of my freshman year, Juliana of Norwich had exhausted me. If it hadn't been for Mother Dunn, a small, soft, apple dumpling of a nun, who involuntarily swayed when she read Gerard Manley Hopkins and thought that it was wonderful if someone wrote a poem about beaches and glued sand onto the cover sheet, I would have suffocated entirely. But by the end of my freshman year, my father's financial situation had taken a bad turn, and it looked as if I wouldn't even have a choice to suffer under Miss Cave at all.

A telephone call from California several weeks before summer break signaled the end of my education.

"I hate to tell you this," said my father, "but I am not going to be able to afford to make up the difference between your scholarship and what it takes to keep you at Manhattanville. Business has been very bad this year—the recession—bills. And if I have to make a choice, and I do," he added, "it's got to be to keep your brother at Saint George's until he graduates."

I saw no flaw in this. My brother would have to support a family some day. Boys came first. I put down the phone, revised my life plan and decided that if I couldn't continue at Manhattanville I would be a ski bum at Aspen. Such witlessness staggers me today, but fortunately I did not have to follow that plan.

I announced the bad news to my closest friends. They reacted with support, tears and last-minute novenas in the hope that something might turn up at the last minute. But nothing did. Manhattanville could not increase my scholarship to full tuition. I did not qualify for that honor, given my academic performance which was dismal that year, and barely qualified me to continue as a sophomore, although a C average technically allowed me to stay on. There were farewell parties and addresses exchanged. Oddly, I did not feel as sad as anyone else. Sketched out in my imagination was a tan, increasingly expert skier who waited on tables, read books between lessons paid for by waitressing, and was destined to have a perpetual holiday for the upcoming year. The last night before I was due to fly home to California, there was a knock on my door after lights out.

I opened the door and found Mother Cavanagh, the college vice-president, on the other side. She has come to say goodbye, I thought, which pleased me. Mother Cavanagh had been my mental lifeline through the entire heart-thumping year, and I loved her best of all the nuns at Manhattanville.

"Dear," she said, "I have something to tell you." She took my hand and led me to a small parlor room at the end of the hall.

Settling herself into one of the chairs, she leaned forward and asked, "Tell me, how much money do you think you need in order to finish up the next three years here?"

The question took me by surprise. I did a rough calculation in my head.

"For the next three years?" I asked.

Mother Cavanagh nodded somewhat inscrutably.

"Uh, I think three thousand dollars."

There was a silence, and then she said, "I have a check in that exact amount made out to you in my pocket right now."

I stared at her. "To me?" I asked, unsure of what she had just said.

"That's right," she smiled, "a last-minute donation to a good cause. But I have been sworn to secrecy. I am not allowed to reveal the source."

I immediately began to grill her anyway. Was it from the college? No. From one of my friend's fathers? No. It couldn't be an Eastern relative of mine? No, it wasn't from a relative. I had run out of possibilities, unless . . .

"It wasn't from one of the girls at Manhattanville, was it?" Mother Cavanagh nodded. "It is," she confirmed.

Gradually, I elicited the name of the girl—an outgoing senior who had been head of student government, in which I was a freshman representative. "It was Claire?" I asked.

"If she finds out that you know," warned Mother Cavanagh, "she will be furious at me, but yes, it was Claire. This afternoon she came into my office, looking very embarrassed, and said, 'Mother, I want to set up a scholarship.' I said, 'Fine, Claire,' and she said, 'Well, but I want it to be a scholarship for a particular person.' I asked who. She said it was for you, that her uncle had given her a graduation present of a lot of money, that she didn't need it, and she wanted to give it anonymously—she stressed that it must be anonymous—to you. Claire is a very wealthy girl, and I've always thought that it burdened her a bit. But I looked straight at her and told her that she was doing an incredibly generous thing that she could be proud of. She could hardly wait to get out of the office. Her face was red as a beet."

Mother Cavanagh patted her black serge skirt, with the invisible check secreted beneath, and smiled. I was stunned, grateful and ashamed. I did not deserve that kind of generosity. I had barely paid attention in class all year. But someone believed I was worth the investment. All thoughts of being an Aspen ski bum evaporated with the speed they deserved, and I stood up and hugged Mother Cavanagh. She said, "I give you permission to go to the senior dorm to thank Claire, but you mustn't stay beyond eleven o'clock. And remember," said Mother Cavanagh, who was fully prepared to take the heat of her own indiscretion, "she will be mortified when you walk into her room."

She was.

The unexpected, outrageously generous gift from Claire was a sign to me that I must think far more seriously about what I did with my life than I had before. Added to the other scholarships that had already come my way, this last one was a kind of proof that I must be slated to repay the gifts in a way I could not at that point particularize. Later on, near the end of my college career, I was clear on how I would justify the investment and redress the balance that weighed so heavily in my favor. But that is another story, one which came after I had graduated from Manhattanville. Prior to that I was far too preoccupied with getting my bearings at college itself. I was very aware, as I walked around the small, lavishly laid-out campus, that I was at the receiving end of the pipe. Every book, lecture and professor was there to develop me. We were, all of us, beneficiaries of an environment which encircled us in a protective horseshoe of academic buildings, dormitories and playing fields. I was not at all impatient to reverse those circumstances.

Chapter
XI

Every spring, brilliantly timed to coincide with the rising anxieties of those seniors whose futures were unclear, Father John Sullivan from Oklahoma descended upon the Manhattanville campus to make his annual pitch on becoming an "Extension Volunteer."

Extension Volunteers took its name and funding from a popular Catholic magazine of that time, which was full of stories about miraculous medals, sudden saves through prayer, and women kneeling in shafts of light coming through chapel windows. *Extension Magazine* financed Extension Volunteers, providing transportation and stipends for young college-graduate women, who would donate a year out of their lives to the Church in Oklahoma, teaching, doing office work and helping the overworked priests in their parishes.

A tall, big-boned man with red hair, blue eyes and a square jaw, Father Sullivan would burst like a prairie wind through the dining-room door, stride toward the microphone, slouch against the wall and start rolling out anecdotes, one after the other, like cigarettes. He was smart with a drawl, the kind of priest who throws a wide but effective lasso.

Oklahoma was the boondocks of the Mystical Body. Father Sullivan always capitalized on this fact. He painted a picture of bookless catechism classes, leaking church roofs, over-worked priests and Catholics scattered like wood quail all over the state. Oklahoma was not exactly hostile to the Church, but it wasn't Massachusetts either. With Manhattan twinkling like a Gershwin theme through the plate-glass win-dows, it was difficult to imagine Oklahoma, but Father Sul-livan tried to fill in the chinks in our imagination. Sometimes he brought along a real Volunteer to give a small talk about what she was doing. She was always bright and attractive, certainly not a wallflower or averse to marriage at a later date. But it was Father Sullivan's show, and he rarely left Manhattanville without lopping off a few vulnerable heads, usually girls who were toying with the idea of being a nun but couldn't decide.

I never had the least desire to be a nun, although it was impossible to be a Catholic girl without contemplating the possibility—awful though it always seemed to me. Sister Dolores had once gazed significantly in my direction during high school and said, "There are some girls in this room who definitely have a vocation." But I always discounted every-thing that Sister Dolores said, and whenever I thought about having a vocation, it was mainly to worry that it might mate-rialize, like a weed I wouldn't be strong enough to yank out once it took hold. The point was to patrol the soil of my de-sires very carefully to make sure this didn't happen, although there was one segment of time when I seriously wondered whether I could keep the nunnery at bay.

Christmas vacation of our junior year at college, I flew with my closest friend to New Orleans to spend the holidays. My friend was part of the old New Orleans social stratum. We were plunged into a round of parties which began at breakfast and ended the following morning. New Orleans, when you're nineteen and love to dance, commands you to fall in love. I did, with a tall, coltish-looking boy whom I rarely saw out of a tuxedo, who treated me like a magnolia and pleaded with me to come back (at my own expense) to visit the following spring. I flew back to college with nothing but love on my mind.

Finances were a problem. I barely eked out an existence on a small stipend each month. I washed sweaters for the next three months, at forty cents a sweater, to pay for the return trip. But Christmas and Easter did not match up. In the interim the boy in the tuxedo had been having severe second thoughts.

"Ah just can't see not eatin' bacon on Fridays," he confessed, as we sprawled by each other's side on a segregated beach in Pass Christian.

"Ah mean," he said haltingly, "Ah just can't imagine mah whole life being married to a *Roman* Catholic."

I thought of all those sweaters. My hands had looked like lobster claws all winter. It occurred to me, as I silently sifted sand through my fingers, that he had never introduced me to his parents. I was being discriminated against by an Episcopalian! I looked over at his face. He seemed to be genuinely suffering. I tried to adjust my own face to look as if I were suffering too! But I must not have been that much in love. Once the bacon issue was raised, the romance short-circuited in my mind.

Shortly afterward back on campus, I met another southern boy who, for reasons best known to him (he was a Methodist divinity student at Yale), asked me out. We went to a local "trattoria," danced under a trellis of plastic grapes and fell under the sway of each other's insights and footwork. At the end of the evening, as we walked back toward his car, I felt centrifugally pulled toward everything about him—his eyes, his voice, his grave southern shyness. Also, he had a lovely name, Lawrence McCullough, a name one could live with.

As we stood rather self-consciously by his car, the moonlight full and promising, he cleared his throat and said, "Uh, is it awl-right if I kiss you?"

It was such a courtly thing to ask. Kissing in those days was still a relatively new art form for me. But suddenly an unbidden series of images passed before my eyes. I saw myself pouring tea in an Atlanta rectory, the wife of a Methodist minister, having renounced Catholicism for a mere southern sect. I shook my head and felt a pain in my chest. I had not counted upon being Catholic being so hard.

Back at college at the end of the evening, I leaned against the bureau and stared into the mirror. Why was God only sending me Protestants to love? Perhaps I was being told that I was supposed to be a nun. Why else would God only offer up Methodists and Episcopalians?

Taking my hands, I placed one on each side of my face to see what a wimple would look like. It would kill me to think that Sister Dolores was right. For the next few weeks I avoided all "occasions of grace," the small, sacramental gestures of faith, holy water, chapel visits, signs of the cross. My fear was that if I let down my guard for a moment that I would be involuntarily suffused with desire—like Saint Theresa of Ávila, who had been dragged kicking and screaming against her own humanity to become a Bride of Christ. I did not want to be Saint Theresa of Ávila unless I could marry Saint John of the Cross.

For several weeks I dragged my "vocation" behind me, a shadow that wouldn't detach itself even though I confided my fear to no one, on the theory that the best way to convert a fear into reality is to discuss it. But I sank into an irritable, absentminded state, cut classes, skipped meals, slept. Finally Mother Cavanagh, the vice-president of the college, called me into her office.

There were many nuns at Manhattanville, nuns I admired

and could have chosen as my spiritual confidantes. But Mother Cavanagh shone like a warm, translucent bar of sunlight. A tiny woman with pale-blue eyes, a droll wit and an instinct for holding your hand which she patted as if patting wisdom into your possession, Mother Cavanagh was not easily shocked. There was no judgment in her soul. Over the years we had become close, although it was an entirely one-sided relationship; I handed her straw, she returned gold. She rarely talked about herself, as if she were reluctant to waste time on that subject. She did not seem to find herself very interesting. Her concerns transcended herself.

During the time in college when I was plagued with thoughts of suicide, she had found a psychiatrist. He was an off-campus flop, who did nothing but talk about how expensive he was, and were my parents prepared to pay his fees?

My parents had no idea that I was anything but sublimely happy all the time. I never wrote letters home unless I could prove this fact, both to myself and to them. But while I returned from the psychiatrist entirely unhealed, I awoke several weeks later to realize that, miraculously, I had not even thought about suicide for at least a week. That burden had been inexplicably lifted. I didn't know why, but I knew I wasn't responsible.

Intercepting Mother Cavanagh in the hallway one afternoon, I told her about this sudden lifting of fear. "Did you do something?" I asked. "Something I don't know about?"

Mother Cavanagh nodded. "It seemed to me that this was a rather desperate situation."

"What did you do?" I asked.

"I had Father say a special Mass for your intentions."

"When?" I asked.

"Last week," she replied.

I had many reasons to trust Mother Cavanagh, but I had not been able to bring myself to tell her about my "vocation," since, as a nun, she would naturally be compelled to rejoice.

"Sit down," she instructed, looking slightly cross. "I haven't liked what I've observed in you lately. You're not yourself. If there is a reason, tell me. If not, you must stop."

The tears began to slide down my face. "There is a reason," I admitted, "but I just don't know if I can tell you."

"Try," she said.

I recounted the saga of the Protestant romances, how in one instance I had been rejected, in the other I had felt forced to cut off a possibility. "And so," I said, barely able to squeeze the rest of the sentence out of the tube, "I think . . . that perhaps . . . I am meant . . . to be a nun." I stopped, stared at my lap and waited for Mother Cavanagh to chop off the rest of my life.

She was silent. I raised my head to look at her. Picking up a small wooden carving of the Virgin Mary that always sat on the edge of her desk, she began to turn it slowly around in her fingers. Then, fixing her eyes at a point over my shoulder, she began to speak.

"There are some girls who are meant to be nuns. It is a very special vocation, but not for everyone. Carole O'Connor, for instance, would make a very good sister, but, in my opinion, a terrible wife. Don't quote me," she added quickly. "Carole is dying to get married, but I don't see it in her future."

She replaced the Virgin Mary back on the desk, carefully aligning her wooden feet along the edge while she lined up her next thought. Then, raising one arm above her head, she pressed her eyes shut and continued.

"I don't usually do this," she said, "but I think I can truly speak for God on His behalf when I say"—she pointed toward the ceiling—"that as far as you're concerned, you are not one of those girls."

I felt enormous relief. I was off the hook, back in the running, free, detached from the shadow that was trying to crawl up my back.

"Are you saying," I said, "that you don't think I am meant to be a nun?"

Mother Cavanagh brought her hands together on her lap, laced her fingers together and allowed a small smile to creep across her face.

"That's just what I'm saying," she answered. "We don't want you."

For these and other favors, my daughter bears her name.

There was marriage, of course, but as college drew to a close, I felt less and less marriageable. I had no fantasies about flying free on the sidewalks of New York, and the word "career" had never seriously entered my mind, but I did want to do something serious. When Father Sullivan swept onto the campus in the spring of 1961, I was ready for him. My entire life had been subsidized by the Catholic Church. It was time, I thought, adding up the convent and college scholarships, free music lessons, and particularly Claire's graduation gift, to pay the Church back.

"Naow," began Father Sullivan, cradling the mike in one large, freckled hand, "Ah want you to know that down in Oklahoma we don't have Catholic schools like Manhattan-ville. We just have Catholics, mostly poor, without any chance to get a decent Catholic education. But you girls," he said, looking out over a sea of Peck and Peck blouses, "you girls have been blessed with the best Catholic education in the country. All right," he continued, "I'm going to come right out and tell you what I want. I want you to give it back."

Having sent his scythe in one direction, Father Sullivan paused.

"Okay," he started in again, "what is an Extension Volun-teer besides tired a lot of the time? That's right, you're going to be tired and frustrated a lot of the time, also out of money. You'd only get fifty dollars a month. Also—I wouldn't want to lie to you—there isn't a great deal of night life in Oklahoma. Oklahoma doesn't feature night life, to be perfectly truthful. But that's just on the negative side."

"On the positive side," he said, sending the scythe in the other direction, "you'll never regret the year you give. You'll learn things and meet people who will stay with you for the rest of your life. You'll have a chance to use everything you've been given and receive a great deal in return. The Church in Oklahoma is very alive, and I don't know one Extension Volunteer who wasn't glad she signed up, or one priest who wasn't glad that she came."

I signed up. My friend Barbara Higgins signed up. After a summer of fending off raised eyebrows in California, I flew to Oklahoma City to meet up with Barbara and the priest to whom we were assigned. If I had had the plane fare, I think I would have flown right home again.

Oklahoma was the driest, flattest, most burned-out-looking state I had ever seen. Gas stations, rusty cars, small, ugly houses with pink plastic flamingoes on brown lawns. And Oklahoma City was the capital. It could only get worse.

Our destination was Norman. It had been decided over the summer that Barbara and I would plow new territory. Up until that time, all Extension Volunteers had been attached to regular parishes in cities or towns. But this year the Church was going to expand its influence on the campus of the University of Oklahoma. We would be attached to the Newman Club on campus. Our territory would be the whole university. I rather liked the idea.

"Most Catholic students on campus," said Father Swett, the priest who picked us up at the airport, "won't touch the Newman Club with a ten-foot pole." I concluded that we were supposed to go out from the Newman Club with ten-foot poles of our own and drag them in. It was all rather vague, but as I leaned forward in the car and looked out the window, I wondered why anybody—Catholic, Protestant or Jew—lived in Oklahoma at all.

Don't these people read *Time* magazine? Haven't they ever seen a picture in *National Geographic* of Switzerland, Yosemite or Cape Cod? All the blue, green, soil-soft alternatives to the wasteland we were driving through passed by my eyes. If this were Russia, I could understand why people didn't leave. But it wasn't. For some reason Oklahoma attracted people. Or was it lack of funds to get out? That was a possibility, but I would hitchhike if I had to.

Then I looked at Father Swett. He lives here. I had instantly liked him the moment I was introduced. I held my inexperienced judgment about Oklahoma in reserve and decided to depend upon his. I had never met a priest like Father Swett before. Like Oklahoma, he was out of my experiential realm.

He was very young. About thirty. I don't know what I noticed about him first—his age, his face, his clothes, probably his eyes. But the impact of all of these things combined was confusing and pleasant. He was waiting for us at the airport, dressed in a pair of bleached chinos, a Madras shirt, and loafers. I had never seen a priest in a Madras shirt before. He had short dark hair, a chiseled face, and his eyes were dark brown, almost black. They were very changeable. In a receptive mood they liquified, as did his voice. In a rage they turned hard as granite. Then he would speak in a clipped, sarcastic way.

He looked us both over skeptically, trying to figure out what he had let himself in for. As we walked toward the car, he made small jokes, about being a "missionary," about Oklahoma, about the other priest on campus, Father Flusche. "Don't forget to pronounce the 'e'," he said. I got the impression he did not like the other half of his team.

Father Swett was a natural, sometimes cruel mimic, and he used to imitate the cardinals and archbishops in a way that fractured me. "Oh, I can just see what's going on in Pope John's mind every time he decides to have a Vatican Council.

Why, just calling in those cardinals is enough to kill off at least three or four making the plane ride over to Rome. Good way to get fresh blood into the Church." He would then limp arthritically across the floor, pretend he was overloaded with rings and vestments and change his face into that of an eighty-year-old cardinal, heavy-lidded and encrusted with his own seniority.

The college students thought he was wonderful. Football players, grinds—all of the fraternity and nonfraternity boys were attracted to his personality. He had no qualms about giving a sermon on masturbation. He once said that if the Church relaxed its ban on celibacy, he would be married tomorrow. He neither flirted with nor turned a blind eye on the pretty coeds who surrounded him. He walked a straight line, frugging one minute, performing the Mass with solemnity the next. I hadn't been in Norman for a week before I thought he was the most extraordinary priest I had ever met, although he carried a vial of anger within him that always made me keep a safe distance away. He had his circumference. It did not tolerate trespassers.

Father Swett was technically the number two priest. His superior was an older, portly priest, who had no particular interest in students, who never went to the local hangouts or had guitar and beer parties, as Father Swett did, and I don't ever remember any students soliciting his advice.

Father Flusche had no feelings for young people, and he seemed to like his air-conditioned office on the second floor of the Newman Club better than any other place on earth. He spoke with a strange, adenoidal accent, which was strange since he was born in Oklahoma. He was a heavy, comfort-loving man, who liked to summon Bertha, the black cook, up to his office for consultations on the menu. I would watch Bertha as she humored Father Flusche, giving him a sleepy look of indifference, one hand propping up her chin, as he went on about how to make a good cream sauce. Bertha was a terrible cook. She knew it. Father Flusche knew it. But she indulged him in his fantasies. At supper, she retaliated.

Barbara and I settled into a small upstairs apartment across the street from the Newman Club. It was furnished with two beds, a broken sofa and a chipped Formica table in the kitchen. We ran around gathering up driftwood for the walls, dried flowers for jam jars and a few second-hand appliances to turn the place into our home. We were rarely there, however, and Barbara and I sometimes didn't speak for days because she hated to be awakened in the morning. Every night she would ask me to make sure she got up. Every morning, until I learned to disregard this request, I would receive a punch, or an alarm clock in my eye. I would proceed to have bruised feelings for twenty-four hours. But Barbara, who was cheerful once breakfast was over, considered any semiconscious acts of aggression on her part not her fault.

For nine months we spent most of our waking moments in the Will Rogers cafeteria at the student union—drinking coffee and talking to anyone who came by—Pi Phis, Phi Gams, Tri Delts or unaffiliated students. You were either a Greek or a barbarian. The purpose of our presence was supposed to unfold as we got a feel for the campus. Father Swett urged us to be creative.

I wasn't sure what being creative ought to mean. We set up seminars at various sorority houses, choosing the improbable subject of Teilhard de Chardin's *The Phenomenon of Man* to study. But it was hard to get a quorum. Most of the girls who signed up came in late or not at all because they had been engaged in the sorority girl's highest moral obligation, which was to make sure that the house float was ready in time for Saturday's football game parade. It took time to stuff crepe paper into chicken-wire floats.

I found the sorority house system intriguing. The small rituals, the things the girls wore, the second floor of the Pi Phi house with its dozen pink hair dryers, which were always occupied, the sorority pins themselves, which were heavy with in-house significance.

The Tri Delts, for instance, wore a pin that was a jeweled trident plunging through a pearl-strewn crescent which seemed almost lethal. One false move and the pin could puncture a girl's heart no matter how many angora sweaters protected her. Yet the pin summed up all the Tri Delt values.

"Here comes Poseidon with his trident in his hand, to lead the sister Deltas to the Promised Land," went the Tri Delt song.

"It's a real-beautiful initiation ceremony," said one Tri Delt to me. "Of course, I'm sworn to secrecy about it, but it's very religious, and everything is tied into the pansy, the pine tree and the pearl—our sorority symbols."

"The pansy, the pine tree and the pearl?" I asked.

"Uh huh," she said. "I mean, there's a part in the ceremony when we talk about Christ bleeding on the cross, and his blood drips down upon the pansy, turning it purple in the middle. It's so beautiful. Just thinking about it makes me cry."

It was ludicrous to try to sell Teilhard de Chardin to a bunch of sorority girls who, at that time in their lives, were making connections between pansies, pine trees and pearls. I hardly knew what Teilhard was talking about myself, and a French Jesuit mystic was as alien to a Tri Delt as France, the Jesuits and mysticism itself. But we slogged on together, the sorority girls and I, out of politeness from their end and lack of alternatives from mine.

There were other people in the loosely defined "parish" surrounding the Newman Club—professors and their wives, grad students, mostly married, and their wives. But it didn't occur to me to form a bond. I viewed them as living in a separate world, coming to church with their children nibbling zwieback in strollers. I fell between the cracks of two social orders.

The Newman Club, like all campus ministries, existed on

the fringes of the university, competing for the loyalties of students whose allegiance to the campus occupied the center of their lives. Barbara and I had a rather impossible task of trying to reverse these loyalties, or at least mesh the two. But it was a doomed mission, perhaps because neither of us were zealots, and both of us sat back and watched the campus population roll by us in waves of "hully-gullying," float-stuffing students, sometimes poking each other in the ribs to prove that we were in Oklahoma at all.

I shouldn't speak for Barbara. She has her own memories, which may be very different from my own. But I remember her as an ally, a comrade, the other person carrying the other tray in the Will Rogers cafeteria on our daily forays to the student union, where we used to sit around doing very little, drinking coffee and waiting for anybody to show up. But even though I rather liked the pointless "kaffee klatches" where students who knew us from the Newman Club would slide in beside us and ask how Father Swett was, I grew awfully tired of them and my own incapacity to think what else I could do with the day. I did not attend classes and had no desire to sit around an empty Newman Club, typing up census cards on students who would be graduating that year anyway.

We just talked, for nine months, to business majors who wanted to make it big in Muskogee, to engineering majors who wanted to go into "solid-waste disposal" in Tulsa, to art majors who dreamed against the odds of getting a job working for Hallmark Greeting Cards in Kansas City. I neither liked nor disliked the students I met, but our frames of reference were radically different, and Teilhard de Chardin was not exactly a bridge.

Being from out of state, not students, and "missionaries" who didn't act like missionaries set Barbara and me apart, made us curiosities that were neither accepted nor rejected. The boys who clustered around Father Swett accepted us. Barbara began to date a political-science grad student. I took up with a law student who came from Chicago, which at least gave us an appreciation of big cities in common. But looking back on that year, I wasn't a missionary at all. I spent an inordinate amount of time loafing around the Sigma Chi house listening to Johnny Mathis records and drinking Coke.

Barbara was quickly slotted in Father Swett's mind as being the quicker, more organized member of the duo. She devised a method of conducting a census of Catholics on index cards. I slogged around getting the cards filled out, losing at least half of them between dorms. Barbara thought of the idea of holding seminars in the sorority houses. I used to show up at a sorority house prepared to wing it on back knowledge. But when a serious problem arose, Father Swett picked Barbara's mind first, mine second. Both of us were anxious to please him, but Barbara was, in my mind, on more equal terms with him.

I noticed, because I could not help but notice, that in my case the distance from Father Swett's side of our relationship was increasing. After a warm, accepting beginning, a valve in his mind had closed. One day we were friends; the next we were estranged. Each day, despite my attempts to warm him up again, the distance increased. He began to glare at me. I began to feel nervous whenever he walked past.

In an effort to make amends without knowing what the problem was, unless it was my entire personality, I tried to think of a way to readjust the scales. He was going away for a week. In the interim I decided to reorganize and paint the Newman Club library. It was football season. I had no volunteers to help.

Every night after supper I hauled books off shelves, dusted and painted. The day he arrived back I was just finishing up the last section of the room. He walked into the library, gazed up at me standing on a stepladder, brush in hand, and said, "What the hell are you doing up there?"

"What do you think I'm doing?" I hurled back, feeling defensive. "Painting your library. Do you like it?"

He didn't answer.

"Well," I persisted, "do you? I mean the colors?"

His face was tight with anger. "You're not supposed to be painting the library by yourself. Your job is supposed to involve the students in projects like this. The fact that you're doing it yourself means that you have failed!"

Suddenly, I was rigid with fury of my own. I threw the brush down and yelled, "If you weren't a priest, nobody would work for you, including me!"

"Oh, is that right?" he said between clenched teeth. "I happen to have a nine-thousand-dollar-a-year secretary who thinks working for me is the best job she's ever had."

Father Swett's secretary was a small, accurate woman who never opened her mouth.

"It's the only job she's ever had," I yelled. "How would she know?"

Father Swett glared at me, swiveled sharply on his heel and walked out. I stood on the stepladder shaking with rage and sorrow. I adored Father Swett. I had killed off my last chance to be a friend. In my most elastic fantasies, I had never imagined getting angry at a priest.

Before the year was out, I had alienated Father Flusche as well, although I fought with him on much sounder ground.

One afternoon, while I was working in the small office across the street from the Newman Club alongside an older nun who had been detailed to Father Flusche to help out with the census, the telephone rang. It was a young professor who had often come to Sunday Mass with his wife, who was pregnant or had been.

"I wonder," he said faintly, "if Father Flusche could say Mass for us. My wife went into labor early this morning, and our baby died at birth."

I took a sharp breath. "Oh, of course," I answered. "I'm so sorry. I'll tell Father Flusche right away and will call you back as soon as I know which Mass it will be."

He hung up, saying thank you.

Just then Father Flusche walked into the office. "Father," I said, "I just got a call from Mr. Pittston. They lost their baby this morning. He wanted to know if you could say a special Mass for the baby's intentions."

Father Flusche said, "Ummm . . . that's too bad. Did he make any mention of a Mass offering?"

"A what?" I said.

"A contribution," he repeated. "It's customary to do that when you ask for a special Mass."

"His baby just died," I said between clenched teeth. "I didn't even think about asking for money."

"Well," said Father Flusche, who began to look irritated, "I'm not about to get up at six in the morning to say an extra Mass without feeling that the family has contributed in some way."

I screamed at him so loudly that the elderly sister working with the index cards dropped her box. "How can you call yourself a priest? It's disgusting! You're disgusting. I will not call him up for money. I will call and tell him you're saying a Mass for their baby tomorrow."

Father Flusche, who routinely filched from the special collections at Mass to make up any deficits in the regular plate offerings, was not impressed with my anger.

"Tell him anything you want. But remind him about the offering. It's a custom that, once he has time to think about, he will remember to do something about."

With an entirely righteous expression on his face, he left the room. The nun looked down at her index cards. I called up the professor and told him that the baby's Mass would be at 6 A.M. tomorrow and that Father Flusche was deeply sorry to hear about his death.

"I'd like to make a special offering if I could," said the professor. "Tell Father Flusche that for me, would you please?"

"Father Flusche wouldn't hear of it," I said. I've never told a lie with more conviction.

Father Swett made a great effort initially to take both Barbara and me around to all the student hangouts: "So this is Oklahoma," I thought, looking at the sorority girls grinding through the "hully gully" with every strand of rolled, curled hair sprayed into place. The room was dark, except for the spotlight tracks which were marbleized with cigarette smoke. The music was loud, pulsating and southern.

"When Ah was a lit-tle, bit-ty baby, mah momma would ROCK ME IN MAH CRADLE." I thought I was hearing an authentic Oklahoma song never heard anyplace else in the country. During the first weeks in Oklahoma, I made a lot of mistakes like this. But one thing I didn't make a mistake about. Oklahoma was a sexy state. The boys wore tight jeans, drank beer on the mud flats behind the university, and behind the Greek-porticoed, curtain-swagged windows of the sorority houses, where girls who got "dropped," "pinned," or "engaged" passed chocolates around the circle, there was one sin that resulted in a quick pack-up and expulsion! If she got pregnant.

If a girl found herself pregnant, she found herself alone, and Father Swett routinely counseled formerly bright-eyed, exuberant girls, now ashen-faced, hugging coats around their soon-to-expand bellies, who had suddenly found themselves on the other side of the moral code. It made Father Swett furious.

There was one girl who regularly appeared at Mass who was an unsolved mystery to me. Every time I asked Father Swett about her he was curiously restrained. Yet I often saw Dawn with her boyfriend talking to Father Swett by themselves, and I could not help but notice how beautiful she was. A honey blonde with soft brown eyes, a flawless complexion and a beautiful, wide smile, she didn't seem to belong to any sorority. In fact, the girls who regularly clustered around Father Swett never spoke to her at all, and her boy-friend, an older postgraduate student, always seemed to have a protective eye on her, as if he didn't want her to get out of his sight.

One day, while I was sitting with Barbara in the Will Rogers cafeteria (everything in Oklahoma seemed to be named after Will Rogers), Dawn walked past with a tray for food and we invited her to sit down.

Perhaps we spent forty-five minutes with her, talking about anything that came into our heads. She was friendly but not confiding, and she mostly asked us about ourselves—where we came from, how long we would be at the Newman Club and what did we think of Father Swett? She obviously thought a lot of him.

That evening the telephone rang. It was from one of the boys who lived next door. Jimmy was a funny, slightly dippy freshman from Tulsa, who had decided that he would look out for us, since, as he put it, "You all are so out of it that somebody has to help you get along." There were two or three boys who felt that way about us. Jimmy was one of them.

"Hi," he said. "Listen, was that you and Barbara I saw talkin' with Dawn at the cafeteria this afternoon?"

"Yes," I said. "Why?"

"Well, listen," he said, sounding uncomfortable at his end of the phone, "I don't know quite how to say this, but you shouldn't really hang around her."

"What are you talking about, Jimmy? I can hang around with whoever I want."

"Naow," he said, "you're gettin' mad. I'm just telling you

somethin' you don't know. It's not good for you to be around her. She's well . . . she . . ."

His voice trailed off and then took up again. He had his duty. "Oh, Christ," he said. "The whole football team's done it with her. Every college kid in Oklahoma City used to line up at her bedroom door. I mean she's what you call 'a mattress.' And I felt like you ought to know about that and keep out of her life. Know what I mean?"

"Yeah," I said, "I know what you mean."

A sigh from the other end of the phone. "Okay then," he said.

"But what about Fred?" I asked. "Isn't she going with Fred now?"

"That's what I hear," he said. "Maybe she's tryin' to go straight or somethin' on account of him. But you couldn't get me to touch her with a ten-foot pole. God, she makes me sick!"

I hung up the phone and informed Barbara of our terrible "indiscretion." Her eyes widened and then she got furious.

"Those little shits," she muttered. "Those Goddamned little shits."

Barbara comes from Rhode Island, where they know how to narrow their eyes. She puffed angrily at her cigarette and stared into space. If an alarm clock had been within reach, it would have smashed Jimmy's brains to mush.

Oklahoma remained too large for me to comprehend the whole time I was there. Too young to understand Father Swett, too old to want to understand the University of Oklahoma, and too nervous to impose any real structure upon this odd free-wheeling assignment of being a missionary to a campus full of students whose minds were full of other things, I simply went from one day to the next, botching orders I tried to follow.

One day I would be trying to wheedle a Pi Phi out from under a pink hair dryer to come downstairs for a discussion of Teilhard de Chardin. The next day I would be sitting in a small, toy-strewn living room, listening to a professor's wife talk about how she and her husband were going to raise their children around the liturgical calendar. "We always plant wheat on Saint Cecilia's Day." I didn't know whether this was a good thing or not.

On a weekend when all the Extension Volunteers met in Oklahoma City for a reunion, I stayed in a damp, depressing orphanage and found myself in a restaurant with three black children from the orphanage who were not allowed to use the rest rooms. I said thank you, waited until the manager had disappeared and took them to the bathroom anyway.

Once, while meeting with several priests and volunteers in Oklahoma City, I listened to one of the priests talk about the extreme poverty in his parish and how hard it was to get the families who needed help to accept it. "It's one thing to be poor," he said, "but another thing to have to take help. They know right off if the person helping them identifies with their poverty or thinks they're doing them a big favor." I thought a lot about that.

One Extension Volunteer died that year, the victim of a faulty gas radiator which blew out during the night. I did not know her. Our own gas radiator blew out one afternoon while I was reading a letter from a boyfriend in Rochester and suddenly felt myself drifting off to sleep. Jumping up, I threw open the window and ran outside, very frightened.

When it snowed, Norman was quilted and peaceful. In the hot weather you fried and died. The surrounding countryside was sere and uninviting in any season except autumn, when the leaves had a brief, brilliant moment before curling into shoe leather. There was no place to go except in circles, although once while driving down a back road I saw a small, abandoned-looking schoolhouse and walked up to the window to investigate. A few chairs were scattered around inside, near a piano covered with a piece of plastic. The following syllogism had been written on the blackboard: "God said it. We believe it. That settles it." It made me laugh.

The saddest, most alive person I met in Oklahoma was a priest who had once experienced God with such painful joy that he had wept. But that had been a long time ago. Now he was teaching in a boys' boarding school outside of a town whose name I can't remember. I had visited him in the science lab and to prove my love of small creatures, had picked up a white mouse from a cage. While I was holding it in my hand against my stomach, the mouse slipped in between two button-holes of my blouse and began running around my midriff. There was only one thing to do and I did it. Fortunately, all the boys were in study hall. The priest laughed until the tears ran down his face.

These are the chief memories of that odd, Godless year. There was no pattern to it. I was perpetually out-of-focus, tripping over my anxieties with the same regularity with which I used to trip over my feet on the outsized cement curbs that lined the sidewalks of Norman.

I could not wait to leave in June. My ambition to repay the Church backfired in my face, and if I had to put a date to when my first doubts about the institutional Church were sown, it was there in Norman, sandwiched between a priest who disliked me and a priest in an air-conditioned office, both of whom gave me an increasingly wide berth.

In the middle of the riddle, however, there was one significant event which sent the next fourteen years of my life in one direction. It was in Oklahoma that I first focused upon the man I was to marry.

He was the friend of my best friend in college. She envisioned us, from afar, in Washington, D.C., as being perfect for each other. Separately, by letter, she told us so and the campaign was launched.

During that year, he began to write letters. They were funny, illustrated with cartoons, and one of them said, "Don't do anything serious, like get married, until we have a nice, long talk."

I was, at that time, receiving letters from a boy in Rochester and feeling slightly disloyal to him because I was also eating hamburgers with a Sigma Chi in Norman. Neither of them seemed quite right.

One snowy December weekend, my future husband flew in, en route to Texas on a business trip, to meet me. He was wearing a navy-blue overcoat with a velvet collar and looked like a prince. I was wearing a navy-blue coat with loose buttons and looked, he told me later, like a waif.

There was nothing to do in Oklahoma City except take a tour of the Anadarko Indian Reservation. A dried-up little Indian, who kept talking about "yesterday's people" in a high, whiny voice, took us around some teepees. We stopped in a restaurant at the outskirts of the reservation, and my future husband stepped on a "Weight-Fate" scale. He inserted a nickel in the machine and out came a small white card. It read, "Love and happiness are within your grasp. Reach for it." He turned around and took me in his arms.

That was it. Well, that wasn't quite it, but against the dry, sere backdrop of Oklahoma I was vulnerable to a feasible escape route. My future husband provided it, although I certainly didn't consciously view him in that way, but I concluded the rest of the Oklahoma experience, which ended in June, knowing I had something wonderful to look forward to—him.

Chapter

XII

The period after college but before marriage was a fast shuffle through a deck of possibilities, husband possibilities, that confused me as much as it confused the men whom I ineptly transferred from the top of the deck to the bottom and back again, as I judged the shifting worth of the hand of cards itself.

I met my future husband while I was still in college. He had been visiting my best friend, Barbara Boggs, who knew him through their mutual student government interests, she as class president for all four years, he as class president in his college, Pratt Institute. It was a brief, unmemorable encounter. He said hello, I took a hamburger out of my mouth and said hello back. Then he was gone. Later, much later, he said that he should have realized how much I liked to eat from that first encounter.

The first time I actually focused on him was on the last day of my college career at a graduation dance in New York. He was escorting Barbara as a "cover" date, masking the man to whom she was secretly engaged and who she had fixed up with her younger sister, also in on the ruse.

He asked me to dance, and from the other side of the floor, Barbara saw us together and thought that she heard wedding bells. I heard nothing at all. At that time I thought I was quite in love with a smart, funny boy from Rochester. I danced the night through, thinking about John and knowing that within several days I would be visiting him, staying with a college friend who lived in Rochester and had invited me to stay for a week to cement the relationship. I remember nothing about my husband, except that I thought he was very nice, very shy, and that he couldn't be having much fun, since Barbara was always conferring with her secret fiancé behind various potted palms, hoping her parents, who didn't particularly approve of him, did not see her at all.

The week in Rochester with John was, I suppose, a confirmation of my intuitions. He invited me to Boston that following Christmas over vacation. I was smitten with his wit, his passionate regard for me, and for the entire summer prior to leaving for Oklahoma, I bored my father royally by reading John's letters out loud as soon as he came home from work.

John had only one drawback, his parents, who were small, smugly affluent members of "better" Rochester, which put me off somewhat. John's father liked to stand by the living-room window and tell me who lived on the street. "That house belongs to the senior vice-president of Eastman Kodak," he would say. "That house is owned by the general manager." Rochester was full of Kodak tycoons, and whether John's father was one of them or not I don't remember. But it was a faintly stifling household, and while John was full of bright ideas (one time he handed me a pound of bacon at the front door to prove that he knew how to bring the bacon home) his parents were not his best feature. They made me feel uncomfortable, which might have had something to do with the fact that I was a Catholic.

Rochester draws and divides itself as clearly along racial

and religious lines as any city I have ever been in. It was considered unusual to socialize with Protestants if you were Catholic, and something of a hidden triumph if you actually knew a Jew. I imagine that it is still the same way. The girl I stayed with was a bright, voluptuous girl called Beverly de Lucia. I liked the De Lucia family a lot. But after a week or more of tripping over John and me on their front sofa at two in the morning, I doubt that they liked me as much.

I carried John's picture, letters and prospects to Oklahoma and continued to write to him, even though I met a boy through the Newman Club who began to ask me out, and I continued to go out with him for the nine months I was there.

Bob was a law student who came from Chicago, and nagging at the back of my brain the entire time I knew him was the question, "Why did he come to the University of Oklahoma for law school?" The answer he always gave me was that he wanted to practice law in Oklahoma, which struck me as a very dull prospect, even in Tulsa, which was the solitaire in the ring of the state. Tulsa was affluent and high-powered, but I couldn't imagine actually living there. Nor, in my secret heart of hearts, could I quite imagine marrying Bob, who had no particular drawbacks but who simply did not fulfill whatever maddeningly vague but stubborn requirements I had for the mythical man I planned to marry.

From his end of the relationship, it must have been a terrible ordeal. He knew about John in Rochester and banked upon my turning him down as a prospect when I went to Boston to see him over Christmas. I did go to Boston and did turn John down, staying a week to do it as the houseguest of a girl he knew. I arrived in Boston, feeling pale and frightened at the prospect, and when I finally uttered my words of rejection, John's first and most logical question was, "But why did you come all the way to Boston to tell me?" In all honesty I had not imagined that there was another honorable way. I flew out of Boston and was met by Bob in Chicago, where

I spent the rest of the holidays with an aunt and uncle who lived nearby.

In February, neither more or less taken by Bob than before but feeling obligated, I spent a weekend in Oklahoma City with my future husband, which added insult to injury in Bob's eyes. As I look back, he was right to be outraged. But I was simply trying as best I could to broker my own future. I did not know who I wanted to marry. There were various alternatives, any one of which might disappear on me if I did not watch my lines, and at the age of twenty-three I felt quite businesslike about my future.

Having not fallen in love in college, I had only a few more years to accomplish that feat before I felt irretrievably threatened by old age. Twenty-three seemed verging on overripe. In fact, I was as green as a cooking apple, had yet to feel any real stirrings of adult female response, and when I thought about romance, it was to project ahead to days of ironing gingham curtains that the sun would shine through, candle-light suppers at which my husband and I would speak of noble things from our noble minds, and uppermost in my nervous mind was the question of who would take care of me in perpetuity.

There was no doubt that I needed to be taken care of, that I would only be able to flourish with the half-dozen or more children I hoped to have if there were a strong, understanding man to sigh against at the end of the day. I was not so singlemindedly set upon marriage that I could envision sighing against my husband in Tulsa, which would cause me to sigh in and of itself, but I thought of marriage as the next and last step before I could stand still and begin real life.

I did not have any sense of whether I was marriageable or even particularly pretty, or someone that anybody would want to marry. But I conceived of myself as being cheerful, having a positive attitude and the potential to be a good mother. No one had ever said I was beautiful, and I tried, secretly, in mirrors, to assess whether I was pretty. I concluded that I had nice hair, an all-right nose, but my eyes were too close together.

My parents had not ever raised the subject of beauty one way or the other. Looking back at old photographs, however, I think the child in the pictures was, in fact, pretty. But in a certain way, I was ignored growing up. It was my cousin Mimi who I thought was admired within the family as the central flower, unfolding her delicate petals in a series of long dresses, velvet evening jackets and summer skirts. But the adjectives "pretty" or "handsome" were rarely used on any of us. "Radiant" or "clean-cut" were more popular ways to describe us.

Years later, when I was married and with children, someone told me that her brother-in-law thought I was a very attractive woman. I had never thought of myself in these terms, but I proceeded to silently fall in love with him, and would stand in the kitchen wishing he would come in the back door, snatch the frying pan from my hands and sweep me away. Taking the fantasy further, however, I saw the two of us walking hand in hand down a beach, asking each other questions like, "Where do you want to live?" and "How many children shall we have?" That would be starting the process I was already in the middle of, and slowly, reluctantly, I closed the damper against the fire.

Having dismissed John (who swore himself to a celibacy I am sure he did not follow through on), fallen partially in love with Bob, and thinking that if I could only drag myself through the remaining months in Oklahoma, I could have all doubts resolved in Gene, I walked a faintly immoral tightrope, discussing love with Bob on the rug of the Sigma Chi house and writing letters to Gene, who was living in Washington, D.C., where I planned to visit Barbara (who also lived there) during the following summer.

Everybody knew about everybody else, my belief being that

245

truth would set me free from being considered manipulative, although I was. When June came and I packed up to leave Norman, Bob drove me out of the state as far as Charlottesville, Virginia. There was a terrific thunderstorm in Oklahoma the night we left in his small sports car. Lightning plunged in terrifying forks on either side of the car as the windshield wipers struggled to keep the rain off. I was congealed with fright, snatched all the metal bobby pins out of my hair and my gold ring from Manhattanville off my finger, and threw them into my lap in an attempt to keep the lightning from stabbing me from the rear. I had no idea about how lightning or love worked, but I was taking precautions with both of them.

Arriving in Washington by train, I was met by Gene, who knew about Bob, who knew about Gene. I didn't know about anything, except that I was immensely relieved to be out of Oklahoma, and I am afraid to say I had no feelings about Bob once I exited from that state. Such callousness shames me now. But it is an indication of how tremendously important I felt it was never to be without a masculine protector, and I traded one for the other, trading up, trading away, and several days later, while walking through the willow trees on the back lawn of Barbara's house, I asked Gene a highly significant question:

"What would you do if I ever got sick?"

"I would take care of you," he said.

Later on, just weeks before our wedding, when I was having an attack of premarital nerves, I asked him another highly significant question:

"What would you do if we didn't get married after all?"

"I would survive," he answered, calmly.

I packed away my nerves and did not raise that question again.

The year I got married was the last year that our family

assembled for a decent picture. There we are, lined up on the brick steps of the last large house my parents owned, a Carmel frame house covered with bougainvillaea, several blocks from the Pacific Ocean, where I forced my prospective husband to repropose to me—so we would have a sunset and ocean setting for the memory album.

My father is a bit heavier but still electrically handsome with curly eyebrows, a crooked front tooth and an expensive silk scarf in his breast pocket—probably plucked off the top of a pile of silk scarves from the shop he currently owned in Carmel. Next to him is Mother, wearing her "good" dress, a tweed hand-me-down from a sister-in-law in Chicago, with a matching sweater with tweed buttons. She is smiling.

Then the rest of us—I am wearing a kilt skirt and sweater and looking hearty, sitting next to my almost husband, wearing tie and sport coat, looking young. I am holding Tony, only three at that time, on my lap. Tony was a blond, chiseled child, with a curling half-smile, the Infant of Prague in short navy-blue pants, sweater and Peter Pan collar. Wendy and Cindy, oafishly preadolescent, are all legs and inexperience, not yet beautiful but laughing. They are in jumpers. My brother John, handsome in a Kennedy-esque way, in pressed flannels, oiled loafers, shirt and tie (the East Coast image later sacrificed for the Michelangelo-in-leather look) beside his wife (also sacrificed seven years later), a slim, high-cheekboned blonde with cornsilk hair and blue eyes.

The clothes seem more important than the people in them. I am struck by how definite we all look, just as several years after, when I lined this photograph up with another later one, I was shocked to see how far and fast we had declined in style. Blue jeans, flyaway hair, everyone seated on aluminum chairs, without organization or thrust. The light is bright and bad. An unprofessional shot. But in 1963 when I got engaged and married, the family was still doing things right.

As luck would have it, there was another cousin, Tony, getting married on the same day as I was. The family split up, my Uncle Ed and Aunt Dorothy flying south to Los Angeles for that ceremony, my Aunt Irene staying home to prop up Mother, who was stricken with a prewedding case of bursitis, which even she knew was psychosomatic but she still couldn't get out of bed.

The wedding made no attempt to model itself after my cousin Mimi's. Finances dictated a smaller occasion. We no longer lived in San Francisco, which cut the list by 80 percent, and with the exception of my future husband's commanding officer who assumed that he was invited ("It's just a family wedding," my husband had said. "Wonderful," said his commanding officer, "I love family weddings."), there were only about twenty people there.

Perhaps I should have taken certain jokes as omens. The photographer who took our engagement pictures for the papers was an artist who said he only did these kinds of jobs at the moment because he had inadvertently poisoned his trout farm on the Big Sur. Ordinarily he photographed kelp formations or his third wife.

The wedding photographer, an enlisted man (who was later courtmartialed for using Army equipment to take pornographic pictures), forgot to take a picture of us at the altar of the Carmel Mission Basilica, and forced the entire wedding party back down the aisle just after the ceremony was over so he could snap another shot, an anticlimax so embarrassing that I was forced to laugh.

The priest, a pale, affable man who was not quite as witty as he thought he was, later left the priesthood to get married himself. Of course, we didn't know any of these things at the time, and it did not dilute the immensity of the step I knew I was taking. In fright, I insisted upon a short dress so I would not trip over my feet. Ten minutes before leaving the house, I almost did not leave at all.

"Mother," I called out from my room. "Please come here." She walked in, saw my face twisted in panic and asked what was wrong.

"Do you think I'm doing the right thing?" I whispered.

"What?" she said, startled. "You mean geting married?"

"Yes," I said, tears beginning to roll down my face. "I'm so afraid that I might . . . oh, I don't know . . . be too strong for him."

My mother was mystified. She had not been privy to the thoughts behind this observation. Yet I had, over the months we had been engaged, worried over myself. This gentle, flexible, eager-to-please future husband of mine might be too weak for my strong will, might not assert himself ahead of me, which is where I wanted my husband to be. Might I not, I thought—assembling all the cartoons of rolling pin harridans in my imagination—become a bitch, a nagger, a pain in the neck? Blackmailed by fears of my future irascibility, I hovered on the edge of running away but of course it was too late. My father was already starting the car.

My mother said the only thing she could say, "Don't be ridiculous." I realized that I was just having a case of nerves, and twenty minutes later I was walking through the courtyard of the Basilica on my father's arm. He joked about the pigeon-choked bell tower. "Think of those poor Indians having to ring those bells in their bare feet." I giggled and got married.

I was not in love with my husband when I married him. It was almost a prerequisite that I marry in order to experience that emotion, or at least that was how it developed in my instance. He was, I knew, safe. Only later did I discover, to my surprise and delight, that he was many other things as well. I never knew, until I felt it happening within me, that love expanded, doubled, ebbed, resurged and sloughed off all past irrelevancies, like his Pendleton shirts that I could not stand, and that within the safe, sacramental confines of a binding commitment, all my experiences were intensified because they were shared.

I did not know how to make a white sauce when I got married. He was a reason to learn. I depended upon him greatly.

Several months after the wedding, I stood in the middle of our small kitchen in our first house, a two-room cabin in Carmel surrounded by eighteen pine trees. It was late morning. The smell of bacon grease hung in the air. I was alone, at the kitchen table, gazing at my hands, which were warm with sun and appeared detached from me, in a contemplation all their own. I was content. Utterly so.

The small window over the kitchen table was fringed with Scotch broom, bright-yellow flowers on dark-green stalks which brushed against the windowpane and sent the sun in zig-zag patterns over the new blue-and-white-checked gingham place mats, which had been a wedding present. I mused over the colors—against the white oilcloth of the table. Everything was so pure and primary.

Humming a tune, I gathered up the two breakfast plates and carried them to the sink, where I turned on the hot water spigot. As the soap powder turned the sink into a bubblebath, I admired the way the bubbles multiplied into millions of rainbow colors. Filled with deep happiness, I plunged my arms into the soap suds and, inexplicably, without warning, felt something crack with sorrow inside.

Why sorrow? I lifted my eyes and looked out the window, through the pine trees, into the sky. It was a bright-blue sky, utterly devoid of grief. What? I could barely comprehend the wordless message that poked like a thorn into my heart. I listened to the silence for a further explanation. Then the thorn poked at me again. It was the same message.

"You mean," I asked, my arms still submerged under the soap suds, "you mean, this isn't it?"

Chapter
XIII

They say that it takes about three years after a marriage has terminated before you can sit across the table from your former husband and look at him as he is instead of how he was. I have not tested that theory out. But whenever he comes to pick up the children or drop them off, and for those few brief moments we are reassembled as an ersatz family, I find that I want to do what I always wanted to do—go into another room.

Only recently have I understood why I did this. All those years of diving into a magazine, retreating toward the kitchen, going upstairs, outside, or finding some other place to be happened because I was a coward. I did not feel loved and for fourteen years I fled from that fact—burning the spaghetti sauce, messing up the checkbook, forgetting to roll up the car windows when it rained, misplacing screwdrivers and going into other rooms. Fear made me clumsy, anger I would not acknowledge led me to guerrilla warfare with tools of unkemptness, guilt exacerbated my penchant for self-destruction, and I saw myself through his eyes as a woman who depreciated in value year after year. Ultimately, I could not stand the sight. I chose to live in other rooms, to confirm my own worst fears. Alone there was a chance for perfection. I could think, write, read, assess. Every so often, my "term paper" finished, "footnotes" in order, and "theme" double-checked for error, I would walk back into the room where he was and try for perfection in real life. But I think I was less interested in trying for perfection than trying for him. He was, I thought, real life. If I failed to win him, I failed everything. If I could not convice him of my worth, then I could not convince myself. That was not what I thought but what I felt. What I felt dictated my thoughts, organized my impulses and urged me to wait just a little longer. Something would happen. It would be all right. He would see, I would respond, we would not always live in separate chambers. I was a terrible coward. I was not prepared to risk it all.

Upstairs there were children whose cheeks I used to rob of kisses before I went to bed. I told myself that the children needed to be protected. They could not survive without us.

I thought of the oldest, riding his bicycle, brown bangs flipping over his forehead as he rode his wheels over the pavement. He was the solemn child, the one who lay in bed before he went to sleep and picked out animal shapes in between the tree branches. I would protect him with my life.

The middle child, my daughter, arrived as a bit of puffy dough with two little eyes gazing seriously into my face. She still gazes at me this way, although now she is a slim, arm-circling scrap of vulnerability, so good, so easy to ignore, so anxious to fill in every place that wants filling, out of absolutely unshakeable love.

The third child is the chattery one, the self-confident one, the mystic who sees God by the swing set at the playground. He stands in his outsized underpants, small legs standing barefoot on the floor, solemnly drawing a picture, the picture of grace himself.

I was blackmailed by visions of small children in droopy underpants for years. They undermined my arguments, assaulted my convictions, came creeping into bed on cold mornings to fling their arms and legs over the two of us, like angelic jailers who would keep us together at any cost.

I could not bury my nose in their wind-scented hair as they rushed by the kitchen table, en route to someplace more important than me, without vowing to search for another compromise that had escaped my imagination. But finally my imagination failed. I ran out of term papers to write. I entered into a period of deep silence that, against my desires, filled up with truth. I did not want to hear it.

"I think," I had once said, feeling frightened and wanting him to immediately disprove my thought, "that we are not loving each other enough. I know that you love the children. But I think that our love for each other is bypassing us and going only to the children instead."

He was silent. A sideways glance in my direction informed him that I was looking at him, waiting for an answer. He sighed. An exhausted, exasperated sigh. "It is easier," he said, removing his glasses, "to love children than to love adults." Then he placed his glasses on the nightstand and turned out the light.

The dog outlasted our marriage. He was a large, blond Labrador, the safest, gentlest breed. A family dog who started out as a puppy with too much skin, he turned into an outsized, slightly neurotic giant whom the children adored.

I told my husband when we picked him out that he wasn't going to be my responsibility. I expected others to take him out for the walks he needed. But of course he was my responsibility, not that I honored it, and I was grateful that Sam (a good name for a good dog, I thought) was in the house once the family was split asunder because the children needed him more than ever.

They lay on his back, played with him like a rag doll, used his tail for a microphone when they gave skits, fed him their broccoli from the table when my back was turned. I was determined to keep Sam, despite the fact that he chewed shoes, was only partially housebroken, and frightened old men with heart conditions by jumping playfully onto their shoulders when their backs were turned.

Once Sam stayed away for three days and the children were heartbroken. Fortunately he returned—to chew, frighten and dominate the household once again. I knew we shouldn't keep him. He was too large, too potentially dangerous outside. I saw law suits, and took my last five hundred dollars and put up an Anchor fence. But he would not stay in the backyard. The children kept forgetting to close the gates. The only alternative was to keep Sam inside. Yet he would lie, ostensibly asleep in front of the fireplace, but at the first sound of the front door opening, he would spring to all fours and dash like a greyhound toward the opening. I would flatten myself against the door, try to keep him from muzzling his way between my body and the door jamb, and sometimes be successful. More often I was not.

Sam turned mean on the streets. He bit a Chinese student, who appeared at my door with a bill for a tetanus shot he had had to receive. He snapped the buttons off a little old lady's cardigan sweater as she was peacefully making her way to church one Sunday. Joggers were not safe. I could not count on the charity or understanding of the neighbors any longer. Sam had become a menace. One afternoon, I put him in the car and took him to be put to sleep. Sam thought he was going on a nice ride. His brown eyes were full of anticipation.

The pound was not far away. I took Sam out of the car, snapped a leash around his collar, and was dragged behind him as he walked to the office. Sam had never learned to heel.

"I have a dog that must be put to sleep," I told the girl at the receptionist's desk. I don't know why it is but dog pounds always seem to attract young, attractive women.

"What is the problem?" she asked.

"He has begun to bite people," I said. "I tried to find a place for him on a farm somewhere, but I was told that a dog who bites will bite cows and horses too. I cannot think of any other alternative."

"I'm afraid there is no alternative," she said. "They are too old to understand their limits at his age. He would not be safe for anyone to own."

"Shall I just leave him?" I asked.

"Yes, you can do that," she said, "unless you would like to be with him when we give him the shot."

"Be with him?" I asked, feeling nauseated. "Don't you have rules about that? I thought no one but the technician was allowed inside the room."

"No," she said. "Some places have that rule. But here we don't. In fact, we like to demonstrate that the way in which a dog is put to sleep is absolutely painless. It takes about five seconds and he won't feel anything at all."

I wasn't sure this was a good enough reason. I desperately did not want to watch.

"Also," she added, "it's much better for the dog if you're there. If he is held by someone he trusts, he feels peaceful. He is not afraid."

I couldn't withstand that argument. It was the least I could do for Sam.

We took Sam down the hallway to a room with a white tile floor and white porcelain table.

"He doesn't have to get up on the table, does he? Couldn't we just sit on the floor together?"

"Sure," she said.

I coaxed Sam down onto the floor and put my arms around

him, feeling like Judas. Another young, attractive girl came into the room. I did not watch them as they got a bottle off the shelf and filled up a syringe.

Sam looked inquiringly into my eyes. "Good dog," I said, rubbing my cheek over his silky ears. "That's a very good dog."

A girl knelt down and quickly inserted the needle into Sam's left hindquarters. I tightened my grasp around Sam, waiting for some kind of horrible involuntary shudder when the chemical took hold.

First Sam was looking at me and then his eyes went out. There was no shudder. He simply slipped within his skin into another dimension. I laid his large, noble head upon the floor and began to weep.

He was such a beautiful dog, such an innocent, well-meaning dog. I stroked his head, laid my cheek against his ribs, mourned him, dripped tears that made small points in the fur where I rubbed, and started to talk out loud to nobody.

"I did not take care of him," I sobbed. "It was not his fault that he had to die. I fed him, and I built a fence for him, and I loved him, but I did not know how to take care of him. He wouldn't have bitten people if only I had taken him on more walks. But I never did. I never trained him."

The two girls did not say anything, and suddenly I became aware that they were still in the room and watching a distraught woman on her hands and knees going to pieces over a dead dog.

One of them leaned down and handed me a Kleenex. For a moment I thought she wanted me to clean up their floor. I began to wipe up little spots of dirt on the tile.

"No," said the girl. "You don't have to do that. It's for you."

"Oh," I said, leaning back on my heels and wiping my eyes, "I'm sorry." Then I looked up with embarrassment and said, "I'm not sure what I should do next. I don't know the etiquette of how you leave the euthanasia room of a pound."

Slowly I got up off the floor and took one more look at Sam. He was lying, as he used to lie in front of the fireplace—front paws crossed, hind legs extended.

"Does one say thank you?" Both girls were silent. The only way to leave was to leave. I turned around and walked out.

At the front desk, I handed the receptionist a five-dollar bill, not stopping.

"Don't you want a receipt?" she called out. "Your contribution is tax-deductible."

"No," I answered.

I drove home barely able to see the road. Over and over again I thought of how it had felt to hold Sam's warm body in my arms and how it had suddenly slipped within itself, with my arms still around him. I had watched Sam die, holding tight until the end. It was like my marriage. At the end I had made the decision to let the marriage die, feeling like a criminal, out of choices and assailed by what might have been.

I walked back in the front door, and there was no blond bullet colliding against my knees waiting to get out. The house was peaceful. But I had paid a terrible price.

Chapter

XIV

Dearest Phyllis,

You rightly say in your last letter that 'you fear losing the thread of your life.' That fear is most genuine and must be recognized as to what it is.

Your soul, your invisible life if you'd rather, is yearning to express itself. And can only do so when there is an emptying of self so to speak in order for a new inner awareness to take place. Misplaced needs can take their toll. The emotions rule and hence California in the midst of it becomes California without a zip code and then where is the real thread of life?

I will stop in the middle of this letter from my mother to decode it.

The first Christmas after I was separated, when the children were without their father, I had asked her to come for the holidays, given her the plane fare, and she had arrived, worrying the whole way that she had not brought the right clothes.

Mother had not been back East for five years. Her life after separating from my father had been a hard, quiet period of healing. I only knew of it through her letters. But usually they did not refer to her life as much as mine.

She was, I knew, part of a small group of "students," who surrounded a teacher of cosmic awareness who lived in Carmel. His name was Lawrence. He was an older, contemplative man with a background in metaphysics who gave lectures and private consulting time to several dozen people, including my mother, my cousin Mimi, my Aunt Dorothy and others. They had benefited enormously from him. I had met him once. As usual, I failed to feel myself in the presence of anything extraordinary. He was, I concluded, not meant to be my teacher. But he was Mother's, and she always spoke of him with a kind of restrained reverence, as if she did not want to reveal the full extent of her feelings because I might not understand or properly receive them.

That first broken holiday in my life, my friends had gone out of their way to share themselves. There were many invitations that would keep us all moving from one house to the next, and as Mother unpacked I told her what we would be doing, who was going to be at various parties, and did what I always do, which was to fan the fires of her enthusiasm to meet people who had already been fanned by me to meet her.

She said very little. She did not seem to want to meet anyone, although she smiled politely when I gave her the itinerary and assured her that she had just the right things to wear, not that anyone would care if she did or not.

"Let me stay home with the children tomorrow evening when you go out," she had said. "I think I would rather be with them, just for that evening. But you go. It would be good for you."

I went and returned early, finding Mother sitting in the living room next to the fire with a book in her lap.

"Well you were smart to have avoided that particular out-ing," I said, sinking into a chair on the other side of the fireplace. "It wasn't a very interesting group of people, and the only person you might have heard of was Joe Califano. He's the current head of the Department of Health, Education and Welfare."

A look of consternation flicked across her eyes.

"What is the matter?" I asked, wondering whether everything had gone all right with the children. Mother had walked around the house on the first day being very careful with the children, trying to make sure she did not overwhelm them or say the wrong thing, looking into each face to get a better fix on who they were and how she should respond.

"Your friends intimidate me," she said quietly. "They all sound so bright. I'm not sure that I'll know what to say to them. I feel that they are all writing books, or maybe they *are* books. And I don't read very many books at all, at least not the ones anyone knows about."

I looked at Mother and tried not to smile, thinking of Mother sitting between two dinner partners who loomed up as leather-bound volumes on either side, striking her dumb. The fear was unjustified. I tried to reassure her.

"Mother, that's not true. My friends are just my friends. They aren't frightening at all. What you forget is how anxious they are to meet *you*. I've done nothing but talk about you for the past five years."

She sat in her chair, looking very small in her bulky pink bathrobe. "I rarely see people these days," she said, gazing into the fire. "You have no idea how quiet my life is. Mostly," she added quietly, "I watch seagulls."

"Great," I said, leaning toward her. "Talk about seagulls. Nobody on the East Coast knows anything about them. You'll be the expert. I can tell you that I'd rather hear about seagulls than almost anything else that people around here talk about."

She looked up, not quite convinced. "I suppose it's silly," she said, "but I really have gotten to know one family of seagulls at Point Lobos very well. First, there was just the mother and father. But then there were eggs, and then two little baby seagulls. I would walk quietly so they weren't disturbed by me. Their nest was just off the path I always take by the ocean. And every day I would watch the babies as the parents tried to teach them to fly."

Talking about Point Lobos and the seagulls seemed to cheer her up. "One day," she continued, "the smallest of the babies got out onto one of the rocks near the ocean, and a wave splashed over the rock and washed it over. I was very frightened for it, you know, wondering whether I shouldn't jump off the rocks and try to get the baby back. But I couldn't. The surf was too powerful. I was helpless. But then the mother swooped down and plucked it off the top of the foam and brought it back to the nest. I can't tell you how relieved I was."

Her face, as I looked at it, looked very soft and young. My mother then said, "I felt it was such a privilege to have been there."

She looked at me self-consciously. "Do you think anybody would want to hear about that?"

"Of course, they would," I said emphatically. "It's fascinating. You're going to be a large hit."

Mother wasn't sure she could wing through the holidays on seagull stories, and as we sat by the fire she shifted uncomfortably in her chair and said, "Oh dear." She stared at her hands, her face growing more vulnerable as the silence grew, and I sat on the other side of the fire and realized that I had not scotched her fears. She was, in fact, terrified. My first instinct was to be irritated.

Was it not I who needed a mother? Had I not asked her to come to me, at a time when I greatly needed to feel her steadying hand? I never answered the question. Suddenly, I saw her packing her suitcase in California, alone, taking the plane away from the only place she felt comfortable in, and flying East, prepared to be a help, only to find herself sitting in a chair, needing a mother of her own. I was the closest she could come to that. I got up from my chair, went over to hers, crossing a divide that I had too long avoided. Sliding down alongside her, I put my arm around her shoulder. I looked at her face and saw tears quietly running down her cheeks. They were such soft cheeks. I wondered what they felt like to touch. From my position, looking down, she looked ten years old.

"I don't know why I'm crying," she said, shaking her head. "But thinking about being with all those people, trying to keep up my end of the conversation—I'm so afraid that I'll get Califano mixed up with California."

I laughed, gave her a hug, felt a release of love in excess of any other time I had thought I loved her before. My mother never had a real mother as she had been mine. I kissed her cheek, laughed again and vowed that I would be her mother. I had never had the chance before.

"We will brave it together," I said. "Trust me. It will be all right," and it was.

Her letter came several months later, after she had gone back to Carmel and gotten in touch with the cypress trees and the seagulls who kept her spirits high.

> When even for a moment [the letter had concluded] you can attend to what is Real, your mind gets beyond itself. Understanding and clarity begin to come into the whole person, and you start moving with what is harmonious in you. And when you get results from doing this, you begin to rely less and less on the external and conditioned self, which is always so deceptive. As Lawrence once said, "You have to catch the ego napping.

Mother is unclear as to how one hails a cab. She speaks

with absolute assurance on the availability of Infinite Love. Three people at a table are too many for her to absorb. She is totally vulnerable to Truth.

She once told me that as a little girl she had spent long hours behind her house on Long Island, staring into the bottom of the brook that ran across the field. "I wanted so much to jump in and live forever with the water babies who I believed with everything in me were down there at the bottom. But I could never quite get up the courage. I was too afraid."

I'm not sure that Mother still doesn't believe in water babies in some neo-Plotinian form. She is a born believer, although she laughs at the time when she was a teenager and the man playing tennis with her winked at her so many times that by the end of the match she was in love. "It turned out that he had a congenital twitch," she said.

Mother is beyond protection. Sometimes my heart cracks when I am around her. But there is nothing I can do. She is extraordinarily stubborn. If she gets run over by a bus, it will be on her terms. And only recently have I begun to view her as she is, a human being who, only in passionate passing, gave birth to this first, most grasping and mother-draining child. But I no longer stand on her shoulders to face the world. They are too frail to support my weight. They probably always were, but she never let on, and only after I had myself endured the failure of a marriage did I understand my mother and the failure of my parents' marriage, which had been, despite its assets, bankrupted by a lack of understanding that ultimately became total.

Before my parents divorced, almost everything they owned had been broken or vandalized beyond repair. The gallery table was missing a half-dozen struts. The French dancing master under the glass dome had had his left foot knocked off. The tea caddy swung on broken hinges. And my Aunt Irene, who grieved over anything beautiful that wasn't taken care of, once fished a Joshua Reynolds oil painting out from behind Mother's Bendix.

"A Josh Reynolds!" she had cried out as if slain.

"I know," admitted my mother, who had forgotten it was there, "but it's not one of his better things, and anyway it would cost too much to restore."

But the little fox had survived, and I often wonder where it was sleeping now. Probably on one ear in a packing crate in a rented garage in Carmel, where Mother had stored everything she hadn't been able to sell.

Mother never loved her furniture. She respected it but did not love it, although every so often she would square up to the rips in her slipcovers and decide that she must do something about their condition. But once she made this decision, she realized she didn't know what to do further.

"Never mind," my Aunt Irene would say. She would swoop through the door with a thousand swatches from Jackson Square, fling material over the backs of all the chairs and then wait, toe tapping, her mind already made up, for Mother to make up hers.

Mother didn't know what she wanted most of the time, and when she did have an idea, my aunt always felt morally obligated to challenge her because she was ten miles ahead of everybody when it came to color, and my mother would feel silently swamped in her presence.

"Well," Aunt Irene would say, "the chintz from Schumacher's is a possibility. But I don't know if your rug can stand the earth color in the design. There's too much clear yellow in the rug, which needs to be picked up by a slate blue perhaps. There isn't any slate blue in the design you like."

Having delivered herself of that opinion, my aunt would start moving around lamps, and Mother would drift out to the kitchen to put on a pot of coffee. By the time she re-emerged into "swatchland" again, my aunt would have mentally redone the entire room to her own satisfaction. It took the wind out of Mother's sails. She had to admit that Aunt Irene was right.

Over the years, increasingly toward the end of her marriage, Mother would call up dealers and invite them, singly, over to the house to try to get a fix on what the whole lot would be worth if she ever had to sell out.

One by one, the dealers would come—small-town Billy Baldwins in tweed jackets and pressed flannels, holding notebooks in soft, ringed fingers, which they would pass over the wood, subtracting dollars each time they encountered a scratch or cigarette burn.

"This is unquestionably a good piece," they would say.

"Yes, I think so," said my mother, who would feel cheered up at their estimation.

"But it has not been well maintained," they would add reproachfully.

Mother would sigh, not knowing how to respond.

Smiling politely, they would make little jottings in their books, look over her head and agree to display "the bachelors' chest and perhaps the George Moreland print . . . on consignment, of course."

"Of course," my mother would agree, who had been thinking that perhaps she ought to skip the local scene and go straight to Park-Bernet if the going got tough, which ultimately it did.

My father had worked at Vacu-Dry for twenty-five years. It was always on the verge of becoming a large company. My father sensed that he did not have the expertise the company needed. He called in an outside authority, the former vice-president of a large company, and asked him to look the company over and tell him where the weak spots were so that the firm could improve its performance. The ex-vice-president smiled, went to work, told the board of directors that my father was the weak spot, and my father was fired. The former vice-president took his job.

That, of course, is only the bones of the story. But his eviction from Vacu-Dry left him with a house (which was undersold) and some stock, which he used to buy a small men's clothing store in Carmel.

It was one of those elegant, overpriced little shops where Rex Harrison bought his hats when he came to town for the Crosby Pro-Am, and where the local rich, who couldn't be bothered to trek up to San Francisco, usually shopped. You had to be rich to afford the stock. It was heavy on Harris tweeds, Swedish hacking jackets and Alaskan sweaters. "They knit 'em right on the Eskimos," said my father. He sold everything in the store, largely on the strength of these kinds of remarks.

The shop was a smashing success under my father's management. But he had no head for inventory control. The bills were never collected on time, and finally, in desperation, he sent out a notice to all his charge customers saying, "We're no longer using a computer. We're going back to Irving with the two-bit pencil and the green eyeshade." Everybody laughed but nobody paid their bills, and my father's partner, a dour man who used to watch the water cooler to make sure nobody drank from it, finally bought my father out.

With the cash from that sale, my parents sold their last house, staved off some bill collectors who did use computers and moved into a rental. Toward the end, they owned nothing but Mother's antiques and a coffee can full of gold coins that Mother's astrologer in San Jose had advised her to buy as a hedge against inflation.

I have never met Mother's astrologer, Mrs. Wade, although I imagine her as a plain woman in touch with sidereal time who sits at her kitchen table doling out spiritual and financial realities for a fee plus your birth date and hour. At various times, Mother has urged me to use Mrs. Wade, who didn't need to meet you in person and would put all her comments on tape so you could play back her predictions whenever you

267

wanted. But I never got around to it. There is something terrifying about having everything laid out, fore and aft, even though Mother insists that Mrs. Wade "never dwells on negative things." She had been right on target with various members of my family, helped my cousin Mimi to give up smoking in the middle of her divorce, and when she advised my mother to buy pre-1939 gold sovereigns as a hedge against inflation, Mother did.

Together my parents drove up to a coin dealer in Palo Alto and bought as many coins as they could, although they hadn't gotten back to Carmel before they had lost part of their investment.

Stopping in Castroville for a cup of coffee, my mother had suddenly stiffened in the booth, leaned over and whispered to my father, "Don't say anything, but we have to get out of here right now."

The last time my mother had said that she had been in a restaurant and thought a pair of flaming shishkebabs across the room was a fire. But my father's back was to the cash register, and he thought that maybe Mother saw a stickup in progress. Flipping a quarter on the table, he hustled Mother out the back door.

It wasn't until they got to the Prunedale cutoff that he slapped his forehead and said, "Jeez, I think I tipped the waitress with a fifty-dollar gold piece."

Cheap enough, implied my mother, who was sure that the Monterey *Herald* would confirm her instinct to run the next day. But the papers were silent on Castroville. She must have been tuned into a higher frequency and intercepted a murderous thought from the next booth.

They dumped the rest of the gold coins into a Hills Brothers coffee can, buried it in the back of the garage and raked dirt over the top. Every once in a while, they'd dig up the can and use the coins for poker chips. But when they separated, they dug the can up for the last time and split the gold equally between them. I'm glad I wasn't there to witness that scene. The thought of their shooting coins at each other across the table in dead silence tears at my mind.

My father had never managed money very well. He once said with quiet chagrin, "I'm not smart enough to be a crook," which wasn't true. But he did have a one-way feel for the dollar, lacking my Uncle Ed's contemplative interest in the stock market, and it would not be inaccurate to say that he floated above catastrophe almost entirely on the strength of his own jokes.

There was, and is, an almost terrible innocence about my father that has often left him at the mercy of small-hearted, far-sighted businessmen who have capitalized upon his innocence and taken him to the cleaners. To my father's credit, he does not carry grudges. But there are several people, now withered into the insignificance they so richly deserve, whom I wouldn't mind reading about in the obituary column today.

Compared with my father, who couldn't read the financial page without getting nervous, my mother has always loved reading Sylvia Porter's column and has always thought that she would someday earn a great deal of money. She would know how when she knew what. The point was to be true to yourself.

Mother is the only high-school dropout I know who reads on a postgraduate level without knowing what a preposition is. She gets most of her insights from Plotinus and Meister Eckhart. One year she decided to get her high-school equivalency and enrolled in a night program. But she flunked the course because she couldn't get the parts of speech down, although I spent one entire evening confident that I could correct that problem. But she simply stared at me in incomprehension as I tried in vain to show her what a preposition was.

"I am jumping *off* a chair," I said, jumping off a chair.

"Now I am crouching *beneath* the table," I said, crouching beneath the table.

"I see that you are," she said, "but where's the preposition in all that?"

As she grew older and the children emptied from the house, she became increasingly interested in finding a money-making idea that would "go national." "Like the Pet Rock," she explained. Mother is a fairly cosmic thinker, but she's not above trying to figure out what would sell well at Macy's.

Her first attempt to make a job for herself was called Creative Careers, a counseling service that Mother operated out of the kitchen to help people rethink their options about what they wanted to do in life.

Mother had never held a real job herself since she was fifteen years old. At that time, having been pulled out of school in New York because her parents didn't have the tuition money any longer, she had been simply forgotten by them. Mother went down to a Shirley Temple doll factory in Bay Shore, near the summer house where her family retrenched after selling their New York City house, and got a job curling doll wigs. For eight hours a day, she silently wound ringlets around a curling iron across the table from a woman who had just been released from state prison on a murder conviction. No one was allowed to talk on the job, but the murderess never took her eyes off Mother. After a week she was too frightened to return.

But Mother's jobless resumé did not put her off. It simply convinced her that she was more empathetic. And for some time she did have a thriving operation going out of the want ads. People would come to the house, drink her coffee and confess their deepest hopes. Mother would advise chefs to give cooking lessons on TV, physical therapists to take up dancing—I can't remember who she advised to do what, but they were all very grateful for her support, and it was only when Creative Careers turned out to be too creative for the local board of licensing that Mother had to close her door. She was operating a business in a residential zone.

That minor brainstorm went the way of several others, including the "No Sweat Shirt Company" and the infamous "Pat Me" invention, which is still looking for a home, like Mother who doesn't know whose plants she will be watering from one month to the next.

"Pat Me" was born in Mother's mind the same time that my father, having sold his shop, was just getting his Operation Brown Bag with the senior citizens in Salinas County underway. Mother thought Operation Brown Bag was a great idea, with national implications, and at the beginning of my father's new career, their minds were joined together in a way that, as "Pat Me" took shape in Mother's mind, did not last.

"Pat Me" was a small, fuzzy circle of cloth which could be sewn, glued, or placed on anything—a quilt, a pair of jeans, a sweat shirt, even Anwar Sadat's head.

"Sadat's head?" I exclaimed. "Why not?" said my mother. "He's doing a great job. He deserves a pat." Suddenly she was off and running. "You could hand out 'Pat Me's to cabinet members, people in the State Department, anyone who needs to feel appreciated."

After toying with the idea of turning out a line of "Pat Me" sweaters, toys and blankets, Mother decided to simply stick with the circle. She didn't want to get into the marketing end of things. Everybody, except my father, thought that "Pat Me" was a fabulous invention, maybe like the Hula-Hoop. But it turned out to be maddeningly difficult to get a patent on a plain circle. A plain circle was too metaphysically vague.

"Of course," said Mother, who saw vagueness as a plus, "it's supposed to engage your imagination. A circle can be anything you want it to be—a sun, a stepping stone, an island." There weren't enough metaphors around to adequately describe what a "Pat Me" could be, and Mother

271

couldn't understand why my father couldn't grasp the flexibility of the thing.

He was dead set against the idea. It became a source of irreconcilable tension between them, my mother begging for his support, my father seeing no reason why he should bankroll an idea that was too advanced for J. C. Penney's.

"A penny," exclaimed my mother, "it could also be a penny." Suddenly she saw it hanging off price tags, a logo for J. C. Penney's, nationwide. My father would give her a withering look, my mother would respond by withdrawing ever further into herself, a silence would descend between them and ultimately the silence became permanent.

"Pat Me" was not the true straw that broke the back of their marriage. It was only the last straw. But it was an unusually telling one, although it was some time before I made the obvious connection between Mother's invention and the divorce that followed. There was a lot more at stake than a circle of cloth. But on a deeper level, "Pat Me" was a message that my father never got.

Chapter
XV

Strictly speaking, I am not flying home. In the four years since my parents' separation, my father's heart attack, and the dissolution of my own marriage on the opposite coast, the family has dispersed. There is no home. My mother housesits, my father lives with another family as a boarder in a complicated situation. Tina is still around in a supportive role. Wendy has a one-bedroom cottage, Cindy rents a room in a private house, Tony has a place which is all water bed, and John still lives in a wine barrel, a very nice wine barrel but with no guest room. Peter has just moved to 214½ Abalone Avenue. The "½" sums it all up in my mind.

I know all these things. I have no illusions about anyone's capacity to expand. The Gallweys are still providing the hospitality in the family. Their guest room will be free for the entire time I am in California visiting the family. But it is not the same family. It has gone inward, my Aunt Dorothy quietly trying to open herself up to death, my cousin Mimi struggling to remain independent in her own house, my brothers and sisters too young when the family was in full flower to even miss the resource, and my mother quietly separate from everyone.

She rarely sees any of the family now. Everyone is gently estranged, some by choice, others as a result of that choice, and as I lean back against the cushions, the plane gaining on California, I wonder why I am trying to go home at all. To confirm what I already know? To prove, in person, that I too am older, wiser, trying to survive? Or is it simply wanting to die among my own flesh and blood? I am mortally tired. So many hopes have evaporated. I don't know what my purpose is anymore. But if my heart is going to stop beating, it might as well be on Point Lobos, where I can pull the ice plant over my head and stare at the seagulls for a few moments.

I am not sure that I had these thoughts at that time. But I was very tired . . . my mind continued to flip through back issues of *Harper's*, cranking out ideas, shredding them, hauling in more, unstoppable.

"You must not always think so hard," says my mother. "Try to listen to your breathing, open your inner eye and receive what is there to be received."

But the mind doesn't listen. It keeps on collecting data. I feel like a badly defined statistic, a woman with a certain number of credit cards in her purse, bits of plastic which register my comings and goings—a number who was in Washington this morning and will be in California this afternoon.

The plane pulls on, taking me home because I don't know where else to go. But I expect nothing, the first time I have ever felt so utterly, calmly reduced in hope. As I think this thought, I am mildly appalled by it. Hope has always been a trump card.

Whether it was instinct for self-preservation or self-annihilation, I don't know, but I planned my trip home by starting at the periphery of the family—Los Angeles. Perhaps from the materialistic outer edge, I could work into the mystical core of the family more slowly. Perhaps I simply wanted to be reunited with the three cousins I had grown up with in San Francisco. Now that the family was collapsing with age from the top, I wanted to link arms with the ascending generation. Tony, Tim and Johnny were part of my generation. We would need each other more now. Perhaps it was none of these things. But I wanted to see them, all the better to feel surrounded by three boys who would stick up for me. I felt weak. Los Angeles itself would be a tonic.

Los Angeles was never mentioned as a city when we were growing up in San Francisco. Yet all three boys now live there, leading lives that nobody could have predicted back in the days when everyone was hurling dirt clogs in Presidio Terrace.

Tony, the shambling, private, slightly out-of-pocket cousin, is now a rich man, a computer company president, who claims to be the only company president who personally goes around and fixes all his machines when they break. That isn't true, but Tony is a self-deprecating man who lives in Westlake Village, with two boats in the backyard off a fake lagoon ("Like your place in Belvedere," he confessed. "I always wanted to duplicate that environment."), and a guard at the entrance of the community which is six-figure and affluent. He still lopes like a friendly bear looking for garbage pails in Yosemite, but his face has a responsible look on it now. He is married with four children, and lives with a high-strung, honest, beautiful wife who thinks Tony is a slob but wonderful, which is true. She vacuums behind him and is getting her Ph.D. They lead busy, lesson-planned lives. Tony claims to have succeeded out of laziness, which other people interpret as genius. That's not true. He masks his anxiety behind geniality, but his stomach is the victim. I spent an evening with him when I was in Los Angeles. I'm not sure he knew who I was.

I never got to see Tim. A gigantic boulder was due to crash over Highway One, which was closed off to traffic and jammed with television crews waiting to film the rock smashing a famous director's house that was in its path. Tim lives on the other side of the rock in Malibu Beach with his wife and stepchildren, in a state of semi-isolation from everyone else.

Tim has managed to do what nobody else in the family has, which is to weld together its two dominant forces—spirituality and athletics—and make a fortune. A dreamer, absent-minded professor, natural teacher, and yogi, Tim came up with the idea of psychic tennis, where the emphasis is on cooperating with the life force, which knows how to execute a backhand if only the ego would shut up for a few moments. The idea caught on like wildfire. His book *The Inner Game of Tennis* became a national bestseller. The idea works, although I don't "love the ball" (as Tim instructs in his book) enough to play tennis at all.

Lean, charismatic and a mystical replica of his businessman father, Tim bounced around between alternate life-styles until he finally met up with the guru Maharaj Ji, the boy prophet who flies around the United States imparting "the knowledge" to his devotees. Tim met him while he was in India. From that trip was born the idea for "the inner game," and Tim now divides his time between The Inner Game Institute, talk shows and the guru, who doesn't play tennis but indirectly inspired him with the idea. It is a winner, although wanting to win is precisely the villain that Tim skewers in his book.

"A rock has come between us, Tim," I told him over the phone from a gas station on Highway One. "I can't get to you from here," which is how I have always felt about Tim in general.

The last time Tim stayed at my house, having just returned from India, I was spellbound with the stories, but most of the time he sat backward in a chair upstairs in the guest room meditating, while I stayed downstairs trying to keep the children quiet so he wouldn't lose his train of thought. Tim burns but with a different fuel than most people use. I'm not sure what it is, but I am resigned to, and respectful of the difference.

"I'm sorry you can't make it," said Tim, who sounded distracted as he said it. "Me too," I replied. "Maybe next time." I hung up, wondering when that would be.

The third cousin has always been my favorite, and as the plane landed and I disembarked, Johnny came loping down the corridor, arms outstretched, looking like a handsome, steak-fed Jesus who wasn't sure he was up for being divine. Johnny is twenty pounds overweight, with sideburns, a concession to L.A., I suppose. I hoped he wouldn't notice that my skirt zipper was broken. He didn't. He collided against my ribs, lifted me off the ground and said, "Hi, Griss, welcome home. How many chapters have you given me in your next book? I'm prepared to do whatever outrageous thing I have to do in order to get in."

Tim was the serious cousin, the one who got himself up at 6 A.M. to pound tennis balls against the backboard. Johnny had beautiful form and footwork. I can still see him leaning with consummate grace into the ball—just before it hit the net. I had neither endurance nor form. We grew up and grew apart. Johnny is a dealmaker, into real estate, advertising, whatever flies fast. He has one marriage down, another in the offing. He, too, has made some money, not a pile but enough to look affluent. When he laughs, it starts at the beltline and works up—strong, genuine and naughty. Johnny is the most sybaritic of my cousins. He radiates comfort. I had wanted to marry him when I was seven but was told, to my sorrow, that it wasn't possible.

We piled my luggage into his car, and I watched his hands expertly guide the wheel of his Thunderbird onto the road. I can never look at Johnny's hands without thinking of the way he used to walk conspiratorially around 36 Presidio Terrace, a plump Lone Ranger in mask, hat and holsters, pushing the fingers of Grandmother's leather gloves down upon his fingers.

I was anxious to get a reading on the family from Johnny as soon as possible. Who was sick, who was well, was my father in good shape? and my mother? what about Mimi? and how was his mother, who had not been well for at least fifteen years? My Aunt Dorothy, Johnny's mother, had—since her husband died—suffered a series of illnesses, lung cancer, cataracts, heart attacks. She is seventy-six and serene except for the fact that she is always about to die. It doesn't worry her half as much as it worries my Aunt Irene, who is her emotional reverse—the artist as opposed to the logician. I have often thought of myself as having somehow been conceived by both of them, with my own mother being somewhere else at the time. My Aunt Irene's fears and sensibilities, my Aunt Dorothy's urge to transcend the earth and talk to the North Star—I have sometimes worried that I might wind up as an exaggeration of one or the other, but I am drawn to both, as water to its twin source, feeling closeness with one and drawing inspiration from the other. Whenever I see something particularly beautiful, I want to share it with my Aunt Irene, but it has always been my Aunt Dorothy who moved, like a self-confident prioress, into the various vacuums of my life, blessing, reaffirming and sustaining my faith. Aunt Dorothy is less self-confident than she appears. My Aunt Irene is more intellectually acute than she will take credit for. Both are highly opinionated. They compete but I'm not sure for what, other than for each other's love.

"How is your mother?" I asked.

"Fine," replied John. "Of course, she's not supposed to be fine, but so far she's buried all her doctors."

As Johnny and I talked about his mother and the family in general, we lapsed easily into our favorite discussion—the family's attitude toward each other.

"In many ways," he said, "they're no different than they

were when everybody was in Moral Re-Armament. Only the names have changed. But they are still convinced that all of us are improving every day in every way."

I laughed. How many times, I thought, had I heard my mother say, "Well, you wouldn't know her." Or "he is entirely different now." I had become used to these telephone reports of someone being born again, even though two weeks later a meaningful sigh might sum up the same person who had recently gotten it all together. "Whenever I go up to Carmel," said Johnny, "it's all so wonderfully the same. 'So and so has just blossomed!' or 'All that has gone now!' "

"I'd forgotten about 'all that has gone now!' "

"If only anyone knew what 'all *that*' was," said John, who has been the center of enough family dissections to be inured to all the rebirths they've tried to pin on him.

"It's a wonderful family, isn't it?" I mused. "They just never give up."

"That's right," said Johnny. "Too bad we can't be as wonderful as they know we are." Both of us laughed.

We turned onto the San Fernando Valley freeway, and within an hour we were soaking in John's new Jacuzzi whirlpool ("just installed today," he said exultantly)—under the starry California skies of the valley.

"I feel like I'm in Hell," I said as I looked at my body, turned red by the filter glass. The steam from the Jacuzzi rose into the sky, red clouds that floated past grapefruit trees toward the sky.

"This is just a small-town Jacuzzi," joked John. "Only four jets. If you've really arrived, you have at least six and can hardly hear the person at the other end of the pool."

The ruby water from the Jacuzzi spilled quietly into the violent emerald-green water of an L-shaped swimming pool. We lay back under the stars, drinking gin and tonics, and as the water jets pushed against my spine, I knew—despite the oddness of the environment—that the jets couldn't dissolve the tension. I stretched out in the whirlpool, beyond hydro-massaging. Johnny could not set my failures right for me, but we passed our lives back and forth for inspection, floating in the water and feeling comfortably washed up.

We went inside to discuss his life. Maybe he would leave Los Angeles and move to Phoenix to work for a guy who sold ticket-selling franchises. Maybe he would get married. Maybe he would get into real estate. Maybe he would stay where he was and suck his thumb. He didn't know, but what did I think? I didn't know either. In California, people build up empires and smash them like sandcastles tomorrow. Johnny moves in these kinds of circles. I've sometimes spent two weeks working on a lead paragraph. The pace in California is different.

Over the past year and a half, I had been moving slowly through quiet rooms, struggling to interpret the changing shapes of strong, obscure, complex feelings, clinging to the trumpets in Handel's *Messiah* as I searched for a way out of myself into broad daylight. But I had been right to ease home through the back door of Los Angeles, which clapped its hands in an explosion of Taco Huts, popsicle-shaped shrubs, green lawns, and beautiful, tan women who sulked at stop-lights in their Mercedes-Benzes. I didn't have to interpret anything.

Los Angeles is like a digital clock, telling you what time it is every minute of the day. Then it was time to go. I passed another credit card through the airport computer, waved good-bye to Johnny and flew to Carmel, my anxiety undissolved. I still didn't know why I was coming home except to prove that I had flunked Mysticism I.

I am the only member of the family to live on the East Coast, with all those sharp faces and umbrellas that poke you in the ribs. Nobody says it, but I sense that they don't understand the attraction. My family considers the East cold, crowded and full of people who grind their intellects over nothing, reading magazines which, by and large, miss the point of life altogether.

The point, on the West Coast in my family, has shifted over the years. Simplification has set in. Health food, small walks, simple gifts and quiet understandings. In my family one can hear a pin drop these days. The sound of a rose unfurling is easily heard. To drop in on this environment, reeking of cigarette smoke and loose ends, is to feel—as I sometimes have—defensive and shut out, the only person who hasn't seen an aura, who wants to listen to roses unfurl but is too tense to settle down for the experience. On the other hand, a hot Jacuzzi leaves me cold. Where, I have often asked, is my truth? Nobody will say. In retrospect, I am grateful for that.

Over the years the family has migrated together. San Francisco, Marin County, Santa Cruz, Carmel. My father and his two sisters with their families have never wound up apart from each other for very long, although forays into different communities were made, and it was almost happenstance that where one family settled the other two followed suit. Carmel is now the receiving center. Thirty-six Presidio Terrace has simply moved south.

A quaint, offensively quaint some think, town a hundred odd miles down the coast from San Francisco, Carmel was originally an artists' colony, a collection of cottages sunk among the pine trees, perpetually damp with fog.

Then, in the 1950's Carmel was discovered by the rest of the state. It is now jammed tight with shoppes and boutiques, small, expensive, geranium-hung businesses full of candles, pottery, sheepskin rugs, English leather goods and good food. The tourists swing down Ocean Avenue, cameras dangling, credit cards at the ready, until they reach the bottom of the street which dead ends into the Pacific Ocean. There commercialism is overwhelmed by God.

There is no more beautiful beach in existence. On the grayest, most windswept day, the ocean tears at the ears like the climax of a symphony. At evening, with the air sharp with seaweed and chimney smoke from town, the waves break in jade rolls, sucking the seaweed into pale arches that break into foam where the sandpipers waltz along the wave line. The dunes are edged with ice plant, which blooms with magenta flowers in the spring. The sand is almost flour softness. Old ladies doing wind-sprints, sockless soldiers from Fort Ord, T'ai Chi enthusiasts, hippies, divorcées, dogs—the Carmel beach attracts everyone to its edge in any kind of weather. The mountains surround the entire town in the background— an enormous backdrop cradling the Carmelite monastery, a pale chalk square fronting the ocean beyond the Odello arti- choke fields. There is something for every eye. My eye is al- ways overwhelmed.

"Here," I had said to my future husband many years ago on that beach, "is God." I stuck a twig in the sand. "And here's you," I continued, putting a twig beneath the God twig. "And here," I said, taking a third twig and lining it up directly be- hind his, "is me."

"No," said my future husband. "Here's you," and he had taken my twig, pulled it out of the sand and lined it up parallel to his own.

I had smiled but not been convinced. I knew my place. So much for twigs.

Back and forth the family had moved, but eventually we had gathered, or what was left of the family had gathered, by that beach, my father to own a clothing store and then work for the Senior Citizens, my uncle to retire, my cousin Mimi to raise her three children on her own.

A quietude had descended over the core. Everyone was older now. There was yet another generation beneath mine, second cousins who romped and had moods and tried to run away and thought that only the latest rock group understood them. But they largely lived apart, in other places. We were scattered, even over the holidays, like embers away from the main fire, although the Gallweys' still provided the one solid hitching post where everyone from out of town came to stay when they visited.

I cannot remember who I saw first; Mother at the airport, I think. But I was dropped off at the Gallweys' to have supper with Mother later on, and as I stood in the middle of their living room, surrounded by my Aunt Irene's taste—apricot and yellow slipcovers, small Chinese lamps, fabulous candlesticks that were artfully held together with chewing gum, Ming bowls painstakingly glued and reglued so you would never know that one small shudder would make them fall apart—I knew I was among real kith and kin. Who else throws car keys on the floor of the car? a capital offense in any other family. What other family wastes electricity so joyfully, keeping rooms lit just in case someone might go into them? The house bloomed with light, and as I looked around I saw the array of silver-framed pictures along one long windowsill: Mimi in her wedding dress, Tim and his wife at their own wedding, a grandchild in underpants and a wedding veil, my grandmother, posing in newly blued hair in a dinner dress, holding her lorgnette in her lap. They were all lined up behind the sofa in various states of equipoise. Some dead, some fled, some simply more realistic. The fire was lit.

Aunt Dorothy, who recently decided to move—a metaphysical choice, she had never lived alone—came out of the kitchen. When I embraced her it was like embracing tissue paper. She felt very frail. Over the years all the solid flesh she used to lament had melted. Uncle Ed, damnably handsome, ageless and walnut brown, with those perpetually brimming-with-tears eyes, moved in to have his own embrace. Aunt Irene, the beautiful sister, now plump but still Byzantine of thought and expression, my vulnerable aunt. I kissed her as I always do, wishing I could take her place and give her some relief from that continually working mind. Everyone arranged themselves loosely in a circle to greet this latest arrival. But why was I here? I did not know. Fortunately, nobody thought to ask.

I put my suitcase in the guest room and fell onto the bed. "Just a short nap," I called out to my aunt and uncle. I would be up before six. Somehow I could not think what I wanted to do now that I was here. The family in the flesh seemed like so many photographs that I did not have to have in order to see them. So I would sleep.

It was a restless, foot-faulting sleep, neither deep nor shallow. I slipped around the greased bowl of my subconscious, gripping the pillow, shutting my eyes against a certain sense of isolation, and woke, finally, into the pre-evening, a netherland, which coincided with my state. I must, I instructed myself, change for supper. I moved slowly around the room, looking for something to put on. I had packed with distraction. Nothing matched.

From behind the closed door, I could hear the Gallweys talking to each other in the living room. It was a comforting sound. First, Uncle Ed's deep voice, making a statement. Then Aunt Irene's laugh—a small, silvery laugh, as if my uncle had said something delicious and funny and she wanted to hear more.

He must be telling a story, I thought. The two sounds went back and forth—his voice, her laugh. I could not help but think what a triumph that muffled conversation was. After all these years, I thought, those two people still have something to say to each other. I felt indirectly warmed by it, as if by a miracle that I was hearing about second hand. I opened the door to eavesdrop.

Now my Uncle Ed's voice could be plainly heard. So, he was reading something. I listened to hear what it was that made my aunt laugh so often. The words had a familiar cadence to them. I knew, before the words came out, what the next sentence would be. They were, as I listened disbelievingly, my sentences. My uncle was reading out loud from a scrapbook of my essays. They were entertaining themselves, in my absence, with me.

I cannot say precisely what this meant to me. But there was a healing in it as I listened to those two people I loved, quietly sitting together, reading those small essays. Each time my Aunt Irene laughed, the burden I had been carrying lifted a cubit further off my shoulders. Each time my Uncle Ed resumed his reading, the weight I was bearing lightened, and new confirmation came into the room.

I had traveled such a long distance to come home, not knowing why, except my instinct at an exhausted moment. Most of my life had been spent apart. The family I had originally adored had turned, in part, into a curse that I fled from, afraid I would catch it and freeze to death, the victim of too many ideals that I was incapable of fulfilling. Yet how far can anyone really grow above their roots? We struggle, rebel and rise above them, like a sunflower craning its neck toward the sun. But even the sunflower, heavy with seeds, ultimately bows its head in humility back toward the source of itself. I bowed my own head over and felt the seeds drop back onto the earth. The burden I had come with was, in that moment, gone.

I kept a journal, into which I now dip, during the ten days I spent visiting my family on this last trip. Thoughts are entered as I had them, about this person or that one, about my confusion or struggle to understand who each person was, and how we were bound together, or kept separate, as individuals and as a family. And the notes are as diverse as who I saw.

Here is my Aunt Dorothy, whom I went to visit in her small, perfect little cottage one afternoon for tea. We spoke of my sister Wendy. "There's a solidity about her," said my Aunt Dorothy, "that wasn't there before." We moved on to talk about the meaning of family. "Well, when you think about it," she mused, "from a spiritual angle . . . and, of course, what other angle is there? . . ." "Of course," I answered, loving her for reminding me from whence I came. I don't remember if we ever got off the "spiritual angle." Only if forced would we do such a thing.

The next day, according to my journal, I saw my father. He had driven in from Salinas in a new sports car. "I call it my covered skateboard," he said. We went to lunch. Sitting across from him, I realized he was not who I was looking at. It was a shock to know that I did not even notice that he was an old man, with lines and wrinkles and a faintly white face. The man I was talking to lay behind that mask. Perhaps I, too, was wearing a mask. Do fathers and daughters freeze the frame at a certain point and disregard wear and tear after that point?

Together we drove to Mother's current house in which she is sitting. I had not seen them together for a long time. But the tension was gone. My father walked into the living room and waved an envelope, her monthly support check.

"Here's your chewing-gum money," he said.

"Oh," said Mother, clutching the envelope dramatically. "I'm so glad you came."

"Well, I couldn't afford to mail it," he said.

We settled down for a cup of coffee. I did not feel strange. Nobody seemed to. Enough time had passed.

"Jack," said my mother, "we must think about our funeral plans. Do you want to turn over in an urn?"

"I don't know," he answered. "Are you going to get fried or buried?"

"I can't decide," she said. "Getting cremated seems a little hot."

They left that topic, still undecided. My father started to tell us about having taken up art classes. "A life drawing course," he said.

"Whoo-whoo," I teased.

"Actually," said my father, "I didn't really need the course. I could have drawn from memory . . . and it would have been cheaper too."

Even as I reproduce this joke, I cannot keep from laughing. I have thought long, hard and sometimes angrily about my father. But when I looked at him then and think of him now, my conflicts with him have always revolved around the unshakeable conviction that I think he is the most marvelous man I have ever met. I cannot dispense with him any more than I can dispense with myself. I suppose that his originality got the best of him. It has controlled him more than he ever controlled it. But to sit around a kitchen table when you're sixty-nine and joke about being so broke that "I have to get my teeth in the mail" is a kind of end-run control. He's always had that. Mother thinks he is as funny as he ever was. They don't have a marriage anymore, but they have something. I don't know quite what it is.

My sister Cindy is running, meditating and eating good food. She looks beautiful. Somehow all the dross has disappeared, and only pure Cindy remains. She is cleaning houses, trying to pay off her car.

Gazing with those impossibly liquid brown eyes at me, she summed up all her achievements and then giggled, "I'm trying so hard to be mellow. My art class is wonderful . . . so is my art teacher."

(I repeated Cindy's remark to my father. "Our family," he said, "seems to be in a constant state of arousal.")

"No," said Cindy, "I'm really off men at the moment. I've made a lot of new friends, girl friends. I want you to meet Chris and Wanda. I met them at an A.A. meeting."

"Cindy," I exclaimed. "I didn't know you have a drinking problem."

"Oh, I don't," she said. "I just go to the meetings for moral support."

She giggled again. Cindy is the only person I've ever met

who uses Alcoholics Anonymous as a launching pad to make new friends. But I think she's onto something.

For one whole day I drove around with Tony, who hustles liquor for a package store between Carmel and Pacific Grove, delivering whiskey to old ladies who live in dumps. What an awful life for a seventeen-year-old, I thought. But Tony doesn't think so, and we swung around the curves in his truck, with the door on the driver's side only vaguely held together by a rubber book strap that didn't keep the door from opening when he turned sharp corners. Tony is in love with a fifteen-year-old girl who takes reservations at the Pine Inn. They fall silent in each other's presence. When he introduced me, they put their hands on top of each other's on top of the reservation desk and stared silently into each other's eyes. I felt a little uncomfortable, standing to one side. Finally, I put my hand on top of theirs to unlock their gaze. Tony is quite handsome and very smart. He snatched his high-school diploma out of the registrar's office during summer vacation, even though he had a few credits to make up. He is fiercely independent. He has survived the dissolution of the family, sometimes I think just a little too well.

Wendy is learning the piano, from scratch, living in a small brick bungalow that is covered with her art work. She works days at the television studio as the anchor woman for a news program to support her two habits—piano and therapy. Both are peeling old layers off the onion. We spent an afternoon racing through Clementi sonatinas, talking about Handel, becoming sisters again.

One supper with my cousin Mimi. She was preoccupied. I did not know until the next day that for some time now Lawrence—her teacher, my mother's teacher, my Aunt Dorothy's teacher—lay dying in Santa Fe. All of them were carrying him closely inside, not speaking about it except among themselves. It explained my mother's wistfulness, her quietude during those days. "I am, of course," she said as she curled up in a chair one evening, "feeling terribly sad. But on another level everything is fine."

I did not know what to do about Lawrence dying. He had been to Mother a tremendous source of light. We went to Lawrence's old house, a dramatic, steep-shingled house that overlooked the ocean down the coast for several miles. She seemed to gain peace just sitting in his garden. I went inside and played his piano, "The Moonlight Sonata," trying to console her the only way I knew. "That was lovely," she said, coming inside. "I wasn't sure I wanted to break the quiet. But I feel that you playing his piano has somehow brought you into his spirit. I am glad you did."

Several times I went for a walk along the ocean. Often, on the opposite coast, I have lain in the dark and made the waves break in my mind, as they were doing before me—in curling, turquoise breakers, tumbling into foam, spreading their creamy, lace bubbles along the sand. The knowledge that the Pacific exists and breaks upon itself even though I'm not there comforts me, like my family which tumbles at a distance, at the edge of my life.

It was a different visit this time. The family had been like a symphony orchestra that had fallen in love with its own music. Too much so, I suppose. Now they are like so many instruments playing separately. The music is purer but more plaintive.

On the final day of the visit to Carmel, I sought out the place I am attracted to beyond all others, a small Carmelite chapel near Point Lobos which sits on a hillside overlooking a small bay. I have gone there many times for the same reason. It is neither heaven nor earth, but inside that chapel I am conscious of being in a kind of antechamber between the two. Something always happens when I am there. I never know what it will be.

The road leading to the monastery is lined with acacia trees, which in February are thick with yellow bloom. The sisters do not garden *in extremis.* Small paths are allowed to choke over with sour grass. Mustard plant makes a brilliant yellow bush against black apricot trees. The chapel is buff-colored stucco, slightly moldy from the fog that never allows it to dry completely. Chiseled in stone over the front of the cloister chapel are the words, *Voce mea ad Deum*— "let my voice rise to God."

It is a Sunday. I realize with a chill that it is also my former wedding anniversary. Father Juan, the resident priest who has been there as long as I remember, enters to say Mass.

Often in the past I have been so struck by his face that I have fallen out of sync with the Mass itself and simply meditated upon what I saw in that face. I do not know Father Juan. He appears every other year in my life, like a Hernandez sculpture, a suffering, suffused piece of wooden art that one might see in Ávila. He is a Spaniard. Perhaps that is why I think of Ávila instead of some other place.

His eyes are bright, full of humor. His mouth a straight, comical line, as if he is repressing a joke. A self-aware man, not capable of physical humility, he stands before the congregation in his white cassock and bright red stole, a brown priest in an amber light. I imagine he has had his dialogues with God over the state of his life. But he has stuck with it. I am not inspired by his appearance. What inspires me is that he continues to appear at all.

The gospel is a reading from Saint Mark on divorce. I stiffened. They are hard words. Father Juan reads them, makes no comment, shuts the book and steps away from the lectern.

"My friends," he begins, stretching out his hands, smiling as if it were somehow a joke to call us friends. "My friends, I have been reading from the Book of Sirach. It has nothing to do with the gospel we have just heard. But in Sirach, he speaks of friendship. And he says that the test of a real friend is two things, loyalty in time of stress and a shared faith in the mercy of God.

"Eh? I think this is right." Father Juan raised his hands, like a man who is empty-handed of further wisdom. "I do not have anything to add to that. But there is not one of us here who has not felt, in our hearts, that we had lost everything, even perhaps our faith. Yet God, in His mercy, is never far from us. We can think so, but no, He is here. I know it. More so each year. I wish for you to know that too. As much as I can wish anything. And now, my friends, may God's blessing be with you."

He leaned forward, cocking his ear.

"God bless you, Father," people murmured.

"Good," he said. "Thank you. Let us pray that we may all be instruments of Christ so that others may recognize him in us."

That evening I spent the night with my Aunt Dorothy. She had spent the entire day—insisted upon it—reading everything I had brought of my work. In my journal I have taped a page ripped from her notebook, where she had written, in a fine, sharp penmanship, her thoughts for me before I left. I will not reproduce them, but she read me her thoughts, each one more generous than the last, and concluded with "You are surrounded by guardian angels."

I could hardly bear the gift. It was offered almost in passing, without thought. Yet I gazed at her in plain disbelief. She had not had to do what she had just done. "Will you let me have that piece of paper? I want to keep it to remind me of what you said."

My Aunt Dorothy is seventy-six. She seems almost translucent to me, a collection of wisps and straight lines, with only her blue eyes to buckle everything together. She is beautiful and almost but not quite at peace.

"Tell me," I asked, "do you see Mary very often?" (Mary is her ex-daughter-in-law, Johnny's former wife, with whom she corresponds regularly.) "Ah, Mary," said my aunt. "My dear, you wouldn't recognize her! All inhibitions have been lifted . . . thank God!"

I did. The following year, on Thanksgiving Day, my Aunt Dorothy died.

She had been straddling the edge of death with equanimity for many years, although death did not frighten her any more than life did, and it was a source of puzzlement to her, as well as to her doctors (several of whom died, closing their own cases before hers), that she continued to remain in this dimension, given her eagerness to experience the next one.

But remain she did, the house philosopher always stretching "to be" with as much patience as her basically impatient nature allowed. And when she mused out loud on the subject of her own longevity, she used to say, with a smile, "Well, I don't quite know why I'm still here, but I must be meant to accomplish something else before I go."

True, we would agree, although nobody, including my youngest sister, Cindy, in whose arms she died, knew what that "something else" might be. Until the end. Then everyone knew.

If one were to choose two women within the family who were diametrically opposite (although not opposed) to each other in every way, it would be my sister Cindy and my aunt. Both of them were, in entirely different modes, highly feminine. There, however, the similarity ends.

My Aunt Dorothy was a Mother Superior, a doyenne, a rigged ship that sailed through rooms in pearls, Paisley scarves and fine wool dresses that matched the fineness of her thoughts. A cosmic thinker, with a pair of pale blue eyes trained to spot excellence (sometimes where it didn't quite exist), she read Plotinus and Meister Eckhart, studied the *I Ching*, and was fond of saying about almost everything, "Well, that's the point, isn't it?" In this last, of course, she mirrored more family members than herself. Collectively, the family has always had a penchant for beating the point of life to death.

Cindy, on the other hand, has never shared that penchant. A teenager during the 60's, who hitchhiked in cutoffs, ironed her hair and supported the Beatles with enough emotion to fill up a stadium, she has always been the one member of the family who could be guaranteed to giggle when everybody else was trying for solemnity. She is easy to love.

Cindy did not sail, she romped into a room, like a beautiful filly at the end of her tether, swinging a full makeup bag and a roster of men who hadn't read Plotinus either. Artless, without intellectual pretensions, and entirely unsure as to where she would find her next ten cents for a phone call, she bolted through adolescence and her early twenties, not sure where she was going, although whenever she had a thought on that subject, she would consult my aunt.

Cindy would talk. My aunt would listen. A temporary fix on the universe would be drawn. And then Cindy would be gone again, to test her strength in a world of part-time jobs, lapsed car payments and clothes on lay away, a world that my Aunt Dorothy knew very little about, unless Cindy filled her in. Their lives, except when Cindy rushed in to lay her own life at my aunt's feet, were somewhat out of sync. Or so it seemed.

When my Aunt Dorothy was partially paralyzed by a stroke, she who had always been so strong had to learn to be helpless —a new form of being, the last lesson in the book.

She needed twenty-four-hour care, a full-time companion, someone (nobody in the family knew who) who would feed her, bathe her, change the bed and perform the large and small duties that would keep her as comfortable as possible. It was Cindy who eagerly volunteered for the job. Several years ago, she would not have been the first person to spring to anyone's mind.

If my Aunt Dorothy inspired you to be strong, my sister

Cindy inspired you to be protective. One handled life so handily. The other seemed to find life too difficult to hold at all without a lot of outside help. Yet over the past several years, Cindy had refocused. There was an order to her life that had not been there before. Healthy food, exercise, meditation and clarity were beginning to characterize her existence. She still giggled, she was still beautiful. But she was no longer quite as unsure of herself, with reason. The chief fetter of her life, that of being too dependent, was loosening its grip. And when my aunt was rendered entirely dependent, Cindy, the original "free-lancer" who never wanted to be tied down, willingly tied herself to my aunt. For two months she rarely left her side.

It was a grueling schedule, demanding patience, fortitude and open-ended commitment. Cindy wrapped her strong arms around my frail aunt, lifted, bathed, fed and dressed her. Twice a day she was relieved by another member of the family. She would explode upon the beach nearby and jog several miles and then return to her assignment, ready to take over again. At first the family was mildly amazed. Then the amazement turned to respect and gratitude. She was doing what no one else in the family could do. And despite the long hours, Cindy grew more "radiant," an adjective that my Aunt Dorothy often used to describe people who are totally in tune with their own music.

Cindy's strength grew in proportion to my aunt's need for it. And on Thanksgiving Day, when my Aunt Dorothy drew her last breath, it was Cindy who held her, talked to her, stroked her hair; and when she finally died, Cindy looked up at my mother, who was also in the room, and said, "It's over now."

And so it was. Although for Cindy, it was a beginning. In the last two months, there had been a transfer of power. My aunt was, from all reports, serene in her weakness. As for Cindy, she was quite simply "something else!"

*   *   *

Somehow I feel called upon to wind up this chronicle with a flurry of trumpets. The trumpet never fails to remind me what a piece of brass can do, in the right hands. Yet to exit with trumpets would be to exit to an applause that the facts of this particular life don't warrant, or lead the reader to assume that all large questions have been triumphantly resolved, which isn't quite the case.

Well then, what instrument, playing what notes? Or is there, when all is said and done, a theme worth playing? I think there is; it relates to vision.

A child does not know if he or she truly exists without someone to confirm it. "Watch me," a child implores, "as I go off the diving board." "Watch me, as I jump off into the water; watch me, as I run, hop, draw, sing and do all those things that I would not have the courage or belief to do if you were not there." We watch, applaud, say "good, very good," and children begin to know what goodness is because we have confirmed it in them with our eyes.

Then a child grows up, becomes one of us. Who is watching us now? The ego takes the parents' place. We become self-critical, self-examining, self-doubting and self-applauding. Our eyes are upon ourselves, watching. I would also maintain that if we stay in this contorted position too long, we lose our sight. It is a necessary business, self-examination, but it should lead somewhere else. To be egocentric too long is hazardous and unfulfilling, and cuts one off from just plain looking around for its own sake.

I come from a family of mystics, although it is my particular cross to have never seen an aura, experienced an electrical transmission of energy, endured a fast, or gone into a deep meditative trance. I believe, without having seen or experienced these things, that they are real. But every once in a while, the curtains are parted as much as I can bear, and I glean some new intuition of another dimension which was

295

there for the looking if only I had had my eyes open.

Bringing in the cushions from my Aunt Irene's patio one night, I happened to look up at the sky and was startled by the moon. It hung like a pearl, aeons removed from the clouds, which passed in serried wisps back and forth across its face, now obscuring it, now brushing past so the moon hung once more, perfect and alone.

I was caught up by the moon and the utterly black space around it. How windless it must be up there, the realm of pure spirit moving unobstructed back and forth across the void without sound. How different from the earth, where the wind encounters obstacles—clouds, grasses, mountains, men. Down here it is so noisy, full of sound, different sounds as the spirit passes through different configurations. No two throats utter the same laugh or cry, yet the breath passing through them is from the same source. Ah ha, I thought, so that is how it is! Each of us an instrument, with no two instruments alike. Yet we are not quite estranged from each other. We are bound together by a common breath. We can communicate and complete each other with that. I stared at the moon for some time—struck, startled and at peace.

I admit this is not a high-class mystical experience, but it fulfills the requirement of being a moment of perception where the eyed gazed outward and silently beheld something as it was, not as I wanted it to be for my own egocentric sake. Which returns me to the theme.

Not long ago I asked someone who was blind why she didn't act blind. Or was I wrong? Had she not just lugged my suitcase down a dark path she had never been on before? Had she not just explored a house that was strange to her and not once bumped into a wall, window or door? Perhaps she could see more than I had heard.

"No," she said, "I'm blind, but I have what doctors call 'compensatory vision.'"

"What is that?" I asked.

"I think I can see even though I can't. I don't believe I'm blind, and because I don't believe it, I don't act blind. Most blind people have some compensatory vision, but I have quite a lot. But it's something I could lose."

"How?" I asked.

"There are two ways," she replied. "If I try too hard to prove I'm not handicapped in any way, then I wind up stumbling up stairs, bumping into walls."

"What is the other way to lose it?" I asked.

"By giving up, by not trying hard enough. If I let myself get overwhelmed with the difficulty of being blind, if I despair or give up, then I start to act blind."

She looked into my face, the face she could not see, and continued. "The trick is to try to stay in the middle of these two extremes, to be just relaxed enough to stay in a state of . . ." She paused to try to pick out the right word from her mind. A word popped into mine.

"Grace?" I volunteered.

"That's the word I wanted," she exclaimed. "The trick is to stay in a state of grace."

Aknowledgments

A book is the last link in a connected chain of links. If any of them break along the way, the book would not be written. The linkage was particularly strong in my case. All along the way there was help, crucial help, from people who donated time, inspiration, and encouragement. My worry is, as I begin to thank them here, that I will omit someone who I will later remember as having been very important indeed.

My children, who think that books are secondary to themselves, which is true, were taken into the families of various friends and parented to perfection when I had to leave them to travel on book business. Sherry and Bob Dunn, Merrill and Ray Hare, Mav and Colman McCarthy deserve more than thanks. They deserve royalties.

Certain friends had to endure continual reading sessions. Mary Carll Kopper and Steven Hofman bore the largest brunt of that necessary (to authors) burden. They were brave enough to tell me what they didn't like as well as what they did. Steven not only played editor, but also nursemaid, budget director and general morale booster, a role that others also filled. They know who they are.

Nancy Newhouse and Jim Greenfield at the *New York Times* know what parts they played, as do Lou Rosen, Mary and Tony Smith, Maralyn Wheeler, and Jill Merrill.

My editor, Julie Houston, should be everybody's editor. Ann Buchwald, Molly Friedrich and Aaron Priest were agents of grace, and I cannot go another line without thanking Molly's parents, Priscilla and Otto Friedrich, who twice provided me with a room of my own in their house so I could finish the book in peace, which is what they provided, along with yogurt, Schubert sonatas and the Long Island Sound.

Finally, there is my family who, in their innocence and trust, opened themselves up to my probing, never blinked during the entire process and were, despite what must have been secret nervousness on their part, largely supportive of what I was trying to do—which was to write about them. "Perhaps," I said to my mother, "I have written something that will hurt your feelings."

"That's all right," she answered. "I can learn from it." This sentiment was almost everyone's sentiment, confirming my belief that the family itself is extraordinary in certain ways.

My mother, when asked for suggestions on what to title the book volunteered, "A Feather of Truth." My father, when asked the same question said, "If I Holler Let Me Go." Ultimately I chose my own title, which is neither as profound nor as funny as the other two. But then, neither am I. My parents have always been the two strongest links in my life. I don't see this changing, although they have changed themselves. Not many children, when grown, can claim that their parents continue to inspire them. I can and, in this space, I do.